SUSAN LEWIS

Just one more day

PENGUIN BOOKS

PENGUIN BOOKS

UK | USA | Canada | Ireland | Australia
India | New Zealand | South Africa

Penguin Books is part of the Penguin Random House group of companies
whose addresses can be found at global.penguinrandomhouse.com

Penguin Random House UK,
One Embassy Gardens, 8 Viaduct Gardens, London SW11 7BW

penguin.co.uk
global.penguinrandomhouse.com

First published in the UK by William Heinemann 2005
First published in paperback by Arrow Books 2006
Published in Penguin Books 2025
001

Typeset by SX Composing DTP, Rayleigh, Essex
Printed and bound in Great Britain by Clays Ltd, Elcograf S.p.A.

The authorised representative in the EEA is Penguin Random House Ireland,
Morrison Chambers, 32 Nassau Street, Dublin D02 YH68

A CIP catalogue record for this book is available from the British Library

ISBN: 978–1–804–95458–4

PENGUIN BOOKS

Just one more day

Susan Lewis is the internationally bestselling author of over fifty books across the genres of family drama, thriller, suspense and crime. She is also the author of *Just One More Day* and *One Day at a Time*, the moving memoirs of her childhood in Bristol during the 1960s. Following periods of living in Los Angeles and the South of France, she currently lives in Gloucestershire with her husband, James, and her dog, Mimi.

To find out more about Susan Lewis:
www.susanlewis.com
www.facebook.com/SusanLewisBooks
@susanlewisbooks

Praise for Susan Lewis:

'A multi-faceted tear-jerker' *Heat*

'Expertly written to brew an atmosphere of foreboding, this story is an irresistible blend of intrigue and passion, and the consequences of secrets and betrayal' *Woman*

'Utterly compelling' *Sun*

'Spellbinding! You just keep turning the pages, with the atmosphere growing more and more intense as the story leads to its dramatic climax' *Daily Mail*

'One of the best around' *Independent on Sunday*

'Sad, happy, sensual and intriguing' *Woman's Own*

Also by Susan Lewis

Novels

A Class Apart
Dance While You Can
Stolen Beginnings
Darkest Longings
Obsession
Vengeance
Summer Madness
Last Resort
Wildfire
Chasing Dreams
Taking Chances
Cruel Venus
Strange Allure
The Mill House
Missing
A French Affair
Out of the Shadows
Lost Innocence
The Choice
Forgotten
Stolen
No Turning Back
Losing You
The Truth About You
Never Say Goodbye
Too Close To Home
No Place to Hide
The Secret Keeper
One Minute Later
Home Truths
My Lies, Your Lies
Forgive Me
The Lost Hours
I Have Something to Tell You
Who's Lying Now?
No One Saw It Coming
I Know It's You
A Sicilian Affair
Nothing to See Here

Memoirs

One Day at a Time

To Eddress and Eddie's grandchildren,
Grace and Thomas

Just one more day

Chapter One

Susan

I'm very brave. No-one else knows I'm being brave, because I haven't told them. It's a secret – between me and my dad.

I'm sitting at my desk now, in my classroom, watching the teacher chalk things up on the blackboard. It's something about poetry, but I'm not really paying attention, which would make Daddy cross, because he loves poems. I've got a lot to think about though, because it's not always easy being brave, and I have to make sure I'm doing it right.

As I think about it, I stare up at the big, oblong window with twelve square panes, where I can only see milk-coloured sky outside. If I stood on a chair to look I'd see the library next door, Warmley Hill and the petrol station opposite where my friends and I sometimes sneak into the ladies' toilets to play doctors and nurses. But that's another secret and I'm definitely never going to tell anyone about that – not even Daddy. And if Mummy ever found out I know she'd tell the police, because she already nearly did once. That was when she caught me and my friend Janet in the garden, pulling down our swimming costumes to show the boys our chests. We were so scared when Mummy came storming out of the house, telling us we were wicked and that she was taking us to the police, that we ran and hid in Mr Weiner's shed.

Mummy wouldn't look for us there, because Mr Weiner's German and Mummy doesn't have anything to do with him because she still hasn't forgiven him for the war. Daddy has, but Daddy forgives everyone for everything.

Today my hair is in plaits with two white bows at the end of each one. Grown-ups are always going on about my hair, saying how lovely it is, all thick and red and curly, but it's all right for them, they don't have to put up with Mummy's brushing every morning, or the horrid, smelly boys in my class who call me Ginger and pull it. Granny told me once that Mummy, whose hair is the exact same colour (I bet Granny never used to be so mean with a brush when Mummy was little), used to beat people up if they called her Ginger, or worse, Ginge. I've never done that, but I do get *really* angry, especially on the days when Mummy forces my hair up into a high-topped ponytail that the boys keep swinging on, then running away before I can punch their noses.

I've got freckles too. I hate them. But even worse are the glasses I have to wear. As if they don't make me look stupid enough, the right lens since I was six (I'm seven now) has been covered up with a white patch to make my left eye see properly. It doesn't though, so I have to keep peering over the top so I can read my books and watch the telly. When Mummy spots me she puts her fingers under my chin and tilts my head up again. She's very strict and won't ever let me take them off. But even she laughed when we first got them from the optician. I was sulking and wanted to cry because I knew already how stupid I was going to feel in them, and how much fun everyone was going to poke at me. Then the optician gave us a pair of round National Health frames, which came for free, and when I put them on Mummy split her sides laughing. I love it when Mummy laughs, because it always makes me laugh too.

I think I'm being quite brave at the moment, because I don't mind that Mummy won't be there when I get home after school. The first time she wasn't there I was more frightened than when Daddy took us across the Clifton Suspension Bridge and we looked all the way down at the river. I was little then and hid behind Daddy's legs. I still don't like looking down when I'm high up, and I don't really like it when Mummy's not there, but I'm being brave, so I won't cry. I expect Gary will though. He's my brother, who's four years younger than me, which makes him only three, so he's allowed to cry. If I feel like crying too, I'll wait till I'm on my own so no-one will see, because I don't want Daddy to know I'm afraid in case it makes him afraid too. You see, it's all right to be scared of the dark, and of spiders and witches and things, and to make Daddy sit at the bottom of the stairs singing and telling his silly jokes while I go to the toilet, but it's not all right to be scared about Mummy not being there, because that's just silly when we know she's coming back.

Five and twenty ponies,
Trotting through the dark –
Brandy for the Parson
'Baccy for the Clerk;
Laces for a lady, letters for a spy,
Watch the wall, my darling, while the Gentlemen go by!

The teacher's reciting my favourite poem now. I recite it to Granny sometimes, though I keep forgetting bits, which makes her chuckle and then she hugs me to her chest, which is like a great big fluffy pillow. Granny is Mummy's mummy and is very old and lives in a house full of ornaments and photographs and bottles of stout that she likes to drink. She plays bingo a lot too, either at the Regal in Staple Hill, or the Vandyke in Fishponds, or near us, at the Made-for-Ever youth club. When she goes there Mummy usually goes with her, and if it's Saturday, and I've been good, they take me for the first session, and let me have my own card to cross off the numbers. I won a pound once, but I can't remember what I did with it now. After the first session Daddy comes to pick me up and take me home to bed. Later, Mummy and Granny walk back to our house, then Daddy drives Granny home in his blue Morris car.

Daddy doesn't like bingo very much. Or telly. He prefers books, which he reads under a lamp in the front room, while Mummy watches her favourite programmes all snuggled up by the fire in the dining room. It's lovely snuggling up with her, but she doesn't let me stay up very late. I have to go to bed earlier than everyone else on our street, probably than everyone in the whole wide world, which is horrible, because in the summer I can still hear my friends playing outside. But Mummy won't give in. She's really strict, and sometimes I don't like her very much. She makes me want to go and live on an island where no grown-ups are allowed, and children can do anything they want whenever they want. Daddy read me a story about it once, and I've always remembered it, because that's where I'm going to go if I ever run away. My dad's the best story-reader in all the world. He sits out on the landing every night, between my and Gary's bedrooms, and tells us all about Alice, or Pooh, or Brer Rabbit, or my absolute favourite, Naughty Amelia Jane. I want to be like her, but Mummy wouldn't put up with it.

Five and twenty ponies
Trotting through the dark –
Brandy for the Parson

'Baccy for the Clerk;
Laces for a lady, letters for a spy,
Watch the wall, my darling, while the Gentlemen go by!

Mummy's going to miss *Coronation Street* tonight. She hates missing it, and never does, unless she has to go away, like now. I wonder if there are tellies where she is. Children aren't allowed in, so I don't know. Usually, Gary and I go to Granny's while Daddy visits her. Sometimes I go with Daddy, but I have to wait outside in the car.

It's half past three now, because Mr Dobbs, the headmaster, is ringing the bell, which echoes up and down the corridors, and we all stand up to say 'goodnight' to Mrs Taylor, our teacher, which seems a bit silly when it's not night at all.

Me and Sophie (she's my new best friend) go to get our coats from the cloakroom, and even though it's going to be May next week, it's still a bit cold outside, so we make sure all our buttons are done up. Then, with our satchels strapped across us, we join the crowd gathering round the lollipop lady who's always there to see us across the road.

'Got any money for sweets?' Sophie asks me. 'I spent all mine on tuck.'

'My dad gave me tuppence this morning,' I tell her. 'I've still got a penny ha'penny left.'

'Hey, it's Ginge with the one eye!' Kevin Milton shouts, and he pulls so hard on one of my plaits that I scream and try to bash him with my fists. I always miss though, because he's too fast.

'Cry baby, cry baby!' two more boys start singing. Then some girls chime in, 'Cry baby! Cry baby! Susan's a baby.'

'One-eyed monster, you mean,' someone else shouts.

'Ginger biscuit.'

Sophie puts her arm round me, but I push her off.

'I hate you!' I scream at the grinning Kelvin Milton. 'I'm going to tell my mum about you.'

Kelvin merely pokes out his tongue and waggles his hands either side of his head. He looks like a cabbage flapping its leaves.

'Come on, come on,' the lollipop lady shouts. 'I can't hold the traffic all day.'

Sophie links my arm as we cross over. 'It's all right, they're just stupid,' she says. 'Let's go in the shop and get some sweets.'

I can't find my clean hanky so I dry my eyes with my coat sleeve. I hate Kelvin Milton so much that I'm going to think of something really evil and nasty to do to him. If I was a witch I'd turn him into a slug, then my brother would eat him, because my brother eats slugs. Or he did once, before Mummy snatched it away then stuck her fingers down his throat to make him sick.

The queue inside the corner tuck shop isn't very long, and no-one horrid is in there, because the horrid children never have any money. I just hope they're not waiting outside to steal our sweets. As we move up the queue Sophie and I greedily eye all the jars, mouths watering. What shall we have? A sherbert dip? A lucky bag? A packet of Smith's crisps with a little blue bag of salt? A penny-ha'penny would buy us three sticks of red liquorice, or six fruit salad chews, three white chocolate mice or six mojos. We end up getting four mojos, and two aniseed twists, which are Sophie's favourites. Even though Sophie's parents are rich, I don't mind paying for her, because she shared her potato puffs and Wagon Wheel with me at playtime.

She lives in a really big house with a tower and a weathercock on the top, and hundreds of rooms which are great for hide-and-seek, but I'm a bit nervous of the secret passageways and trapdoors under the rugs. If one of them opens up I could be swallowed down into the centre of the earth and might even end up in Australia, where Rolf Harris comes from, and I wouldn't be able to find my way home then. The paintings on the walls are really scary too, because the eyes move. It doesn't matter where I stand, they're always looking at me. I'm glad we don't have any paintings like that in our house, which isn't nearly so big as Sophie's. We don't own ours either. It belongs to the man from the council who comes round to collect the rent every week.

Kelvin Milton and his gang have gone when we go outside, so we're safe to share out the sweets. Sophie nudges me, and tells me to look. Marilyn Caldwell and Ruth Myers are crossing the street. They're in the fourth form and are exactly like me and Sophie want to be when we're eleven – pretty, popular, lots of friends, and all the boys after us. It'll probably happen for Sophie because she's already really pretty, but not for me with these *stupid*, *horrible* glasses and *freckles*.

'See you tomorrow then,' Sophie says, sucking on an aniseed twist and pocketing her mojos. She lives in the opposite direction so we can't walk home together.

I start walking along the road between the shop and the petrol station, going down Holly Hill, past the prefabs that were put up after the war, then the phone box outside Jackie Wilshire's house, and the small rank of shops where Mummy sometimes goes to get her cigarettes in Smarts, the newsagents, or some pork chops and chitlings in the butchers. I don't like the butcher much, he's always making rude jokes with Mummy and winking, and looking like he wants to kiss her.

Once I get past the shops I run up to the top of the tump then all the way down again. I like doing that, and

I would have done it again, but then I remember that Mummy isn't going to be home and I don't feel like it any more. I skip on down the hill being brave and feeling very different from all the children swarming down the hill too. Their mothers will be waiting when they get home. They're lucky, but I bet they don't feel like a heroine in a book, the way I do, because I have to be grown-up now and take care of Dad and Gary. I'll cook their tea, make their beds, scrub the floors, chop wood, darn socks and vacuum up after them, because they always make a terrible mess, and wear my fingers to the bone, and what thanks will I get?

I asked Sophie once, 'Do you ever feel different to everyone else?'

'In what way?' she'd answered.

I didn't know how to put it into words so I just shrugged and didn't ask again.

The cul-de-sac we live in is called Greenways. It's a bit like a clock with the hands poking out the wrong way. The face is the green, where the boys play football and the girls do leapfrog. The hand that sticks out from nine o'clock is the way into the street, and our house is almost at the bottom of the hand that pokes off of six o'clock. I'm still skipping as I turn into the street, plaits flying as I bob past Julie and Adam Prentice's house – Adam, who's a year older than me, has iron things on his leg because he had polio when he was little – then I speed past Mr and Mrs Weiner's because he's foreign, and also past the Crofts' house because they're a bad bunch whose garden is scruffy and whose uncle has been in prison. Sally Croft is three years older than me and already smokes and goes out with boys.

'She'll come to a bad end, that girl,' Mummy always says when we see her. 'I don't want you going near her.'

A lot of our neighbours are scared of Mummy because

she's tall and always speaks her mind. They're her friends too, because they're always coming in our house for cups of tea and a fag and a chat about the kids. Most of the houses down our bit of the street have children about the same age as me and Gary, so there's always a lot for the mums to discuss.

Since no-one's in at our house I skip on by, still brave, and go next door to Mrs Williams, who's looking out of the window, holding Gary up in her arms so he can see me coming. I give them a wave and push open the yellow gate to carry on skipping down the front path to the front door. Gary immediately drags me into the living room where he's been playing cars in the cardboard garage that Mr Williams, who looks like the film star Robert Mitchum, made for five-year-old Nigel.

I'm not really interested in his cars, so he says, 'Where's Mummy?'

'I don't know,' I tell him.

He looks at me with his big blue eyes and I think he's going to cry.

'Daddy'll be home soon,' Mrs Williams tells him. We like Mrs Williams. She's Mum's best friend, they even went to school together, and when I grow up I'm going to talk over the fence to my best-friend neighbour while hanging washing on the line, the way Mrs Williams and Mummy do.

Gary looks up at her. He's got freckles too, huge great big ones like cornflakes, and crew-cut hair the same colour. Everyone loves him, Mummy especially. I know he's her favourite, but I don't mind – he's my favourite too, when he's not getting on my nerves.

Mrs Williams gives me a glass of milk and a strawberry-jam sandwich which I take to the kitchen table to eat, while watching her wipe the dishes, making everything shine and clink as she puts them away. When

I'm old enough I'm going to marry Geoffrey Williams, who's the same age as me, but in a different class at school, and who always dawdles home. We'll go courting, like my older cousins do, and I'll take a long umbrella with a crook handle to the pictures when it rains.

When Geoffrey comes in his mother tells him off for not even saying hello to me which I mind about quite a lot, but don't say anything. Gary and I watch as he shouts back at her, and stomps off upstairs. If we ever spoke to our mum like that we'd be put in a home, or get the hiding of our lives. Mrs Williams looks upset. She stoops down to give Gary a hug and tickles my face with the end of one plait.

After that we do a jigsaw, but Gary gets it all wrong, because he's too young and his fingers are clumsy. He tries to look important though, by resting his chin in his hands and waggling his feet, the way I do, when I'm studying where to put the next piece.

'Daddy's here,' Mrs Williams eventually calls out from the kitchen. By then Gary and I are huddled in one of the armchairs watching *Blue Peter* on the telly, which he doesn't understand, and I don't like. I'm feeling grumpy now because Daddy's taken longer to come home than I expected, and Geoffrey's still upstairs in his bedroom, avoiding me.

Gary springs up and charges outside.

'Aren't you going too?' Mrs Williams asks me.

'I want to see the end of this,' I tell her.

I stay where I am, feeling angry with Daddy. Mrs Williams goes outside to talk to him over the fence, then Geoffrey comes down and sneers at the puzzle that I didn't manage to finish.

'This piece goes there,' he snottily informs me, pressing it into place.

'No it doesn't!' I cry.

'Yes it does. Look!'

I leap to my feet. 'It's a stupid puzzle anyway,' I shout.

'It's you who's stupid,' he calls after me.

'You won't say that after I've smashed your head in.'

'You and whose army?'

Anyway, I'm going to marry a smuggler when I grow up.

Later on, I'm standing in the doorway of our dining room watching Daddy giving Gary a cuddle. They're in one of the big brown armchairs either side of the fireplace, but it's not cold enough for the fire to be lit. Gary, like the baby he is, is crying for Mummy, but I'm still being brave. Anyway, I don't care that Mummy's not coming home, because I don't care about anything. I just stand and watch and think how stupid everyone is.

Daddy's face is handsome and pale and his hair is fair. His blue eyes always twinkle, and crinkle at the corners when he laughs. He's not quite as tall as Mummy, and he doesn't have a bad temper either, but it's still frightening when Mummy threatens to tell him if I've been naughty. I don't think he's ever smacked me though, not like Mummy, whose hand really stings my legs when she lets go. I don't like Mummy tonight. I don't like her at all.

'Want a cuddle too?' Daddy offers, holding out a hand to invite me onto his other knee.

I want to, but I shake my head and say, 'No. I've got to go and give Mandy and Bonnie their supper.' Mandy and Bonnie are my two favourite dolls, along with Teddy who I've had since I was a baby.

My bedroom is the prettiest of anyone's in the street. It has a pink padded headboard with flowers all over it, and the curtains round the dressing table match those at the window and the seat of the stool. I've got quite a big wardrobe for all my clothes, a fold-up doll's push-chair and cot, and a bright orange record player that I have to wind up. It doesn't play grown-up records like the one downstairs, only the nursery-rhyme children's kind, but that's all right, Mandy and Bonnie prefer them anyway.

My Bonnie lies over the ocean,
My Bonnie lies over the sea,
My Bonnie lies over the ocean,
Oh bring back my Bonnie to me.

I stand watching the record go round and round, then suddenly I snatch the needle off. I don't want to listen to it any more. Not that one, so I put 'Bobby Shaftoe' on instead. Daddy sings that song sometimes, or 'Row, Row, Row the Boat', or silly songs that he makes up the words to. Because he's Welsh he's got a lovely voice. Not like Mummy and me, but I still want to be in the school choir one day. I'm quite good at ballet though, and I'm learning to play the piano. Daddy's probably going to call me downstairs soon to come and practise my scales. He might have forgotten though, and I won't remind him, even though it'll make Mummy cross if she finds out, because she's always saying that I have to practise every day – and ballet too.

Three weeks ago I started going to elocution classes. They're really embarrassing. The teacher talks all posh, and I feel really stupid saying things like *How now brown cow* the way the Queen does. Last week I saw Mummy, out of the corner of my eye, trying not to laugh, and in the end we had to leave because we couldn't stop laughing.

But that wouldn't be the end of it, Mummy warned me as we ran home through the rain. 'You're going to learn to talk proper, my girl, and make a real lady out of yourself.'

There was some talk, a while ago, about me going to a school over by the Downs, which is the *really* posh part of Bristol, where everyone lives in big houses and has servants, and all the snooty kids wear silly uniforms and ride horses at weekends. I hate horses and I'd rather die than go to one of those schools because I'd miss all my friends and get teased even more, which I told Mummy, furiously, stamping my feet and clenching my fists. I got sent straight to my room, and wasn't allowed to come out again until I could mind my manners. Fortunately no more's been said about it since, so I think she listened to me.

Taking off my glasses, which isn't allowed, I put my nurse's uniform on over my dress, then I hook the heart-beat listener around my neck to check on Mandy, who's been a bit off colour lately. She's lying on the bed with Bonnie and Teddy, propped up by a cushion. I'm probably a bit old for Teddy now, but I let him sleep with us still because I know what it's like to be afraid in the night. When I get like that I usually creep in with Mummy and Daddy, so it's only right that Teddy has someone to make him feel better too.

Mandy is still looking peaky. 'You've got to get better,' I tell her crossly. 'I don't want you always being ill.'

'Bobby Shaftoe' finishes so I go to wind up the record player again. When it's ready I decide I don't want to be here any more, so I tear off my nurse's uniform and run down the stairs, shouting to Daddy, 'Can I go out to play?'

'Five minutes,' he calls back. His head pops round the kitchen door. 'Don't I get a kiss?'

I want to say no, but it might hurt his feelings, so I

go and kiss him, then skip back down the passage to the front door.

'Beans on toast for tea,' he calls after me.

'Yeah!' Gary cheers.

I stop and turn round. 'It's Wednesday,' I remind Daddy. 'We have corned-beef mash on Wednesdays.'

He puts down the knife he's holding and comes to lift me up in his arms. I don't want to let him, but I don't stop him either. 'How was school today?' he says, rubbing his stubbly chin over my face.

I want to ask when Mummy's coming home, but that might not be brave, so instead I put my head on his shoulder and my arms round his neck. 'It was all right,' I say.

He gives me a squeeze and kisses the top of my head. 'It won't be long,' he tells me.

My head comes up. 'Tomorrow?' I say eagerly.

He laughs. 'I hope before that.'

I'm just starting to get excited when I realise he's talking about tea, not Mummy, so I wriggle down and go off outside to play.

Chapter Two

Eddress

This is me taking me wedding vows to Eddie, back in '53, at the ripe old age of twenty-one. 'I, Eddress Betty Price, do take thee, Edward William Lewis, to have and to hold from this day forward, for better or for worse, for richer for poorer, in sickness and in health, to love, cherish and to obey, till death us do part . . .'

Eddie and Ed get wed, our Gord joked at the time. He's the brother who gave me away. Our dad couldn't do it, because he went and died back in '47. Deaf as a coot, he was, so he never spoke much. Just sat in the corner of the kitchen reading his paper, or pottered about his allotment where he grew the flowers he sent us kids out round doors selling on Wednesdays to make a few extra bob to tide us over till he got paid on Thursday. He was a clean man, always took his bath in front of the fire on Fridays, and had a good wash and shave every morning before he went off to work on the buildings. His funeral shouldn't have been anything to laugh at, but it was, on account of just about everything going wrong, from the horse bolting off with the coffin on the way to the church, to trying to drop the bloody thing in the wrong hole. Even our mam was splitting her sides in the end, and none of us have ever had the nerve to show our faces in the church since – till the day Eddie and I got wed.

15

I'm no beauty, but I was a radiant bride, they said, surrounded by me brothers (we might have been less of a spectacle if three of 'em hadn't been in plaster casts thanks to a fight they got into on Eddie's stag night. Thank God Eddie was already passed out drunk by then. He never could take his drink, but his mam had told me he was a champion fighter as a boy, working down the mines, so if he'd been conscious who knows what part of him might have been strapped up for the big day). As it was, he had on a smart black pinstriped suit, a red tie and starched white shirt. Very handsome, even if he is an inch and a half shorter than me. And I had on a beautiful white lace dress, with a long white veil and the biggest bouquet of flowers any of us had ever seen. Cost our mam a fortune, it all did, but she was as proud as Punch when our picture was in the local paper after, saying how much I resembled our lovely young Queen when she'd got married, the same year as our dad popped his clogs.

It has to be said Eddie was a bit out of his league with our family. There's a lot more of us, you see, and our edges are a lot rougher than his. Not that his family's any better, mind, it's just Eddie himself who's different. He's, how can I put it? more gentlemanly than most. He hardly ever swears, or shouts. He don't get drunk on Fridays and then throw up after being chucked out of the pub. He's not all that keen on drink really. He prefers politics and poetry, and bleeding philosophy, I'll have you know. And he loves to draw, which delights the kids no end, and being Welsh – though he don't have much of an accent – he can sing. The best thing about him though is that he worships the ground I walk on, even though I'm bossy, loud, not interested in hardly anything that interests him, and, well, if the truth be told, a bit common I suppose, though you better never let me catch anyone else saying that, or they'll be more than sorry. No, he really thinks I'm the bee's knees. Course I've got a lot of feelings for him too, I just don't go round talking about it all the time, never could abide all that lovey-dovey stuff. He drives me mad though, I can tell you that, with his head always stuck in some book, and the way he blathers on about Marx or bleeding Lenin. He's a bit of a Commie, you see, which is all right I suppose, just as long as it don't stop him bringing home a wage at the end of the week.

You could say he's a bit of an old brainbox in his way, but he's a good laugh when we go out with my brothers and their wives on a Saturday night. He's a good dancer too, and he never carries on about me going to bingo with our mam whenever I want. He works as a cutter-grinder at an engineering factory in Fishponds, where he earns about fourteen guineas a week before overtime, and he goes up Soundwell Technical College every Tuesday night where he's studying to become a draughtsman.

My first job after leaving school was down the pottery, but after a couple of years I went out the British Aircraft Corporation, which was where me and Eddie met, because he was working there then. Since we had our Susan I haven't worked, and now we've got Gary too, a nice three-bedroomed semi-detached council house in a cul-de-sac right on the edge of Kingswood, which is in Bristol, and a garden big enough for the kids to play cricket at the front, and for Eddie to grow vegetables at the back. Eddie's proper soft on those kids, he is, lets them get away with blue murder, so it's left to me to stop them running riot. They're not bad though, except I reckon our Susan would be a bit of a handful if I allowed it. Has a mind of her own, does that one. She's like me, I suppose, strong-willed, outspoken and doesn't

17

always think before she speaks. Her teachers tell me she's doing well at school though – Eddie and I always keep a check – and she's already won two awards for ballet. I don't think she likes the piano much, but she'll thank me later if I make her keep it up. As for the elocution lessons, well, she'll thank me for those too, one of these days, if we can stop laughing long enough for her to make some progress. Eddie has to take her now, because I can't keep a straight face with all that how-now-brown-cowing, nor can he, half the time, but he's better at covering it up than I am.

As for Gary, he's the apple of my eye. I always wanted a boy, and now I've got one. He's going to grow up to be just like his dad. He might even be a writer. Eddie would like that, as he wants to be a writer himself. He's had a couple of things turned down by a publisher though, which hasn't done his confidence much good. I tell him to keep at it, because not everyone makes it straight away, and I like reading what he writes. It makes me feel proud of him. No-one else I know has got a husband who can write – half the silly buggers can't even read!

He hasn't written much lately, which I have to admit I'm relieved about, because I haven't much been in the mood to read it. I've got a lot on me mind, you see, what with our mam's legs playing her up so she can't get around as well as she used to, and now this business with me. I wish I'd never watched that bloody documentary, because that's where it all started. Right as rain I was, then they go and put something like that on the telly, telling us all to check ourselves for lumps and things, and this is where I end up – in bloody hospital having an operation. They shouldn't be allowed to put that sort of rubbish on telly, should they, it just frightens people. Why can't they just leave well alone? I've got two children at home who need me, so I shouldn't be wasting my time hanging round here having things done to me that would never have had to be done if I hadn't watched that bleeding programme. That lump had been there for ages, not causing any harm, and I swear if I hadn't said anything, it would have gone away on its own. Bit bloody late for that now though, innit? Bit bloody late indeed.

I've just left the ward, on me own two feet (the rest of them in there look like they'll be going out in a box), and now I'm walking down the hospital corridor with Eddie on our way out to the car. He's smiling at everyone as we pass, because he's that sort of bloke, but I'm ignoring them, because I don't feel like being nice to anyone. I know that's not very noble and brave of me, but you try having your bosom cut off and see how you bloody feel. I didn't even say cheerio to the nurse who offered us a wheelchair. I felt like telling her what to do with the bloody thing. I mean, what the hell do I need a wheelchair for – it wasn't my sodding leg they amputated, was it? Oh no, it was my right bosom along with all the other things around that part of me body, so I've got no more need of a wheelchair than I have for a brassiere with two cups now. Silly cow.

Honest to God, you'd never believe it was May. We walk out the door and nearly get blowed straight off our feet. It's like bloody winter. Low grey skies, drizzle in the air and a wind to slice the skin right off your bones. Good job Eddie thought to bring my big coat. It's just draped round me shoulders because I can't get my right arm in, but it's better than nowt.

'It's bloody cold,' I grumble, as he opens the passenger door of our old Morris for me to get in.

'It's supposed to brighten up tomorrow,' he assures me.

I don't really care about the cold, I'm just glad to be going home. First though, I have to get in the car, and after me operation it's not very easy to move. Me legs are all right, it's me arm and that. I can see Eddie's not sure how to help me, and I'm not sure how he can either, so I just plonk me bum down then bring me legs in one after the other. It annoys me that he didn't help, even though I know he couldn't.

He gets in the driver's seat, turns the ignition key then pushes the starter. The engine coughs like our mam's dirty old lodger, then catches.

'That's a bloody relief,' I comment, knowing Eddie was afraid too that it would let us down, because nine times out of ten it does.

'Shouldn't take long to get home,' he says, steering us out of the car park onto the main road. The little orange arm flicks out after a while for us to turn right. Susan's always tickled by those arms. I'm not sure why, but her laughing makes the rest of us laugh too.

'So,' I say, as we chug along towards Old Market, 'what did Michaels have to say for himself?' I don't talk to the doctor meself, you see. All that medical malarkey gets on my nerves, especially when I don't understand what the bloody hell he's talking about half the time.

'He says,' Eddie replies, giving a quick glance over as I unclip the top of my handbag to take out me fags and matches (Embassy tipped, if you're interested, and Swan Vestas), 'that you have to give up smoking.'

'Then he can just sod off, can't he?' I say, lighting up. 'Want one?'

'I've given up.'

Annoyed, I turn to look at him. 'What for?'

'I thought it might help you to.'

'I don't need any help. I can give up any time I like, thank you very much,' and taking a drag, I pull out the

20

little drawer ashtray. 'So what else did he say?' I prompt, a few minutes later. I don't really want to know, but I suppose I have to ask. I mean they don't cut off someone's bosom then have nothing to say about it, do they?

Eddie carries on looking at the road, but I can see his hands on the wheel and they're clutching it a bit too tight. I wonder how he's feeling about me only having one now. Is he dreading seeing it? Well, he's not the only one, and anyway, he doesn't bloody have to, because no-one's going to force him.

'You have to go back for a check-up next week,' he tells me. 'They'll provide transport.'

I know exactly what that means, and I'm having none of it. 'If they think I'm getting in that bleeding cripple wagon then they can bloody think again. I'll get the bus. Our mam'll come with me.'

He goes on driving, not saying anything, which makes me even madder, because he always does that, goes quiet on me when I need to have a bloody good row. I suppose he thinks I'm scared, or something, but it's not that. I just don't want all the neighbours seeing me being carted off in an ambulance that comes round every week to take the old codgers in for their check-ups. I'm thirty-one, for God's sake. I don't want to be lumped in with the gerries. I just want to stay at home and have everything the way it was before.

'How're the kids?' I ask, looking out the window. We're going through Old Market now, so we're quite close to where all the blackies live in St Pauls. You can't go there any more, it's too dangerous, but we've got no reason to anyway. They live in their part, we live in ours, and that's how we all like it. Don't want them coming moving in on us, lowering the tone of the place. Ha! You should try saying something like that to Eddie. Goes berserk he does, because wouldn't you just know it, being Eddie he likes the wogs, even goes out of his way to try and get to know 'em. Got no time for 'em meself, all those drugs and killing each other, but I have to admit the nurse who did nights while I was in hospital was all right. Bloody great fat thing she was, but talk about cheerful. Nothing could get her down, and let me tell you, some of those miserable old gits had a bloody good go. The things they said to her, called her every bloody name you could think of, but she just kept right on smiling. Had to admire her really, because if it was me I'd have turned off their bloody life-support and let 'em croak.

Where was I? Oh yeah, I want to know how the kids are. (And I don't mind blacks really, always put some money in the collections for Africa.) 'Did you tell them I was coming home today?' I ask Eddie.

'Gary knows. Betty's got him next door. I didn't tell Susan just in case . . .'

'In case of what?' I want to know. 'In case I didn't come out? Is that what you were going to say?'

'I didn't want her to be disappointed.'

'Well, she won't be, will she? But I suppose you are. Thought you got rid of me, didn't you? Thought I'd go in that hospital and never come out again.'

'Don't be daft. I knew you'd come out, but when I rang up last night they still weren't sure if they were going to let you go today. I only knew after Susan had already gone to school this morning. She's auditioning for the choir today.'

'Oh God.' Disaster's looming. 'She'll never get in and it'll be tears all over again.'

'She likes to try.'

'What about her piano and ballet practice? You've made her keep it up, I hope.'

He nods.

I finish me fag, grind it out in the ashtray and have

a bit of a struggle to stop meself lighting another. It'll only upset him, and I'm doing a good enough job of that already. I steal a quick look over, and now I've got a bloody great lump in me throat instead of in me right bosom. I turn and glare out the window. Bloody sodding hell. Why did it have to happen to me? What have I ever done to anyone to deserve getting cut up like this?

I remember that the doctor gave Eddie something in a bag, just before we left, so I ask what it was.

'Clean dressings for the nurse when she comes,' he says. 'She'll be in every day.'

'Well it better not be that Cissy bleeding Weiner, is all I can say, because if it is, she can just bugger off.'

'She means well.'

Just like him to be nice about everyone, and I'm right in the mood to argue some more, but I'm afraid my temper might burst the stitches, so I just stare down at my hands, where they're resting on the top of my handbag, and wish I could stop meself wanting another fag and being so horrible to Eddie.

We don't talk again until we're almost home, which is when he chooses to tell me that I might have to have some radium treatment.

My heart turns over in me chest. 'What does that mean?' I say.

'The doctor explained it the other day. Don't you remember?'

I do, but I don't want to. 'I'm not having all that messing about,' I tell him.

'They have to be sure they got it all.'

'They got a whole bloody bosom and half my sodding armpit,' I remind him stroppily. 'How much more do they want?' I take out another cigarette and light it. 'I wonder how many nosy old cows are staring out from behind their curtains,' I snap as we drive into our street.

'They've all been really good with the kids,' he says, and I want to punch him. Can't he say anything bad about anyone for once in his life? 'They're concerned about you.'

It's on the tip of me tongue to tell him where to stick their concern, but I manage to rein it in. I wouldn't mind asking why it couldn't have been one of them, instead of me who had to go through this, but you can't say things like that out loud, or people'll think you mean them, which I do, if the truth be told.

We pull up outside our gate, and Eddie's hardly opened the door when my boy comes bounding across next door's lawn, yelling, 'Mummy! Mummy!'

His lovely freckled face is all flushed with joy, and I think I'm going to cry again, because I love him so much. But I manage to laugh instead, as he whizzes straight past his father to come round to my side of the car. Eddie's right behind him, sweeping him off his feet, before he tears open the door and dives in on me.

I get carefully out of the car. 'How's my best boy?' I say, pinching his cheek. 'Have you been good while I've been gone?'

He looks at Eddie, who nods.

'What's that?' Gary asks, pointing at my sling.

'I hurt my arm,' I say. 'But it'll get better.'

Eddie puts him down at the gate and he reaches for my hand to walk up the path. 'I made a Lego garage,' he tells me. 'We put all my cars in there, didn't we Dad? And Aunty Phil gave me a fire engine.'

He continues chattering away as we go round to the back door, which is at the side of the house, and into the kitchen. It's my pride and joy, this kitchen, with our big gas stove that has auto-light burners and a compartment for warming plates next to the oven. There's sliding cabinet doors under the sink that Eddie put in where I keep me white tin bucket and bowl, along with all the cleaning stuff, shoe polish and washboard, and our lovely big pantry with stone shelves to make sure everything stays nice and fresh. We were the first in the street to have venetian blinds at our kitchen window, and we've got a fridge too, that's taken the place of the Flatley, over in the corner between the living room and passage doors. We were also the first to have a fully fitted carpet going all the way down the passage and up over the stairs to the bathroom door. Dark green with black and white swirls. Proud as Punch of it I am.

I have to be honest, I'm not feeling all that proud at the moment. I know Eddie's done his best, but he just doesn't have the knack of keeping the place spick and span the way I like it. There's a dishcloth still on the draining board, a tea towel hanging out of a drawer, breadcrumbs on one of the worktops and the floor could do with a damned good scrub. I wonder if he's been able to keep on top of the washing. He's promised me a new washing machine, because now me arm's like this I won't be able to manage all that scrubbing on the washboard, never mind turning the mangle.

'So how's about a nice cup of tea?' Eddie says, sticking the kettle under the tap.

'Can I have a jam tart?' Gary asks him.

'You know where they are.'

I watch my boy go into the pantry and feel strange that I haven't been consulted. It's always me the kids ask when they want something. Seems it hasn't taken them long to get used to asking their father.

Eddie's lighting the gas under the kettle. 'You're not looking bad,' he tells me.

'My hair needs a wash. I'll have to get our mam down here to give me a hand.'

'I can do it.'

I don't meet his eyes. 'We'll see,' I mumble. 'Now Gary

25

Lewis, I hope your toys aren't all over the floor in the dining room. If they are, you've got until I come back down again to put them all away.'

'Will you count?' he cries. 'See how long it takes me?'

'All right,' I laugh. 'Off you go. One. Two. Three . . .'

As I go upstairs I get this funny feeling that our Susan's not very happy with me. It's strange that, innit, with mothers and daughters? You seem to know what the other's thinking, even when they're not there.

Susan

I've just walked round the corner and there's Daddy's car parked outside our house. At first I feel excited, because I always like it when he comes home early, but now I'm not very sure. My friends Janet and Sarah, who live opposite, are with me. We're talking about French skipping, and whether or not it's one of the games in the Olympics, because if it is, we could stand a chance of being world champions. We'd have to use knicker elastic though, because the rubber bands we tie together always pinch our legs. I'm good at ordinary skipping too. I can even do a hundred doubles straight off.

'Will your mum let you come out when you get home?' Janet asks me.

'My mum's not there,' I remind her. 'My dad's home though, and he always lets me come out.'

'See you in a minute then,' they say, and linking arms they skip across the road to their own houses.

I want to run down the street to ours, but I just walk. Granny should be there, I remember. I try to spot her face at the window, but there's no sign of her. I wonder if Daddy's round the back, digging the garden. He should be at work. I wish he was, because it's not right for him to be home.

A horrible thought is in my head, that Mummy might have other children somewhere who she's gone to live with. I think she's only pretending to go to the hospital, and when we're not looking she goes to be with another family. It would make Daddy really sad if she went and I don't want Daddy to be sad. I want her to come home and be with us. All of a sudden I start running. I didn't really think about it, I just started. I go down the street, in through the gate, across the lawn – which isn't allowed in case we run a groove in it – and round to the back door. If Daddy's sad I have to make him feel better.

'Dad! Dad!' I shout, bursting into the kitchen.

'In here,' he shouts back.

I run to the living-room door, panting and scared. Then I stop dead, because I don't really understand. Mummy's there, and she's smiling.

'Look who it is,' she says. 'How's my girl?'

I just stare at her.

'Cat got your tongue?' she teases.

She's got bandages over her arm and her face is all white. I wonder if the bandages are just pretend.

'How was school?' she asks.

I go to lean against the arm of Daddy's chair and feel his hand on my head as I hook one leg up behind me and begin twisting from side to side. I feel funny, because I'm glad Mummy's here, but not glad too. We'd been managing all right without her and now I want to shout at her for going away and leaving us alone. It's not fair, she shouldn't do things like that.

'Still peering out over the top of those glasses I see,' she says.

'I can't see otherwise,' I reply crossly. 'Anyway I hate them and I don't want to wear them any more.'

'She's got an appointment at the optician's next week,' Daddy tells her. 'A card came.'

'And they're saying Gary might have to have an operation on his lazy eye,' Mummy adds. 'So maybe one of these days we'll all be seeing straight in this house.'

I don't really want to laugh, so I duck my head to hide it.

'How did you get on with the choir?' Daddy asks.

My lips start to wobble as I remember. 'They won't let me in,' I whisper.

'Come here, you daft old thing,' Mummy says and holds out one arm for me to go to her.

I'm about to, but then Daddy sits forward. 'Are you sure, Ed?' he says.

'Course I am. I need to have a cuddle with my big girl, don't I?'

I look at her bandages, and feel scared. What if she's really hurt and I make it worse? 'I've got to go and see to Mandy,' I tell them, and spinning round I run out of the room.

On my way down the passage I get a thump from Gary for knocking over his bricks, so I thump him back, really hard so he cries, and run up the stairs to my bedroom. Mandy's where she always is, lying on the bed with Teddy and Bonnie. She's got her pyjamas on because she's still not very well. I grab her and throw her across the room.

'You're just pretending,' I rage. 'You're not really ill.'

I plonk down on the edge of the bed, and start banging my heels against it. I never want to sing again. Who cares about the stupid choir anyway? They're all just dumb and horrible and Lucy West is a much worse singer than anyone else in the whole wide world, so I'm not going to cry just because of them.

Someone's knocking on my door.

'Can I come in?' Mummy says, putting her head round.

I shrug. I'm not really looking, but I can tell she's not walking the way she normally does and it makes me angry with her. I don't say anything though, because I don't want to hurt her feelings, or do anything to make her go away again.

'What's Mandy doing over here?' she says, going to pick her up from the corner.

'She was naughty. She tells lies.'

She sits down on the bed next to me and puts Mandy on her lap. She doesn't say anything, but I think she's going to tell me off for hitting Gary. We can hear the children next door out playing on their swings and see-saw. I wish I was out there with them, except if I stay here Mummy might stay too. It sounds like Daddy's mowing the back lawn now, which means we can roll around in the pile of cut grass after.

I look up at Mummy.

She looks down at me.

I can see by her eyes that she isn't cross about Gary, so I duck my head and bury my face in her.

'That's better,' she murmurs, putting her arm around me. 'It's all going to be all right, don't you worry.'

She smells of medicine things and cigarettes, instead of Parma violets and cigarettes, the way she usually does, but I don't really care how she smells, I just want her to stay here now and never go away to her other family again.

'Sssh, ssh,' she whispers, stroking my hair as I cry. 'We'll get that choir sorted out. We'll show them what a good singer you are.'

I look up at her face, which is round and freckled. She's got big brown eyes and a big red mouth – except today it's not very red. She kisses me on the forehead, and says, 'Shall we sing the walls? Just you and me?'

I nod and sniff. We always used to do that when I was a baby, but I don't mind doing it again now, so we lie down, side by side on my bed, and sing the nursery rhymes on the wallpaper. 'Baa Baa Black Sheep'; 'Mary Mary Quite Contrary'; 'Mary Had a Little Lamb'; 'Three Blind Mice'.

We're quiet for a while after, just lying there, until Daddy comes in.

'Was that two angels I heard singing just now?' he says.

I giggle.

'He's cheeky, isn't he?' Mummy jokes.

'You've got a couple of friends at the door,' Daddy tells me. 'They want to know if you're going out to play.'

'Can I?' I ask Mummy.

She nods.

'I've cleared the stage out the back,' Daddy informs me as I get up, 'so you can use it again now.'

I'm immediately excited, because the stage is where we rehearse our pop band, the Orange Crystals. 'Is it Janet and Sarah at the door?' I ask. They're the other two Crystals.

'It is.'

'You see,' Mummy says, 'you're going to be a famous pop singer, so who cares about the silly school choir?'

'Not me! They sing all dumb songs anyway.'

I get all the way down to the kitchen before I remember my tambourine, so I dash back up again, taking some of the stairs two at a time. Mummy's still lying down when I go back in my bedroom, and now Daddy's lying down with her. Her face is turned into his shoulder so I can't see her, but I think she's crying.

'Ssh,' Daddy whispers, 'we're listening for the fairies.'

I roll my eyes, because I know there's no such thing

as fairies, except when you leave a tooth under the pillow and they take it in exchange for a sixpence.

'Do you know where my tambourine is?' I say, pulling open a drawer, and starting to feel a bit cross again.

As I find it Mummy says, 'Can I come and watch?'

'Yes,' I squeal, jumping up and down. I can hardly wait to show her how good we are now.

I charge down the stairs ahead of her, wanting to make sure everyone's ready when she gets there. We've got a really good song. I wrote the words, and we all made up the tune. It goes like this:

Janet: You are my lucky guy,
Me: My one and only lucky guy,
Sarah: Lucky guy.

We haven't got any further than that yet, but it'll be really good when it's finished. Gary thinks we're rubbish. So does Geoffrey, next door, who comes to watch over the fence. But we don't care what stupid boys think. We're going to be on *Top of the Pops* one day, and they'll be laughing on the other side of their faces then!

'Tea'll be ready in ten minutes,' Daddy says, coming out to put a tea towel on the washing line 'Egg and chips tonight.'

I look at Mummy, who's been singing along with us, and I feel really happy. It's Thursday, and we always have egg and chips on a Thursday.

Chapter Three

Eddress

Eddie and I seem to be rowing all the bloody time lately. Course, we always used to, because I can't stop meself, it's just in me nature. But it feels a bit different now, and I know it's my fault, I'm so bleeding irritable all the time. I don't want to be mind, but everything about him's getting on my nerves, from his politics to his poetry, to his own special way with the kids. I know I should feel glad he's so good with them, because he's having to do a lot while I'm like this, but I keep getting the feeling he's trying to prove he's a better parent than me. I know he's not really like that, but I've got it stuck in me head that that's what he's doing, and I can't get it out again. I hate meself, honest I do, but I can't help the way I'm feeling, can I?

Anyway, truth is, left to him those two blighters would run wild, and I'm not having anyone say that about my kids. They're the best dressed, politest and cleverest on the street, and if I have anything to do with it, they'll be the best behaved too. I don't care if the other kids are allowed to stay out until it gets dark. I want mine in bed at a decent hour, and I don't want them hanging out of Susan's bedroom window either, moaning to anyone who'll listen about their wicked mother who beats them and starves them, and only ever lets them stay up on Thursdays to watch *Top of the Pops*. (That girl's

32

imagination is going to get her in trouble one of these days, you see if I'm not right.)

Eddie and I are in the kitchen at the moment, washing up after tea. (I got to take it a bit careful, but I have to do something.) He's just informed me that he's told Susan she can stay out playing for ten more minutes, when she knows very well she should be in by now. I can see her out there, bouncing up and down the hopscotch they've chalked on the pavement, ponytail bobbing, cardigan slipping off her shoulders, socks bagging round her ankles, making her look a right little scruff. She hasn't got her glasses on either. She's becoming too sneaky by half, that girl, getting round her father while I'm giving Gary a bath, creeping out and leaving her glasses behind. My boy's a bloody joy in comparison to her! I only wish she had his easy-going nature, though I have to admit, it's a blessing she's not as loud. Typical boy, he is, hurtling fearlessly through life at top speed and full volume, always on the go, morning to night. He's in bed now, still not asleep. I left him playing Thunderbirds in the dark with his hands. I stood on the landing listening to him just now, trying not to laugh, and fighting the urge to go back in there and squeeze him till he squealed. Susan used to be more like him, but lately I've noticed how much more like her father she's getting – moody and defensive, and seeming to look at me with eyes that see too much.

Eddie breaks the silence. 'Ten minutes isn't going to hurt her, Ed,' he says. 'They were in the middle of a game.'

'She's always in the middle of a game,' I snap. 'Left to her, the games would never end and she'd be out all night.'

'That's a stupid exaggeration.'

My hands tighten on the plate in the water. I want to

break it over his head. It's all right for him to have patience, innit, and to be Mr Nice all the time. He doesn't have to put up with what I'm putting up with, having to go off in a bleeding ambulance tomorrow, watching the neighbours looking out from behind their curtains, feeling all sorry and pleased it's not them. He's off to work like normal, isn't he? His life hasn't changed. He can pick the children up and play their games. He doesn't have to avoid the mirror when he gets undressed at night, or try to scratch a bloody bosom that's not there any more. There's a nasty little trick, innit, reminding you it's gone by making it itch. Well I don't need bloody reminding, thank you very much. I know it's not there any more. I could never make any mistakes about that.

I stack the plate behind the others in the dish rack and reach for another. I start to wash it, but my temper's rising up to a point where I know I'm going to explode.

'Don't you ever call me stupid again,' I shout, and grabbing a towel I storm off to the front door, drying my hands and shaking with rage.

'Susan!' I yell.

She doesn't even look up, just throws her stone into a square.

'*Susan!* Get in here! Now!'

'But Dad said . . .'

'I don't care what your father said, you get in here now and straight to bed.'

Her face floods with colour. I've embarrassed her in front of her friends and she looks so angry I think she's going to cheek me back. She'll be sorry if she does, and she obviously knows it, because she comes stomping down the garden path, pushes in past me and thumps up the stairs.

'It's not fair,' she protests, close to tears. 'Dad said I could stay out. No-one else has to go to bed this early.'

'That's enough of your lip. Now get up to bed.'

When I go back to the kitchen Eddie's finishing the washing-up. He doesn't say anything, and nor do I. I can't even bring myself to look at him, so I go into the dining room and light up. Summer's struggling in at last, so there's no fire in the grate. The windows are open, but I'm still too hot. I'm always too hot, because unless I want everyone to see I've got nothing to fill out the top of me frock, I can never take off me cardy. They've given me a couple of falsies to pad out me brassiere, but they're not the right size and they keep slipping out. Susan found 'em a couple of weeks ago. Eddie caught her marching down the garden path with 'em stuffed up her jumper. He whisked her in again pretty fast, probably hoping I wouldn't see, but I did. Funny, but it made me smile and think of her growing up, sprouting breasts of her own. Then the dark clouds came back and had me praying to God that hers don't take after mine. The thought scares me even more than the dread of it coming back again to me. It was the first time I'd allowed myself even to think it, and that was when I made a deal with God, letting Him know that I would accept it if mine came back, just as long as He spared my girl.

She drives me mad when we have our ups and downs, but until I had her, honest to God, I didn't have any idea how deep the love could be for a child. Nothing matters more than her, except Gary now he's here too. That's what's going to save us from this, you mark my words. My children need me, so I have to be here for them, and I damned well will be.

The radium treatment's going well, the doctor said. The operation was a success, and they're finding out new things all the time. It's going to be all right. I'll be out of the woods before I know it. Eddie believes it, or he says he does. I just wish I could too. I mean, I do, sometimes, but then I get afraid again and I can't sleep, or think, or even talk to anyone without getting all worked up inside. You want to try it, one minute you're laughing your head off at something, the next you remember it all, and it's like the gas has run out in the middle of baking a cake. I suppose it's going to take a lot more than two bob in the meter to get me cooking again though.

I can hear Eddie putting the dishes away. Any minute he'll go upstairs to Susan, dry her eyes and read her a story. She probably hates me now, after I showed her up out in the street. Daddy the hero will make it all right though. Daddy can never do any wrong. She loves him more than she loves me. I heard her telling Gary that. Gary loves me the best, he says. I love them both the same, but in different ways. Our mam says I push them too hard to do well, especially Susan, but I'm determined they're going to make something of themselves. I've got plans for their education that might even take them on to university. They'd be the first in our family to go that far. Eddie wants that for them too, but he doesn't push them enough. He's too soft, lets them get away with too much.

'Cup of tea?' he says, putting his head round the door.

I shrug and grind out my cigarette. 'If you want to make one.'

'The kettle's on. I'll just go and tuck Susan in and make sure Gary's asleep.'

While he's gone I go and empty a new packet of Typhoo into the caddy and stand watching the kettle on the stove. Z Cars'll be on in a minute. I wish Eddie would watch it with me, but he doesn't like telly much. He'd rather sit in the front room and listen to the 78s he buys in the second-hand shop, or read a book, or do his homework. I wonder if we're really meant for each other. We're so different, and now, since all this, we're not even close in that way any more. I just can't get in the mood, and I don't expect he's all that keen to do anything anyway, with me only having one now.

By the time he comes down again I've made the tea and carried the pot into the room. I pour him a cup and pass it over, knowing he doesn't want it really, that he's just drinking it to keep me company.

'Is she all right?' I ask him.

'Yes. She's got her mother's temper, I know that, but she's calmed down now.'

'Yeah, well, just don't ever call me stupid again,' I say. 'We can't all be as brainy as you, and if you hadn't got me dander up she wouldn't have gone off to bed crying.'

'I'm sorry.'

We drink our tea. I look at the telly and think about turning it on.

'What time's the ambulance picking you up tomorrow?' he asks.

Why does he have to go and bring that up now? I want to forget about it for five minutes, except it's always there, innit, in the back of my mind. I got the bus the first time, but can't do it again. It's not so bad going, it's coming back that's the problem, even though I'm only having to go up Cossham to get me treatment, not all the way downtown to the General. That's a blessing, that is, because I hate the General. Never want to go there again in me life. If all this radium they're giving me now works, I won't have to. Takes it out of you though, going up there, having to wait around for hours, then getting prodded and poked about, marked up for X-rays, taking all kinds of tablets, then having to wait for the ambulance to bring me back again. I always make sure it picks me up down by the garages, so no-one will see me getting in or out of the bloody thing.

Betty keeps an eye out for when I come back, making sure I manage it up to the house all right. Bit weak on me legs after I've been through all that, see, and tired right out. She's a good friend, and I know I can rely on her not to gossip. Eddie takes the children to our mam's for tea on those days, so they're out of the way, and don't see me coming in and going to bed. We've told them I've got a part-time cleaning job at the sack factory on Warmley Hill once a week, so that's why Gran makes their tea on Wednesdays. They don't realise when they come home that I'm already in bed. They think it's a night job, and I come in long after they're asleep. It's best that way. They're too young to understand what's really going on. They'd only get confused and afraid, and what's the point in that, when it's all going to be over soon. No more radium, no more cripple wagon, no more secrets. We're all going to be right as rain come the autumn.

I answer Eddie's question about the ambulance time, then we talk about other things for a while: his night school, new shoes for Gary, whether we can afford a holiday this year. Normally we rent a caravan at Chesil Beach for a week, but lately we've been thinking about getting a chalet in Dawlish. We probably won't be able to though, because it's June already, so they'll be all booked up.

'I'll give them a ring tomorrow and find out,' he says. 'If there's one free I think we should take it.'

'Can you get the time off work?'

'I expect so. If I can't, I'll drive you and the kids down on Saturday, spend the weekend, then come and pick you up the following Saturday.'

'We should take our mam too.'

'All right.'

I know it's daft, but instead of telling him I don't really want to go without him, I just sit there lighting up another fag. The thing is, he might not want to come, and sod him if he doesn't. I don't bloody well care. Let him stay here on his own. We can manage without him. It'll be a blessing not to have him in the same bed for a week, I won't have to pretend I'm asleep when I'm not.

'Are you all right?' he asks.

'Course I am. Why?'

'Just thought you seemed a bit . . .'

'A bit what?'

'Nothing. It doesn't matter.'

I could go on arguing, but I don't. I'm tired and getting het up about tomorrow again. I finish me cigarette, light another and stick it in the corner of me mouth while I pick up the jumper I'm knitting for Gary. As I draw the needles out of the ball of wool a small voice comes from the top of the stairs.

'Mum!'

My eyes go to Eddie. 'What do you want?' I shout back.

'Can I come down for a minute?'

'What's happened to the magic word?'

'Please.'

I look at Eddie again. 'Come on then,' I say. 'But just for a minute.'

Moments later the door opens and Susan pads in. She's in her pyjamas, her lovely curly hair cascading down her back, her eyes red from crying.

'What do you want?' I ask her.

Her mouth trembles. 'I'm sorry,' she whispers.

I put me knitting and cigarette down and pat me lap for her to come and sit down. Poor love, she doesn't even really know what she's saying sorry for, and to be honest, nor do I. She's sobbing her little heart out now, so I hold her nice and close to try and make her feel better. After a while I tilt her chin up so I can see her. Her little freckled face is all blotchy and swollen. 'Oh, what a fright,' I tease, pretending to jump.

She looks at me warily.

'Is that my Susan, or is it someone else?' I say.

A smile wobbles on her lips.

'I think it's her, Dad, but I won't know till she laughs.'

A giggle works its way out and I gasp in surprise. 'It is her! It's our Susan.'

She laughs again and rests her head back against me.

'Want something to eat?' I ask. 'A salmon-paste sandwich?'

She nods. 'With the crusts cut off?'

'All right. And a glass of milk. Did you drink your milk in school today?'

'Yes. And I ate all of my apple.'

'Good girl.' I kiss the top of her head. 'Now, off you go up to bed and I'll bring your sandwich.'

'Will you read me a story?'

'I thought you liked Dad to do it?'

'I do. But I like it when you read them too.'

I glance at Eddie. 'Shall we ask Dad if he'll read one to both of us?'

'And me!' Gary cries from the other side of the door.

We all burst out laughing. 'How long have you been out there?' I call. 'Come on. Come in here.'

The door bangs open and in he jumps. 'Can I have a sandwich too?' he says, climbing up on my lap. 'I want the crusts on mine.'

'You're a scallywag,' I tell him. 'You should be asleep by now.'

'But Susan's up.'

'I'm older than you,' she reminds him.

'Enough,' I say, as he pokes out his tongue.

'Bed, both of you,' Eddie says, scooping them up, one under each arm.

They squeal and start wriggling, pretending to escape. Then he lets them ride up the stairs on his back while I light meself another fag, and go to take the bread out of the bread bin. The milk's in the new fridge, which makes me feel proud as Punch, because we've always had the devil of a time trying to keep it from turning. By the time I put the empty bottle on the doorstep with a note tucked in the top for the milkman to leave two pints in the morning, I can hear them up there, squabbling over whose bed they're going to go in for the story. It turns out to be Susan's, I find when I get up there, with her blackboard spread out on their knees as a table.

After the sandwiches and milk, the blackboard's put back on its easel, and a space is made for me, leaving those two nincompoops barely hanging onto the edge of the bed. Eddie perches on the padded stool that matches Susan's rose-patterned dressing table, and once we're all settled, he starts us on the long, magical journey down the rabbit hole.

At the end of the first chapter he quietly puts the book down and carries a sleeping Gary to his own bed, while I tuck Susan in and kneel down next to her. Looking sleepily up at me, she says, 'Goodnight, Mum.'

I kiss her, and settle her arms in under the covers. 'Goodnight, God bless,' I say softly, and after stroking her face I go to turn out the light.

Eddie's on the landing, drawing the curtains. We give each other a bit of a smile, and I wonder what he's thinking. He's a decent man, so it won't be bad thoughts. Even if it were, he'd never let me know. He'll stick by me, I reckon, if only for the kids. Men need a bit of the other though, don't they? But I can't do it. I just can't, not now I'm like this, so I go on into the bathroom to start cleaning up the mess after the kids, while he goes back downstairs to do his homework.

Susan

That slug Kelvin Milton has been whispering to his friends about me since assembly this morning. He's not even trying to hide it, the pig. They keep looking at me and snickering. It's not as though I've got new glasses, or anything, so I don't know what they've got to laugh at. I've poked my tongue out a couple of times, but I got told off when Miss Taylor spotted me. It's not fair, because I'm not the one being naughty. It's them, and they're so dumb that none of them even knew what the capital of France was when Miss Taylor asked. (It's Paris.) My new best friend, Belinda Watts, isn't in today, so I haven't really got anyone on my side, unless you count Frances Clark, but her breath always smells. I might sit next to her in the canteen at dinnertime though, because I know what that Kelvin Milton's like, him and his stupid friends will keep throwing things at me. I'm going to tell Mum about him tonight. She'll sort him out. He'll be scared stiff then, ha ha!

The bell rings so I close up my geography book and tuck it inside my desk. After dinner we're going to do some ink writing with fountain pens. I can do joined-up letters now, all in italic. I wanted to be ink monitor once, but I don't really care now. I'm getting too grown-up to do babyish things like filling up inkwells, so let Caroline Thompson do it. I hope she squirts herself in the eye and goes blind. Last lesson of the day is PE which I can't stand. We have to do it in our vest and knicks, and Kelvin Milton always looks at me and pretends to be sick. Anyway, I don't blame him because I look horrible in black PE daps, big green knicks, white vest and glasses. But I still wish Gary was my older brother so he could come along and bash Kelvin Milton's face in.

School dinners are always disgusting, but you have to eat them or you'll just go hungry. Today we're having roast beef, which is like a torn bit of cornflake box covered in cold, thick gravy, with boiled potatoes, soggy cabbage and carrots. Ugh! I don't even like jam roly-poly which is what we've got for pudding. Frances Clark eats mine. She's quite fat, so she would.

Kelvin Milton and his gang are coming my way, so I keep my head down and hope the dinner lady is watching them. If they're naughty she'll make them stand in a corner, and they won't get any playtime. That would be good because then I can play chase without them trying to trip me up.

'Your mother's a *cripple*,' Kelvin hisses as he gets close.

I get all enraged, even though I don't know why he said that. 'She is *not*,' I hiss back.

'Then why does she go off in the cripple wagon every week?'

'She does not. She's never been in the cripple wagon.' All his friends are sniggering and I want to jab my fork in their faces, leaving rows of gooey holes like Mum does in her pastry.

'Oh yes she has,' he snorts, just like he knows every-thing. 'My Aunty Beryl told my mum. She goes off in it every week with all the other cripples.'

His Aunty Beryl lives in one of the old-age-pensioner bungalows at the bottom of our street. Mummy hates her and so do I. She's nasty to everyone and even beats her dog with a stick. Once Mummy threatened to take a stick to her if she ever saw her hit the dog again, and even Daddy had been angry enough to say he'd report her to the RSPCA. 'Your Aunty Beryl's a witch,' I tell him. 'And she's a liar too.'

'Oh no she's not. And she says your mother's just a big mouth who's got everything she deserves.'

I leap up and punch him so hard in the face that he goes sprawling back across the table behind him.

Everything goes quiet.

I'm all out of breath and dizzy. Then I notice his nose is bleeding. Good. I hope he bleeds to death, because I hate him.

'*Susan Lewis!*' the dinner lady shouts. 'I saw that. You bad girl. You're going straight to the headmaster.'

'But miss, it was him . . .'

'Don't answer me back. You just thumped that boy and now look what a mess he's in. Come here, Kelvin, put your head back. Susan, go and stand outside Mr Dobbs's office. Now!'

'Please miss. I'm really sorry. I wouldn't have done it if he hadn't said . . .'

'Susan, do as you're told.'

'Yeah, go and do as you're told,' Kelvin sneers from behind his bloody hanky.

I'd happily smash him again, but I can't while the dinner lady's watching. Nearly starting to cry I take myself out of the canteen and along the corridor to the headmaster's study. I'm really scared. I've never been in this much trouble before, and if Mum ever finds out I'll get the hiding of my life.

I make myself very small in a dark shadowy corner, across from his door and as far as I can go behind a pillar. If I'm lucky no-one will see me. I used to think if I closed my eyes I became invisible. I wish it was true. I can hear cars and lorries roaring up and down the main road outside, and the sound of all the other children charging round the playground. Sometimes there are footsteps and voices coming from other corridors, but no-one comes to Mr Dobbs's office. I don't think he's in there, because I can't hear anyone. There's the smell of his pipe though. I've never been sent to him before. What if I have to have the cane? I look at all the paintings on the walls around me. Mine have never been good enough to be hung up. I'm rubbish at art. Some of the pictures are quite good, of houses and fish and trees and dogs. There's one of a lady who looks a bit like Cilla Black. *Top of the Pops* is on tonight, but I won't be allowed to stay up, not if Mum finds out about this.

I'm feeling really unhappy now, because I'm going to make her angry and I like it much better when she's proud of me. I wish she didn't have to go to work at the sack factory. It's horrible when she's not at home. It doesn't feel right, and Dad always talks in a whisper on those days. I think he can't speak loud because he's too upset. No-one admits it, but I know she's going to see her other family on those days, really. I wonder if she loves them more than us. I hate her if she does. I wouldn't care if she went off in the cripple wagon then. I'd want her to go and never come back.

'Hello, and who do we have here?'

The voice makes me jump, but I know who it is. 'It's me, sir,' I say in a whisper, still keeping in behind the pillar.

'And who is me? Step out so I can see you.'

I take a miserable step into the light.

Mr Dobbs is as tall as a giant, with greased black hair and a floppy double chin. He canes everyone, even the girls, so I know I'm in for it, and it's just not fair.

'It's Susan Lewis, isn't it?' he says.

'Yes, sir.'

'And why are you standing here?'

'Miss Phipps the dinner lady sent me.' I keep my head

down and look at his black shiny shoes. They're so big I can't imagine how his feet fill them up.

'Why did she send you?'

'Because . . .' I don't want to tell him, because I really, really don't want to be caned.

'Come on in,' he says, and pushes open the door.

I think I might run away instead, but I haven't got the courage, so I follow him in and stand in the middle of his dark, musty room that's filled up with books and is bound to be haunted. There's a picture of the Queen behind his desk, which I notice as he sits down. She looks nice and kind. I wonder if I'm supposed to curtsey.

'So what have you been up to?' he says, folding his hands together. His mouth is small, and his moustache is a bit like Hitler's.

'I – I hit Kelvin Milton,' I tell him. My fingers are crossed and inside I'm saying, *Please God, don't let him cane me. Please, please, please. I'll go to bed early without making a fuss. I'll be nice to Gary. I'll even do the washing-up after tea.*

He opens his top drawer and I know the cane's coming out. I start to sob. 'No, please don't give me the cane,' I cry. 'I'm really sorry. I'll never do it again.'

His eyebrows go halfway up his forehead. 'Why did you hit him?' he asks.

'He said my mum goes in the cripple wagon, but she doesn't. He's a liar. He said nasty things about her, and he shouldn't do that about other people's mums. I don't ever say anything about his.'

'What is a cripple wagon?' he asks.

'It's an ambulance what comes round for the old people.'

'That,' he corrects. 'That comes round.'

'Sorry. That comes round.'

'Does your mother get the ambulance?'

'No! Kelvin Milton's a liar. He shouldn't say things like that. His tongue'll fall out. He'll grow warts and he won't go to heaven.'

'Maybe I should have a word with your mother.'

'No, sir. Please, don't tell her I've been in trouble. I'll stand in the corner for five weeks. I'll write ten million lines . . .'

His hand comes up so I stop. Just as well, because I can't think of anything else to offer to do. I can't stop crying either. I want my dad.

He gets up and comes round his desk to stand in front of me. He's taller than Big Ben. Not that I've ever seen Big Ben, for real, I've just seen pictures where people standing in front of it look as small as ants. I wish I was an ant, but if I was he might stand on me with his big feet and kill me.

'Here, dry your eyes,' he says, and gives me the hanky from his top pocket. It smells horrible and bits of tobacco fall out, but I do as I'm told.

After he takes his hanky back he picks up a ruler and tells me to hold out my hands. He brings the ruler down really tight over my palms. It stings so hard that I start crying again.

'Go on out to play now,' he says, 'and make sure you don't hit anyone else.'

I leave his office, but I'm so morbidfied and upset that I go to the girls' toilets and shut myself in. I'm all alone in the world. No-one cares about me. I've got no friends and my mum loves her other children more than us. So why should I care if everyone's saying she goes off in the cripple wagon? It's better than them knowing what she's really doing. And anyway, I'm going to tell her that I know the truth, about her other family, and that I think she's wicked for telling lies.

When the time comes though I don't have the courage,

because when I get home she's already looking cross. Gary's done something naughty, so he's upstairs in his bedroom, sulking and banging things around. I try to think of something to make her laugh.

'What did the earwig say when he fell over a cliff?' I ask her.

The hot fat whooshes as she drops in the chips to start cooking. The first time I told her this joke she laughed her head off. So did Dad.

'Go on, what did he say?' she answers.

'Earwiggo,' I shout.

She pulls a face and rolls her eyes. 'Very funny,' she says. 'Now come on, out of the way, before you get burnt.'

I go and stand by the door, torn between staying with her and going out to play with my friends. She hasn't asked how I got on in school today yet, so I should go out before she does, but for some reason I don't seem able to.

'Do you have to go to work tomorrow?' I ask her.

'Yes. Why?'

I don't answer.

She looks round. 'What's the matter with you? What's that face for?'

'Nothing.'

'You don't like me going to work, is that it?'

I shrug. I'm not going to tell her that I know where she's really going, just in case I turn out to be right. I don't want her to tell me, because I won't be able to pretend it's not true. 'How do you manage to work with a bad arm?' I say.

She looks a bit surprised. 'It's not that bad any more,' she reminds me. 'It's getting better all the time.'

'The nurse still comes though.'

'Only to help me change the dressing. And not as often any more.'

48

I shrug again.

Gary shouts angrily from the top of the stairs. 'I'm being good now.'

Mummy looks up at the ceiling, then winks at me as she shouts back, 'Come on down then.'

'I said I'm being good,' he rages.

'And I said you can come down.'

'Oh.'

Mummy and I start to laugh. She holds out her arms, and I go to her, careful not to knock her bad one, that's getting a lot better.

'Ugh! Soppy girls,' Gary snorts, coming into the kitchen. 'Can I have a jam tart?'

'No. And you, madam,' Mum says to me, 'can go and do your piano practice.'

'Oooooh. I hate the piano.'

'Off you go. Fifteen minutes, tea'll be ready by then. I've made some cream and jam horns for afters.'

'Oh yes!' Gary and I cry together. Our mum's the best cook in the world, and this is the first time she's made cream and jam horns since she went to hospital. So she must be getting better. The baker's going to be worried though, because he says she does him out of business when she gets baking. Sometimes, during the school holidays, he comes round in his van in the afternoon with all his custard tarts and jam doughnuts and chocolate eclairs, and no-one wants any because we're already full up on Mum's jam and cream horns.

'Here, Gary, go and put this empty milk bottle on the doorstep,' she says, 'and mind you don't fall. On second thoughts, you'd better do it, Susan.'

'I can do it,' he angrily declares, and shoves me out of the way.

I give him a thump then go off to practise the piano. I'm about halfway through 'The Kookaburra Sits on the

Old Gum Tree', when Dad comes home from work. He starts singing the song as he takes off his greasy over-alls. It sounds a bit silly, because I'm not good enough at playing it, but I like it when he messes about, and so does Mum. Usually. She doesn't join in tonight though, just comes and puts our teas on the table and tells Dad to go and have a quick wash before he sits down.

I'm not sure if she's in a bad mood again, so I decide to have less tomato sauce on my chips than usual to make her pleased with me. 'Can I make a chip sandwich?' I ask.

'Go on then, but make sure you don't get sauce on that cardigan, you've got to wear it again tomorrow.'

'Ah ha,' Dad says, rubbing his hands together as he comes into the room, sounding like a wizard about to do a trick, 'what do we have here?'

'Sausage egg and chips,' Gary tells him, with a sausage bulging in his cheek.

'What have I told you about talking with your mouth full?' Mummy snaps.

Gary merrily goes on eating. Dad sits down and picks up the brown sauce, which he prefers to the tomato sauce. Mum only has salt and vinegar. She likes chip sandwiches too, and the top of the bread for toast.

'So, how did my girl get on in school today?' Daddy asks, tucking into his tea.

I'd forgotten all about it, and now I don't want my chip sandwich any more. 'All right,' I mumble.

'Do anything special?'

'No, not really.' I can feel Mummy looking at me. She pours herself and Dad a cup of tea from the pot, and settles it back on the stand. I knitted the cosy. It took me a long time, because I'm not a very good knitter. I'm a good skipper though.

'We've got jam and cream horns for afters,' Gary informs Dad.

Dad's face lights up. He turns to Mum. 'You've been baking?' he says.

'It's nothing to get excited about,' she answers.

Dad seems to think it is, because he keeps on smiling.

'What happened at school today?' Mum says to me.

Sometimes I think she's a witch, because she always knows everything. 'I'm not telling you,' I say, staring down at my plate.

'No cream and jam horns until you do,' Gary says.

'Shut up, and mind your own business,' I snap at him.

'I'm still waiting for an answer,' Mum says.

I look at Dad, but for once he doesn't seem to be on my side. In the end I admit that I thumped Kelvin Milton.

'Where did you thump him?' Gary wants to know, bouncing up and down in his seat. 'Was it in the face? Smash! Bang! Biff!'

I look at Mum.

'Why did you hit him?' she asks.

'Because he tells lies.'

'What sort of lies?'

'Just lies. He tells them all the time.'

'But what about?'

I really don't want to tell her, but then I realise, if she thinks I was sticking up for her, she might not get too cross. 'He tells lies about you,' I say.

She seems a bit surprised about that. 'What does he say about me?'

I feel miserable again. 'I don't know. I'm not telling you.'

'Susan.'

'*I'm not telling you.*'

She's looking at Dad. If he tells me off too I'm going

to cry, because I don't want to say anything about the cripple wagon. I know it's not true, she doesn't go in it at all. She's better now, but then she might have to tell the real truth about her job in the sack factory, and her other family, and Dad will be all upset. And then there's the ruler, she'll be really cross about that. And then there's Kelvin's Aunty Beryl . . .

'I want to know what that boy's been saying,' Mum demands in an angry voice.

'That's enough now,' Dad tells her. 'Let's just leave it,' and he puts a hand on my head to smooth my hair. 'Get on with your tea,' he says.

We don't say anything again until we've finished eating. For once even Gary is quiet, if you don't count the way he scrapes his knife and fork on the plate, and smacks his chops as he eats. He ends up with tomato sauce all over his face and in his hair, so after we help carry the dishes out, Dad takes him upstairs for a wash, while Mum does the dishes and I do more piano and ballet practice. My friends are all outside playing, because they've got really kind mums who don't make them do things they hate.

Top of the Pops is on soon, but no-one's said anything about it, and though I think of all different ways to ask if we can stay up to watch, I haven't tried any of them yet. But then Mum comes in and puts the telly on. It takes a few minutes to warm up, and by the time the picture's there Dad's brought Gary down in his pyjamas, and Mum's brought in a plate of cream and jam horns for us all. As the programme starts I sit down at the side of her chair where she can't quite see me, so I can peep over the top of my glasses to watch. The Kinks come on first. I don't like them much. Then it's Roy Orbison who's blind, but he can sing anyway. This one's called 'Pretty Woman', and Dad sings along because he knows some of the words. Sometimes we dance to *Top of the Pops*, but tonight we don't, not even when Herman's Hermits come on with our favourite song, 'I'm Into Something Good'. I think we're going to for a minute though, when Mum gets up, but she just goes out to the kitchen. Then Dad goes out too. If Gary wasn't there I'd go to the door and listen, but if I do, he'll come too and give us away. I wish I knew what they were saying though, because I've got a feeling it's something to do with me thumping Kelvin Milton, so if they end up having another row it'll be all my fault.

I don't ever let on that I know about their rows. Mummy would say I was spying, which I suppose I am really, because I sit on the stairs listening when I'm supposed to be in bed. It's horrible, because they shout and say horrible things to each other. I want to do something to make them stop, but I can't let them know I'm there. I say prayers in Sunday school every week, asking God to make them stop. If only Mummy would give up smoking, then Dad wouldn't get on at her so much, but she won't. I don't know why it makes him so angry. It never used to, but it does now. And then there are other things they row about, which I don't really understand, because it doesn't make any sense for Dad to be angry with Mummy for having a bad arm. Maybe he's getting fed up with doing all the washing, and most of the housework. I don't think it's that that makes him mad though, I don't know what it really is. I just hope they don't row tonight, especially not like they did last week, when Mummy slapped Daddy across the face. He didn't hit her back, he just went out for a drive, while Mummy sat in her chair crying and not even watching *Coronation Street* that night. I was really frightened that Daddy might not come back, and I think she was too. I wanted to go and comfort her, but I'd only have got into trouble for being out of bed.

Eddress

'Eddress?'

I'm standing here in the kitchen, wanting to be on my own, but knowing I'd be upset if he hadn't come out to find me. This is my place in the house, our bright yellow kitchen. The window cleaner was here today, flirting, the way he usually does. He got right on my nerves. I just wished he'd shut up and get on with his job.

'Are you all right?' Eddie asks.

I nod, but go on looking out the window, not really seeing what's happening outside.

'Tomorrow's the last one,' Eddie says, perching on the tall stool he made at one of his woodwork classes. 'Then it'll all be over.'

I know he means well, and he could even be right, but he's not the one going through it, is he? He hasn't even come with me for any of the treatments, so he doesn't have a clue what it's like really. It's not his body getting filled up with radiation every Wednesday. It's not him who has to lie under that bloody machine with black marks around his chest and shoulder showing where the radium has to go. It doesn't hurt, but it's radium, for God's sake. It's dangerous. If they get it wrong I could end up as a mushroom cloud. To think, we've even talked about what we should do to protect ourselves from a nuclear war, and here I am getting it fired right at me by a doctor who I swear doesn't know what he's doing. We can't have that argument again though, because it's one I never win, mainly because I

54

don't know what to do instead. Unless I just stop going. I've considered that a lot, but it's a bit late now, when tomorrow's supposed to be the last one. After that, they'll know how successful it's all been, whether they've got rid of it or not. Not the right bosom, of course, they've definitely got rid of that.

'We could all go out on Saturday night,' Eddie says. 'And celebrate.'

'Celebrate what?'

'The fact it's all over.'

'It might not be.'

'It will. You said yourself the doctor's happy with the way it's going. And you're feeling better. Aren't you?'

Yes, I suppose I am. Things seem to be working again. I can move me arm without it hurting too much and I'm not so nervous about rolling over onto my front in the night. I haven't gone as far as picking Gary up yet, he's too heavy now, not a baby any more. I still can't get Susan's hair up into a ponytail either, so she has to have it in plaits all the time. On the whole though, every-thing's improving, providing you don't include things between us, that is. But that's not something anyone wants to talk about, is it? Too private. No-one else's business.

Susan needs a new pair of school shoes. Term's hardly even half over and she's grown out of her others already. Gary'll want some too, now winter's coming on. Where the bloody hell did summer go. Any rate, I've been keeping a bit of cash back each week, so we should be all right for buying his shoes. We can't afford to go out on Saturday night though. I wonder if our mam'll have the kids, so Eddie and I can have some time to ourselves. But he won't want that. The kids are his protection. I don't want him near me, anyway. Not the way I am now. I just want to be how we were. I wish to God none of this had ever happened. I might be past the worst of it, but nothing's ever going to bring my bosom back, is it? That little bleeder's gone for ever, and look what it's taken with it. Everything. We're not who we used to be. None of us. Except Gary I suppose. He's young enough for all this to go over his head. Susan doesn't understand it much either, so she's all right. If she was a bit older I could explain some of it, but she's too young. It's not right to burden children with your problems. If the other kids are saying things at school though . . . I'd like to get my hands on that little bugger Kelvin Milton, I'd make him sorry for upsetting my girl. I can't let her know that it matters though. Kids will be kids, so best to let it all blow over, as though it never happened.

'Thought I'd go to bingo on Saturday with our mam,' I say.

Eddie doesn't answer, but I know I've hurt him by not saying I'll go out with him. But what am I supposed to say? 'It only costs a few bob for bingo,' I remind him. 'We'll need at least a couple of quid if we all go out.'

He could say that we'll make ourselves afford it, but he doesn't. He's happy really for me to go out with our mam. Or relieved. Yes, that's what he is, relieved.

'What about this situation with Susan, at school?' he says.

'What about it?'

'Well, if she's getting into trouble, fighting with the other kids, shouldn't we do something about it?'

'Like what?'

'I don't know. That's what I'm asking.'

'It'll blow over. Kids are always saying things.'

He takes a deep breath and lets it out slowly. I hate it when he does that, because I know he's stopping himself saying what's really on his mind. But I don't want to know what it is, so I don't ask.

'Do you want me to come with you tomorrow?' he asks.

I was about to snap at him again, but then it dawns on me what he just said. I wasn't expecting him to say anything like that, and I'm not sure why he has. 'What for?' I finally say.

'I just thought you might like me to.'

To tell the truth, I would like him to, but we can't afford for him to take the time off work.

'One day won't matter,' he protests when I tell him that. 'I can always do a bit of overtime to make up for it.'

It would mean not having to get the cripple wagon again, which isn't really as bad as I'd feared. The old codgers are all right. Poor sods. We even manage a bit of a sing-song and a laugh now and then. I'd rather go with Eddie though, let everyone in the hospital see I've got a husband who cares. He can talk to the doctor too. He understands things better than I do.

'You don't have to,' I tell him. 'No-one's forcing you.'

'I know. I'm just saying, I'll come if you want me to.'

'Suit yourself. I have to be there at twelve.'

We don't say anything for a while. I'm still standing with my back to him, either staring down into the sink, or out the window where a few kids are playing statues in the street. Sounds like *Top of the Pops* is coming to an end, so our kids'll be out any second. Eddie puts an arm round my shoulder.

'Is it all right if I do this?' he says. 'I'm not hurting you?'

'No,' I say, and after a while I lean my head against him.

'I love you,' he says.

'Oh stop all that nonsense now,' I tell him.

We look at each other. He's got a lovely face. It's kind and serious. His eyes are the same blue as Gary's. He's a bit of a looker when he smiles.

57

He kisses me on the lips. It's nice and makes me want to cry. He won't want to go any further though, so I push him away before he can do it first.

'Come back here,' he says, keeping hold of my hand.

'Oh, go on with you,' I respond, with a laugh, 'you don't fancy me when I'm like this.'

'Who says?'

Just like him to know the right words. 'Then you're mad,' I tell him. 'And the kids'll be out any minute. You don't want them to see us like this.'

'Why not?'

'Because it's not decent. Now come on, let me go.'

He does, and I'm not sure if it's whether he wants to, or because I told him to. I wish he'd tried a bit harder, even though I don't want to do the business really. I wouldn't mind if I never had to do it again, but I expect he would.

We're at the hospital now. I'm keeping me head turned away as the doctor examines me scar, because I don't want to see the mess I'm in. I know it's all red and purple, and still a bit swollen, and there are black marks for the radiographer to show him where to point his lights. The doctor's drawing on some more. The pen tickles a bit, like a feather. I just look at the wall. Eddie's sitting on the edge of his chair, watching everything. This is the first time he's seen the scar as bare as this. I'm glad I don't know what he's thinking. I could easily cry now, but I don't want anyone to know how bad I'm feeling. I could scream, or thump the doctor, or even Eddie. I want to run home to my children. I want us all to be safe and tucked up together, not stuck here, where I'm just a lump of meat they're going to put in a machine in a minute and radiate.

The doctor asks me about the side effects I've been

having. They haven't been too bad, apart from feeling dog-tired after, and sometimes a bit sick. I've had a couple of mouth sores, and some pains under the scar, but I don't tell him about them, or he'll just find something else to do to me, more drugs or injections, and I'm fed up with it now.

'She's had a couple of sores, in her mouth,' Eddie says.

Why doesn't he just shut up? What's the matter with him? I don't know why he trusts these people, when he doesn't even trust the Government. Anyway, they're all out to get us working-class folk. We're guinea pigs for them to experiment on. I bet, if we were rich, I'd still have two bosoms and they'd have got rid of the thing inside me weeks ago.

'That's rubbish,' Eddie retorted, when I'd said that to him on the way here. 'If you'd read something about it, learn what it is and . . .'

'I don't want to know anything about it. It's enough that I've got it, all right?'

'But if you understood it more, you might be able to fight it a bit better.'

'I'm fighting perfectly all right, thank you, so I don't need you to tell me what to do. And as you're not the one having to go through it, you can stop handing out advice and keep your books to yourself.'

'You're a stubborn bugger, sometimes,' he grunted.

'That's right. And that's why it isn't going to get me, because I'm a stubborn bugger who won't let it.'

I mean it when I say that, I am stubborn enough not to let it, and what's the point of reading all those books, when they just end up frightening you even more than you already are. Let the doctors do their job, is what I say, even though I have reservations about that. I know Eddie has too, in his heart of hearts, because as a Communist he's suspicious of most people in authority.

I sometimes wonder if his bloody communism didn't get us into this bleeding mess in the first place. The Government hates Communists, so now they're using the wife of one to carry out their experiments. I haven't actually said that to Eddie yet, but I will if he pushes me. It could all be his fault that I'm being wheeled under the radium machine now, ready to be nucleared.

I look at his face and I want to cry. I love him so much, but I don't know how to tell him. I couldn't do it with other people around, anyway, they'd think I'd gone soft in the head. I think he wishes it was him going through this instead of me. I have to be honest, sometimes I wish it was too, but really, given the choice, I know I wouldn't make him. Would I be as patient with him as he is with me? Course not. I'm just not like that. So it's probably for the best that it's me lying here now, clutching onto his hand for dear life. They make me let go, so I look up at him, then I have to turn away before he can see me eyes filling up with tears. Don't want him to see me crying. Won't do either of us any good.

He has to leave the room while it all happens, and I find out later, as we're driving home in the car, that while I was getting dressed he went in to talk to the doctor.

'He says he's really pleased with the way you're coming on,' he tells me. 'The scar's healing nicely and the treatments definitely seem to be working.'

'Do I have to go again?' I ask.

'Only for a check-up. He'll have the results by then, he said.'

'When's the check-up?'

'The week after next. I'll try to get a couple of hours off again to come with you.'

'Were they all right about you taking time off today?'

'Yeah, once they knew what it was for.'

'You didn't tell them!'

'Of course. I had to. I can't just take time off without a good reason.'

'I don't want people knowing. It's none of their business.'

'There's not going to be anything to know, once you get those results,' he says. 'It'll all be over then. The doctor didn't come right out and say so, but he might just as well have. He was all smiles when I left him. He wouldn't be like that if he wasn't feeling optimistic, would he?'

If I wasn't so tired I could be feeling a bit all smiles meself to hear that, even though I don't want to get my hopes up too much.

For some reason instead of driving us home through Speedwell and New Cheltenham, he goes up through St George and Kingswood. It's the middle of the afternoon, so there could be people around I know. I don't want them to see me asleep in Eddie's car, or all their tongues'll be wagging, him at home in the day, me looking like death in the passenger seat. Bunch of idle gossips they all are. Got nothing better to do than stand around bitching about other people.

Eddie turns to look at me and I give him a wink. I won't complain because he's been really good today. I don't know what I'd do without him.

When we get home he comes round to help me out the car. Too bad if anyone's nosing out their windows as we go up the path. He's my husband, isn't he? I'm allowed to lean on him. I spot Betty in our kitchen window. She must have been waiting, ready to put the kettle on. Gary's up our mam's. I took him there this morning. Eddie came to pick me up on the corner, by the Star, so Gary wouldn't see him.

'How are you, me old love?' Betty asks, as we come in the back door.

'She's a bit tired,' Eddie answers. 'I'll take her up to bed.'

'Kettle's on,' Betty tells him. 'I've just put a shilling in the meter, and there's a cheese sandwich on a plate in the pantry.'

Eddie helps me undress, pulls back the blankets and tucks me in. I love our bedroom with its matching dressing table and wardrobes, and the dark pink candlewick bedspread. It's cosy in here, especially now he's drawn the curtains. It's not cold out, but I'm feeling a bit chilly so he lies down next to me, to keep me warm.

'Once we get the results, and we're sure, we'll go out and celebrate,' I say to him.

He kisses the top of my head. I love the smell of him, and the feeling of being safe that he gives me. I often wonder what the devil he sees in me.

'Do you want some tea now?' he whispers after about five minutes.

I'm nearly asleep. 'No,' I say. 'I just want you to go on lying here with me.'

So that's what he does, reciting bits of poems that I like, until I drift off to the land of Nod.

Chapter Four

Susan

Last weekend me and Gary – oops, I mean, Gary and I – went to stay with our cousins Julie and Karen. Uncle Bob, their dad, is our dad's brother and they grew up in Wales, with an overcoat for an eiderdown that they shared with their two sisters until the girls left home to go into service. My aunties, who are both married now, don't live far away, and my cousin Robert, Aunty Doreen's son, who's four years older than me, is my heart-throb. I'm going to marry him when I grow up.

While we went for a ride on the bus that Uncle Bob drives, and played in the park with Aunty Flo, Mum and Dad went to a bed and breakfast in Clevedon for the weekend. Mum said they were celebrating something she'd explain to me when I'm older. I don't know why she said that, when I know very well what a wedding anniversary is, and theirs is on 21st November, which is the weekend they went away. They've been married for eleven years now. I expect we'll have a new brother or sister next August, because Gary and I were both born in August, nine months after Mum and Dad's anniversary. I want a sister. Gary wants a brother.

Tonight's the first time Mum's been to bingo in ages. I heard her telling Mrs Williams that she didn't really want to see everyone, but Dad's keeping on at her to

63

get out of the house more, and anyway he's driving her bloody mad.

'He's always got his head stuck in a bleeding book, or he's in the front room listening to that bloody wireless of his,' she grumbles. 'Everything's politics or sodding poetry with him. He's in bloody cuckoo land, is what he is, and I'm fed up to the back teeth with it.'

I wish she wouldn't talk about Dad like that because I know he'd be hurt if he knew. He never talks about her to anyone, and he's always nice to her, except when they have a row and she hits him. Then he gets so angry that he shouts and cusses the same as her. He even got her in an armlock once and threw her down on the settee. I thought she was really going to beat him up then, because she could, she's really strong and everyone's afraid of her, but she started laughing and after a bit Dad did too. They were laughing a lot when they came back from Clevedon, but then they had a row about a Chinaman who was in the news and they haven't been speaking since. That's three whole days. Even Gary and I don't go that long without making up.

Now, here we all are, me, Gran, Mum and Mrs Williams, queuing up outside the bingo hut in the dark and freezing cold. Dad's taken Gary to the children's room up the Horseshoe for lemonade and crisps. Gary's even got some empty bottles to take back to the off-licence, so he'll get threepence to spend on peanuts or pork scratchings. Lucky thing. I hope he saves some for me when they come to pick me up at half-time.

'Oh, blimey, Eddress, is that you?' It's Mrs Collins who lives over the back of us. Sometimes I like her and sometimes I don't. Tonight I don't, because I can tell Mummy doesn't want to speak to her.

'How're you feeling now?' Mrs Collins asks her.

'I'm all right. Why wouldn't I be?' Mummy answers, sounding cross.

I look up at her, worried she might start a row, but she just winks at me, and so I relax against Granny whose hands are on my shoulders. Granny's even taller than Mum, and quite a lot bigger. She has terrible bad legs that she has to have bandaged every day, and she has to stick a needle in her bum every day too, because of something to do with her sugar. But she's still the best gran in the world, and I know me and Gary are her favourites even though she has masses of other grandchildren from Mummy's brothers and sisters.

'Here, all right Florrie? How are you?' someone says to Granny. 'How's your Billy getting on?'

Granny's fingers press into me. 'He's all right,' she answers, not even looking at the woman who spoke to her. I expect she's annoyed because she won't want reminding about my cousin Billy, who's twenty-five, and has just been sent to prison for robbing Granny's gas meter. He's done it before, which is why Granny told the police, though she hadn't expected them to put him away. (I'm not supposed to know any of this, but I overheard Mum telling Mrs Williams while they were having a cup of tea in our kitchen the other day.)

'Got your tanner to get in, Mam?' Mummy says.

'Here.' Granny hands it over.

'Eddress! Long time no see,' the man on the door shouts. 'Still as gorgeous as ever.'

'Oh get on with you,' Mummy snorts, though I can tell she's pleased. I expect she's glad she put her lipstick on now, which is cherry red and makes her look a bit like a film star.

'Look who's here,' the man shouts to someone inside. 'Eddress and Florrie. Make sure you keep a couple of good seats for them.'

'Ed! It's lovely to see you.' It's Mrs Burrows, who runs the bingo. She's got all this white back-combed hair, that's piled up on the top of her head like a giant Mr Whippy. She's lucky Mummy doesn't brush it for her.

'Is that you Ed?' someone else wants to know. 'Nice to see you out and about again. How are you feeling?'

It seems like everyone's calling out to her.

'Oh Eddress.' It's Mrs Lloyd from the next street, looking all stupid and soft, as though she's about to start praying. 'You're so brave coming out again after all you've been through,' she says. 'How are you?'

'What's it to you?' Mummy snaps. 'Just mind your own business.'

Mrs Lloyd shrinks away into the crowd. I feel sorry for her and angry with Mummy. She shouldn't speak to people like that, but she always does and no-one ever tells her off.

We move on in through the door, into the warm. My face and fingers are tingling, I can't even feel my toes. Mum looks a bit pale and cross as she stoops to unbutton my coat.

'I can do it,' I say, wishing I'd gone with Dad and Gary now, because I don't understand what's wrong with her.

'It's too cold to take our coats off yet,' Granny warns. 'Let's sit down and wait for this dump to warm up a bit. Oi, Gerald,' she shouts to a man over by the toilets, 'isn't there any heating in this place?'

'Ran out of coins for the meter,' he answers. 'Someone's gone to get some.'

'Hello Sue!'

It's Andrew Fox, the four-eyed twit, who's in our class – the one I usually end up with if we have to be paired as boy and girl. 'Hello,' I say.

He's about to go and join his mum who's talking to someone by the coffee bar when Mummy says, 'Oi, you!'

Andrew looks round.

'Her name's Susan,' Mummy informs him. 'We had her christened Susan, so you can call her Susan.'

Andrew's face is turning beetroot red. I reckon mine is too.

'Sorry,' he mumbles.

'Mum!' I say under my breath. 'All the children in school call me Sue.'

'Well they shouldn't. Your name's Susan. I'm going up there to have a word with that teacher.'

'No! You can't. Anyway, not everyone calls me Sue. Most of them call me Susan.'

Mummy turns round as someone taps her on the shoulder. It's Grace Shepherd, one of Mummy's friends.

'Here Ed, want a fag?' she says, speaking past the one that's dangling from the corner of her lips.

Mummy takes one from the packet, and accepts a light.

'You don't smoke do you, Florrie?' Grace says.

'Never did,' Granny replies. 'Bottle of stout and a pinch of snuff, that'll do me.'

Grace gives a fag to Mrs Williams and they all start talking about boring things, so I wait for a pause and quickly say, 'Can I go and get an orange squash? Daddy gave me threepence.'

Little squiggles of smoke come out of Mummy's nose and lips as she says, 'Go on then, but make sure you're back in time for eyes down.'

I go and stand in the queue, nearly get trodden on a couple of times, until it's my turn. I hand over a penny for a bottle of squash and a straw, make a hole in the foil top and start drinking away. A voice shouts out for everyone to take their seats, so I hurry back to Mum who gives me one of her cards. I want to put my arm round it to stop her from seeing, because I'm not a baby. If my numbers are called I can check on my own.

By half-time none of us has won anything, which is a shame because once when we came we won the first two games. My prize was a washing-up bowl and a bucket. Mummy's was two pound ten, so she bought the bucket and bowl off me for ten bob.

Dad and Gary are waiting outside when Mum takes me out, all wrapped up in scarves and bobble hats, stamping their feet and blowing out clouds of white air.

'Susan, ask your father where the car is,' Mummy says, tying her scarf under her chin.

'Dad, where's the car?'

'At the end of the lane,' he answers. 'Tell your mother . . .'

'Susan, tell your father I've had enough,' Mummy interrupts. 'Everyone's staring, looking at me like I belong in the bleeding zoo. Tell him Granny's staying.'

I look up at Dad.

'Tell your mother I'll go in with Gran,' he says. 'Might as well, seeing as I've got to give her a lift home. I'll take you three home first though.'

'Tell him we can walk, thank you very much,' Mummy snaps.

'No! It's freezing!' Gary wails.

'Come on,' Mummy barks, and grabs us both by the hand.

By the time we get home me and Gary are nearly crying we're so cold. Jack Frost has definitely got our ankles, mine are all chapped and purple, and Gary's have been cut right through by the wind, because one of them's bleeding. Mum quickly shovels more coal on the fire and turns up the back burner. We huddle together in our coats, shivering and holding out our hands to the flames. Mum lights a cigarette and lets it dangle from her mouth as she rubs Gary's legs to get them warm.

As she flicks her ash in the grate Gary slumps onto her, almost asleep. I expect her to pick him up to carry him up to bed, until I remember she can't. But she does anyway.

'Time for you to go up the wooden hill too, young lady,' she tells me.

'It's too cold to go to bed,' I protest.

'I don't want any arguing. You can have a hot-water bottle.'

'How long's it until Christmas?' I ask, following her up the stairs and staring down at the white whirly patterns in the carpet.

'Five weeks.'

'When can we start sending our notes up the chimney?'

'Soon.'

After she's undressed Gary and tucked him into bed, she comes into my room to make sure I'm getting into bed too. I've got my record player on and a big blue winceyette nightie with my socks, knickers and vest underneath to help me keep warm.

'Will Dad tell you off for carrying Gary?' I ask her, as she lights the candle in my night light.

'Not if you don't tell him.'

I slide in under the covers and finding last night's cold hot-water bottle, I push it out the end of the bed to make it plop on the floor.

'Come on, move up,' she says, and unzipping the tops of her furry boots, she gets into bed next to me, still wearing her hairy purple coat.

We listen to the record player.

My Bonnie lies over the ocean,
My Bonnie lies over the sea,
My Bonnie lies over the ocean,
Oh bring back my Bonnie to me.

The next time the chorus comes we sing too, not very loud or we'll wake up Gary. The record finishes and keeps going round until the needle slides over the middle. Mummy goes to put it on again, then comes back to bed.

'Who says my girls can't sing?' Dad teases when he comes home.

Mum gives me a kiss on the forehead and gets up. 'Dad'll read you a story now,' she says.

I look up at Dad as she goes, but he doesn't seem to mind that she doesn't want to make friends. I mind that she's forgotten my hot-water bottle though.

Eddress

Our bedroom's no warmer than Susan's. It's probably even colder, considering she's got the airing cupboard in hers. I start putting away the pile of ironing I left on the bed earlier, only half-listening to the sound of Eddie's voice rising and falling, squeaking and squawking as he reads to his precious girl. I expect his breath is forming little clouds in the air, and he's probably still got his cap on too. It's so bloody cold it's enough to make you think you're in the North bleeding Pole. I still haven't taken my coat off since I came in, and I'm half-tempted to go back into our Susan's room to get my boots. Fancy having to wear coats and boots inside the house to keep warm. It's not right, is it? I bet the poshies up Redland and Clifton don't have to do it. I bet they

70

don't have to rely on their wives winning something at bingo to bring in a bit of extra cash at the end of the week, either.

I don't mind telling you, it's getting on my bloody nerves all this. When I married Eddie I was proud as can be. I'd found meself a good man, I thought, better than all the thickos I knew put together, a cut above us all with his brains and manners. We were going to be rich, me and Eddie. He'd be a famous writer and we'd live in a big house, with a big car and lots of fancy holidays. It seems bloody laughable now that I fell for it all, but I did. Green as grass I was then, and twice as daft. What a long time ago it all seems, though I remember only too well how no-one could believe it when I said I was going to marry him. I could hardly believe it meself, half the time, but once the idea was there it sort of took root, and the next thing I knew we had this big wedding planned and I was off up the aisle.

It was one in the eye for my brothers, who'd said no-one would ever want someone like me. I was too much like a boy, they said, too common and too bloody ugly. Our Gord and Tom never used to say that, it was the older ones, Graham, Ernie and Arthur. Maurice, me half-brother, never said it either, but I was always Maurice's favourite. I think he was a bit jealous when I wrote and told him I was getting married. He still hasn't met Eddie, because he hasn't come home for a visit since going to New Zealand, back in 1950. I miss him. I wish he'd walk in the door now and take me away from all this. I don't suppose I'd leave the kids though. I don't suppose I'd leave Eddie either, if it came right down to it, but I was bloody tempted when he told me the other day I had to start walking up our mam's because I'm spending too much on bus fares.

'You can sod right off,' I told him. 'I'm not walking

in this weather just to save on a couple of tuppenny-ha'penny bus fares, when you're spending ten times as much on petrol for that bloody car of yours.'

'I'm going to ride my bike,' he told me. 'We'll use the car at weekends, for all of us.'

'You think you're so bloody clever, making me look bad, don't you?' I shouted at him. 'Well, I know your game. You'll get a lift from someone, that's what you'll do, while me and Gary freeze to death walking up that bloody hill.'

'I'm not getting a lift, I'm going to ride my bike.' He was looking at the clock. 'I'm going to listen to the wireless now,' he said. 'There's a broadcast from . . .'

'Bugger the bloody wireless. That's all you ever think about, the bloody wireless, or the Union, or books . . .'

'It's from Moscow. They're going to be talking about Chou En-lai's visit a couple of weeks ago.'

'I couldn't care less what they're talking about.'

'You were interested before. We listened together last time . . .'

'That was before you started getting stingy with the money.'

'I don't see how me asking you to cut down has got anything to do with your interest in world affairs.'

'I'm only interested to keep you happy, you stupid sod. You don't think I care about whether or not some Chink drops in on Moscow, do you? As far as I'm concerned they're just a bunch of bleeding foreigners who are more than happy to keep the likes of us nice and poor, while idiots like you believe all their crap about it being for the greater good.'

'You're being deliberately obtuse, and racist into the bargain.'

'Your fancy words don't impress me, so save them for your . . .'

'I'm not listening to any more of this. I'm going to turn on the wireless.'

'Don't you dare walk out of this room.'

'I'll do what I damned well like in my own house.'

'It's my house too, and you can stay right where you are.'

He started to walk out, so I snatched up my knitting bag and threw it at him. It bounced off his head and dropped to the floor.

'You're just being childish,' he told me.

That earned him the ashtray. He ducked and it crashed against the door.

'Eddress, pull yourself together,' he snapped.

'Don't you bloody dare talk to me like that.' I raged. He makes me so mad when he's condescending like that.

'If you throw one more thing you're going to get it back.'

I picked up a book and hurled it. 'Come on then,' I cried. 'Let's have it. Let's see you throw it back.'

He just stared at me, all pale-faced the way he goes when he's angry.

I spotted Gary's toy hammer, grabbed it and threw. He managed to catch it, then before I knew it, it was bouncing off my head.

'You bloody swine,' I yelled as he walked out.

He slammed the door behind him and I haven't spoken to him since. And I'm still getting the bus up our mam's, even though he's riding his bike to work. He's a high-minded bugger sometimes, well now he's a freezing cold high-minded bugger, isn't he, who owes me an apology for the bruise on my forehead.

I have a look out the window as I close the curtains, half-expecting to see snow. There's none though, but I reckon there's a good chance we'll have some by

Christmas. The kids'll like that. It won't be me going out there building snowmen, mind. It'll be Eddie, the perfect dad, the saint, the bloody clever clogs who knows everything. He'll do anything for them kids, so let him. Go on Eddie, show off to the world just how perfect you are, let everyone think the sun shines out your bleeding backside, because that's what they all think, isn't it? They've got no idea what I have to put up with, all your bleeding pontificating and politics, or the shouting and blinding when your temper's up – hardly anyone but me even knows you got a temper, do they? You're a crafty bugger, you are. Never let anyone see what you're really like, accusing me of racial prejudice and not having a proper understanding of what's going on in the world. He goes out of his way to make me feel bleeding stupid when he wants to, and I'm telling you, I've had e-bloody-nough of it. Talking to me like I'm thick in the head half the time. Well who the bloody hell cares what's coming out of Moscow? No-one, that's who – except Comrade Eddie, of course.

I open his wardrobe door, stick his clean underwear on a shelf and start hanging up his shirts. Even my bloody brothers think he's Mr Wonderful. Well, they damned well should. He's always doing things for them, wallpapering their bathrooms, helping mend their cars, or driving them up the betting shop, or the pub, wherever they want to go. Our mam's another who thinks he can do no wrong. Ten quid she won at bingo, while I was in hospital, and she tried to give him five of it. Said he deserved it for the things he does for her. He didn't take it, of course. Not Eddie. It wouldn't be right to take money off an old woman who only had her pension to live on. I'd have given him a right mouthful if he had, mind you, but it don't half get on your nerves when someone always does the right thing.

Susan worships him. Daddy this, Daddy that. It wouldn't bother her if I left and never came back. She'd have her precious dad all to herself then. Well she can have him. Gary'd probably mind a bit if I went, but he'd get over it soon enough.

I close the wardrobe door, turn the key in the lock and wrap my coat tighter around me. He's still reading in there, putting on all the voices, acting all the words. I hit my toe on something and look down. A potato's rolled out from under the bed. I kick it back and think about dragging them all out and dumping them in his side of the bed. You can smell the bloody things, all that earth and damp on my carpet. Why couldn't he have put them under sacks in the shed, the way other people do? No, not Eddie. He's got to be different and put them under our bloody bed. Always different.

Instead of getting ready for bed I find my slippers and go back downstairs to put on the kettle. The heat from the flames is lovely. I cup my hands round them and lean my face in above to thaw out me nose. Wouldn't mind a drop of the beef stew I made earlier. I wonder if Eddie would like some too, before going to bed. He can warm it up himself if he does. There's a bit of an ache under my arm, probably from carrying Gary up the stairs. It'll be all right though. Nothing to worry about. It's all over. Dr Tyldesley says I don't have to go back to the hospital for another six months, and that's just for a check-up. Nothing to worry about, so I won't. It don't matter a tinker's cuss how I got it in the first place, just as long as it's gone now. I don't want to hear about what Tyldesley told Eddie, or what the radium doctor said either. It don't do any good to dwell on it. We just need to put it behind us now and forget all about it.

'All right?' Eddie says, coming in the kitchen.

I don't answer, just go on waiting for the kettle to boil.

'Is that for Susan's hot-water bottle?'

Blimey, I'd forgotten about that. I take the bottle from him.

'She's asleep now, but Gary's woken up. I'll go and sleep in with him, keep him warm. You can have the bottle.'

I sniff and look the other way.

He's got as far as the bottom of the stairs when I say, 'Gary can have the hot-water bottle.'

He comes back in the kitchen. 'Is this your way of saying sorry?' he asks.

'Don't push it,' I warn.

He turns round and starts to walk away again.

'All right, I'm bloody sorry,' I call after him. Honestly, he can be really bloody petty sometimes.

'What are you sorry for?' he says.

'I don't bloody know. Whatever you want me to be sorry for, I suppose. And think yourself lucky I'm saying it, because if you ask me, it's you who should be apologising, not me.'

He doesn't say anything, so I don't either. I just go on staring at the wallpaper, liking the pictures of copper pots and pans, and grudgingly admiring how he managed to get the joins just right when he put it up. After a bit I start wondering if he's still there. I can't hear anything, so I turn to have a look. He's still there, watching me, and I can see he's trying not to laugh. I'm telling you, if he makes me laugh too I'm going to bloody swing for him.

'Come here and give us a kiss,' he says, holding out his arms.

'Don't be soft,' I say.

He keeps his arms out.

I still hold back, but then I think, well, what's the harm?

A couple of minutes later the kettle starts to whistle. He tells me to go on up to bed, he'll sort out the hot-water bottle for Gary, then he'll be in to keep me warm instead. I don't want to do it, but I have to, for him, don't I?

Chapter Five

Susan

Lots has been happening. People are always in and out of our house, our aunties and uncles, my cousins and everyone, but they're here a lot more now that Christmas is coming. My aunties sit round the dining table with Mum, smoking and drinking tea. They all have the same sort of hair, quite wavy, though me and Mum are the only ones with our colour, and they all wear big wide skirts, or trousers with loops under the feet, with spotted blouses and thick jumpers. They gossip a lot, about prices in the shops, knitting patterns, people they know, or us children. They laugh a lot, and say saucy things, and the air gets thick with smoke, so you can hardly see, and biscuit crumbs fall onto the tablecloth with stray speckles of ash and the bits of silver paper from fag packets. Sometimes they shout out rude things to the men in the next room and shriek with laughter when they get a reply. I don't take much notice though, because I'm too busy playing with my cousins, or some of my friends from the street, who're allowed into my bedroom to get out of the cold. Gary's friends come in too, so sometimes we all play together, mums and dads, doctors and nurses or shopkeepers, or schools.

My uncles are a rowdy bunch, and don't seem to listen much when Dad tries to explain about books and political things. They'd rather talk about football or where they work. Because we're the only ones with a telly, they all came to watch the match between Wales and England a few weeks ago. Dad supported Wales, because he's Welsh, so they all jeered and called him a Taffy, but Dad didn't mind. He didn't mind either when England won, because he likes England, and anyway he's a good loser and just laughs when my uncles get on at him.

We've put up all our Christmas trimmings now and decorated our tree. It's not a real one because they have spikes which drop off on the carpet, and it's too much fuss to keep vacuuming them up. Instead, we've got a lovely big silver tinselly one with loads of ornaments and crackers all over it, bags of chocolate pennies and a fairy on top. Piles of presents are building up all around it, wrapped in coloured paper with holly and sleighs and reindeer on. Some are for us to open, others are for us to give. I'm learning to play 'Away in a Manger' on the piano so that Dad and Gary can sing it to everyone on Christmas Day. Carol singers are knocking on our door every night, so we're collecting ha'pennies to give them. Best of all though, we've been to see Father Christmas twice now. The first was in Jones's, the big posh shop up Kingswood that sells great big underpants for men that Gary and I always go to have a look at so we can have a good laugh. Dad took us there while Mum went downtown with Gran and Aunty Phil. (Aunty Phil is Mum's older sister with a sweet shop in Longwell Green, so she's our favourite aunty.)

Father Christmas in Jones's gave Gary some fuzzy felts and me a French-knitting set. Then we saw him in Lewis's down town with Mum and Dad together. That time he gave us a balloon each on a stick, Gary a clockwork train and me a box of paints. After that we went to A.G. Meek where Dad treated Mum to a black handbag, gloves and shoes, then all the way home in the car we sang the advert from the telly:

The matching's unique,
at A.G. Meek.

Oh yes, we had a cup of tea and a cake in British Home Stores before we left, where Gary's balloon got squashed between two fat women and popped. He was so angry he called them bloody buggers. Mum made him say sorry three times, and said he had to go straight to bed when we got home, but after, when we were drinking our tea, none of us could stop laughing, especially Gary, until he said it again, and got a smack.

Now it's only two days, five hours and twenty-three minutes to go to Christmas. We're lucky to be having a Christmas though, because last week, when Gary and I sent our notes up the chimney, you'll never guess what happened. The chimney caught fire. Dad had to charge round the phone box to call the fire brigade, while Mum threw a bucket of water in the grate. We ran outside and flames were still leaping out of the chimney. Dad came back, then the fire engine turned up and all the neighbours were standing in their gardens watching. Mum laughed so much when the firemen left that Dad wrestled her into an armlock and told her she was mad. We were all laughing by then, and when Dad went to get some more coal from the shed and the bottom fell out of the bucket, spilling coal all over the kitchen floor, tears were pouring down Mum's cheeks she was laughing so hard.

They're a bit strange really, because I never know what they're going to laugh at, and half the time it's at things that aren't even funny. It makes me a bit cross sometimes, because it nearly always seems to work out that when I've done something really funny, they suddenly start shouting at me, or each other, and everything turns all horrible. Then, just when I think I'm in dead trouble over something and I'm getting all scared, they start laughing their heads off. Like the time with the rabbit, which definitely didn't start out very funny, because it was in a stew that Mum had made for our tea. I really, really didn't want to eat it, but we're almost never allowed to leave the table until our plates are wiped clean. It was all right for Gary, he'd eat anything, but I was afraid if I ate this stew I'd be sick.

In the end I said, 'Please can I go and eat mine in the kitchen?'

Mummy looked at me in one of her funny ways. 'Go on then,' she answered, sounding as though she knew I was up to no good.

Once I was out there I wasn't really sure what to do. I couldn't open the back door and throw it out, because then it would be all over the garden. I couldn't put it down the sink either, because Mummy would be bound to hear the water running and come to find out why. Besides, I didn't have anything to stand on to reach the taps, and even if I did, what would I do if it didn't all rinse away? Then I spotted my satchel, hanging on the back door. We'd already broken up for the Christmas holidays, so I could put it in there and have a bit of time to work out how to get rid of it.

Quickly I took out the books, hid them in a drawer, and I'd no sooner finished sliding the stew into the satchel than the dining-room door opened and Mummy came out.

'Have you eaten it all?' she asked, putting the dirty dishes on the draining board.

'Yes,' I answered, showing her the empty plate.

She gave me another of her funny looks, but didn't say any more, just squirted some Fairy into the bowl to start washing up. I grabbed the tea towel, certain that God would keep my secret if I did something good.

Everything was going well. All the dishes were put away and I was playing inky-pinky-plonky with Dad on the carpet, while Mum did some ironing out in the kitchen. Gary had vanished somewhere, but then, there he was, coming in the door with . . . *my satchel over his shoulder.*

'Put that back. Put it back now,' I shouted.

He ignored me and carried on stomping about the room, chanting, 'I'm on my way to school, I'm on my way to school.' It's his favourite game, because he's not old enough to go yet, and usually I like chalking on my blackboard and giving him nought out of ten for sums, or telling him to go and stand in the corner or giving him a gold star if he pays me with sweets, or money we get from Grampy, Dad's dad.

'I said put it back,' I raged.

'He's all right, let him play,' Daddy told me.

'I don't want him to.' If Mummy found out what was in there I wouldn't just get a smack, I probably wouldn't be allowed out for a whole year, except for school and ballet and piano. She might even report me to the police.

Then the worst happened. 'Ugh! Yuk!' Gary cried, pulling a hand out of the satchel.

'What's that?' Daddy said.

'Nothing,' I shouted. 'It's nothing.'

'What's going on?' Mummy demanded, carrying in a pile of ironing and putting it on the arm of a chair. 'What's on earth's that?' she said, seeing Gary's mushy hand. 'What have you done?'

'Nothing,' Gary told her, defensively. 'I haven't done nothing.'

'Anything,' she corrected, and lifted his hand to smell it.

With a bumping heart I watched her turn to me. I was sliding in behind the curtains, even though I knew they wouldn't save me. I'd have run if I could, but she was between me and the door. I even thought of throwing myself out the window, but she'd catch me first, so all I could do was stare up at her, knowing I was really for it now.

She started to say something about me being a naughty girl and too crafty for my own good, but then her voice went all strange, and she hid her face with her hand.

I looked at Dad. He had a hand over his mouth too. I didn't understand what was happening, until I realised they were trying not to laugh.

'It's not funny,' Gary shouted angrily.

I started to laugh too, really loud. Gary rushed at me, and shoved his stewy hand in my face. 'I said it's not funny,' he seethed.

'Ugh! Get him off! Get him off!' I wailed.

Mummy whisked him up in her arms. 'Come on, let's clean you up,' she laughed, giving him a big kiss on the cheek. 'And you, madam,' she said to me, sounding cross now, 'can clean out that satchel yourself, because I'm not doing it.'

Dad came up to the bathroom to help me and after we put it in the airing cupboard to dry we did some practice swimming on the tall stool Dad had made. I'm getting quite good at crawl now.

Tonight, which is three nights before Christmas, there's a special edition of *Top of the Pops*. The telly's already on, warming up, and Mum's putting slices of bread on the end of forks so we can toast them in front of the fire. The big lights are off, with just the tree lights on (Dad had to mend them again earlier because they kept going out – he even swore when they went wrong, which isn't like him at all. Mum told him off, then I got told off too for laughing). Last week, 'I Feel Fine' by the Beatles was number one. We're hoping it will be this week too, because it's one of our favourites. I've put it on my Christmas list, so I'm hoping I might get it.

'Oh no,' we all groan as the picture starts flipping up and up. Dad bangs the top of the telly and the picture settles down again.

'Here,' Mummy says, passing me a fork.

I go to sit on the floor between Dad's legs and the fireplace and hold out my piece of bread towards the fire. He leans down and slips off my glasses.

I can see! Without that stupid patch over my eye I can see without having to stick my chin in my chest.

'What are you doing?' Mummy demands.

'Just this once,' Dad says. 'It's a struggle for her with that patch on all the time.'

'It's forcing her bad eye to see right,' Mummy reminds him. 'Put them back on again.'

'No!' I cry.

'I said, put them on.'

'Leave her,' Dad says. 'She's all right.'

Mum looks like she's going to argue some more, but all she does is give me a bit of a look to show she's not pleased, then turns back to the telly. 'You haven't forgotten Gary's got his operation in January, have you?' she says, holding Gary and his toasting fork back from the fire to stop him falling in.

'Of course not.'

'What's an operation?' Gary asks, turning to look at her.

She gives him a big kiss. 'Something to make your eye better,' she tells him.

'My eye's all right,' he says, wiping the kiss off his cheek.

The bread suddenly drops off his fork into the flames. He lunges forward to get it and Mum grabs him back, just in time. 'You silly thing. We don't want roast you for dinner tomorrow, thank you.'

'It was Susan,' he says. 'She knocked it off.'

'I did not!'

'Yes you did.'

'I did not.'

'She did.'

'Did you?' Mum's looking at me.

'I never touched it. You're always picking on me.'

'We'll have less of that attitude, thank you. I'm just asking if you hit his bread off.'

'No, I didn't. Did I Dad?'

'If she did, it was an accident,' he answers.

I want to cry now, because I didn't touch his stupid bread. It fell off all on its own. Everyone always blames me.

When my toast is done Dad butters it and I climb up onto his lap to watch the programme. It's really good tonight, with lots of songs from through the year that we know, so we sing along with some like, 'You're My World' by Cilla Black, and 'Have I the Right' by the Honeycombs. The Beatles turn out to be number one again this week with their song, 'I Feel Fine', so we all cheer and Gary and Dad get up to dance. I look at Mum and hope she's not still cross with me. She doesn't seem to be, because instead of sending us to bed so she can watch *Wagon Train* which is on next, she turns the telly off and puts on the record player. She even puts on my favourite record first, 'Do Wah Diddy Diddy' by Manfred Mann, and holds my hands as we dance together. Gran bought me the record for my birthday when I was eight, back in August, so it's mine. Next Dad puts on 'Twist and Shout'. Mum's a really good twister, but tonight she does a bop with Dad. I want to learn to dance like that. Ballet's rubbish. It's for poofs.

After that Dad takes us up to bed and reads us Peter Rabbit, sitting out on the landing so we can both hear. Mum puts the ironing away then comes to tuck us in and turn out the lights. I wait for her and Dad to go back downstairs. It's bitter cold, but not like it was a couple of weeks ago when the washing froze on the line. We've put the paraffin heater in the hall now, so it helps to take the chill off the bedrooms, and it gives off a lovely inky smell that makes it all cosy and nice.

I tiptoe out to the landing and get as far as the top of the stairs when Gary's door opens.

'What are you doing?' he whispers.

'I'm going to listen. You can come if you want to, but you have to be quiet.'

We go slowly, carefully down one stair at a time, standing dead still and not daring to breathe every time a floorboard creaks. They've turned the record player on again. It's 'Put Your Head on My Shoulder' by Pat someone, I forget now. We get halfway down and peer over the banister. The kitchen and living-room doors are open and we can see them, dancing. Ugh, and *kissing*! I clap a hand over Gary's eyes and shove him back up to bed.

'I want to come in and sleep with you,' he says when we get to his door.

'All right, but you're not allowed to put your cold feet on me.'

We slide in under the covers and I start telling him one of the stories I made up. If I could stop him following me, I'd go back to look over the banister again to make sure they don't end up having a row. I don't think they will though, because they haven't for ages now, not a real one, which means God has answered my prayers.

He's even stopped Mum working in the sack factory, so she's here every night when we come home from school, and Dad's tea is on the table when he gets in from work. I don't think she's got another family any more. She's just got us.

The next day Dad finishes work early and takes Gary up to Grampy's and Aunty Beat's to deliver their presents. The car's broken down so they have to walk in all the rain. Mum and I get a lift up to Gran's with one of the neighbours who's going that way. My cousins, Geoffrey and Deborah, live next door to Gran, so after helping Mum with some of Gran's housework, I go round to play hide-and-seek with them. While I'm lying under the bed in their big sister's bedroom I spot a bottle with a little cork in the top that's easy to pull out. I take a sip, just to see what it's like and wonder if I might shrink, or grow big, like Alice. It's really nice, so I have a bit more, and when Geoff and Deb find me they have some too. We start to get all giggly and silly, and we do rude things like pulling up our jumpers, or showing our bums. We're laughing so much that none of us sees Mummy standing in the door, but even when we do, we still can't stop laughing. She's really mad, I can tell by her face, but it just makes us laugh even more.

'Come here,' she says to me in her strictest voice.

I'm really for it now, I know I am, but I'm still giggling at the others as I go towards her. She grabs my arm, spins me round and whacks me so hard across the legs that I scream. She does it again and again.

'You naughty, naughty girl!' she shouts. 'You're disgusting, do you hear me? Disgusting. I'm telling your father as soon as we get home. Pulling your knickers down in front of boys. And what's that smell?' She looks around, her eyes all wild like a witch's. 'Is that booze I can smell? Bloody hell, have you been drinking?' She spots the empty bottle. 'Deborah, bring that here,' she barks. *'Ivy,'* she shouts to Deborah's mum.

I'm starting to feel really scared now, and a bit sick. My head's spinning round and round and my legs are stinging like bees from where they got smacked. Mum's still holding me by the arm, as she grabs the bottle off Deborah and sniffs it. 'You stupid girl,' she rages, and starts smacking me again. 'What the hell do you think you're doing? Just you wait till I tell your father. Sneaking around in Wendy's bedroom, stealing her booze, pulling your knickers down . . .'

'No, stop! Stop!' I shout, trying to get away. 'I won't ever do it again. I'm sorry.'

'You're damned right you'll never do it again. Now get down those stairs.'

Aunty Ivy's upstairs now, and Geoffrey's getting a smack. Not as hard as the one I got though. My mum always gives the hardest smacks and . . .'I'm going to be sick,' I wail.

Mummy yanks me across the landing, but it's too late, it's already coming up. It goes all over the carpet and down my front. She picks me up and sticks my head over the toilet.

'I'm going to put you in a home, my girl, if you don't learn to behave,' she says.

She always says that, but it still frightens me in case one day she means it.

After I've washed my face and helped her clean the sick off the carpet, I have to go back round Gran's and stay shut up in her bedroom with no dinner, just a cup of water and a piece of bread, until I can learn how to behave like a decent girl. There won't be any Christmas presents for me either, because Father Christmas doesn't come to disgusting little girls like me.

I wait for about ten and a half hours then I call out

to say I'm sorry, but no-one answers. I can hear them talking though, so I know they're still there. I creep out to the landing and listen.

'Let her come down now, Ed,' I hear Gran say. 'It's cold up there.'

'She's got to learn, Mam, and going soft on her the way Eddie does isn't going to teach her.'

No-one ever argues with Mum, not even Gran, so I take myself back into Gran's bedroom and close the door. I want my dad, but I'm afraid he's going to be angry with me too when Mum tells him I showed my bum to Geoffrey. I'm a terrible girl and I hate myself. I'm worried about Gary too, because if Father Christmas doesn't come to our house, he won't get any presents either, and that's not fair. He hasn't done anything wrong.

Gran's bed is so high I have to climb up on a stool to get on it. It's a lovely bed, with big brass railings, huge squidgy pillows and a bouncy mattress. I have a jump up and down for a while, then I sit down to play I-spy with a pretend friend, but she keeps cheating so I stop being her friend. I count the daisies on the wall-paper up to two hundred and five, then I lose my place. I watch the rain running down the window and decide to go and draw pictures in the condescension. As I slide down to the stool it tips over, and I fall with a great big bang, hitting my head on the chest of drawers next to the bed.

Next thing the door opens and Mummy comes in. 'What's going on in here?' she demands.

'It wasn't my fault,' I tell her. 'The stool fell over and I banged my head.' I start to cry because it really hurt and I want her to make it better, not tell me off.

She comes to kneel down next to me and pulls my hand away to look at my head. She smells of Cadum soap and cigarettes. I feel tired and want to curl up in her lap and go to sleep.

'You'll live,' she tells me.

I look up at her. 'Can I come down now?' I ask.

'No. You're staying here until you can learn to behave yourself.'

'But I am behaving myself.'

'Answering me back isn't behaving yourself.'

'I'm just saying, I'm being good now, and I promise to be good for ever.'

'What did I just say about answering back? Now, you'll stay here and I'll let your father deal with you when we get home.'

After the door's closed behind her I stick out my tongue and say, 'I hate you.' Then I climb back up on the bed and cry, because she's turning my dad against me, so I'm going to leave home and she'll never see me again. She'll be sorry then. I'm going to take Mandy and Teddy, some clean knicks and vests, a scarf and some gloves. I'll have to creep down in the middle of the night to make some jam sandwiches. I can put it all in a Fine Fare bag inside my satchel, and carry it over my shoulder. If I go on Christmas Eve I might bump into Father Christmas, who I don't believe in really. But if I do bump into him, he might give me a ride in his sleigh and take me back to the North Pole to live. I'll have all the toys in the world then, and I won't get smacked all the time, or have my hair pulled by horrible boys in school. The elves and the goblins will play with me, and there'll probably be other children there too, whose parents don't love them either. I wonder if I should take Gary, because he'd really like it. He'd miss Mum though and she loves him. It's only me she doesn't love.

When it's time to go she shouts upstairs for me to come down now. She's waiting in the hall with my coat and scarf. I put them on myself and go in to kiss Gran cheerio. When Mummy's not looking Gran pushes a penny into my hand.

'Be a good girl now,' she whispers. 'See you on Christmas Day.'

I don't tell her I won't be there, because she might tell Mum.

It's still raining outside. Mum's got us both plastic rain hats, which tie under the chin, and plastic macs to put over our coats. She makes me hold her hand as we walk to the bus stop and tells me off for splashing in the puddles. I wasn't, but if I cheek her back I'll only get a smack, out here in the road.

We wait for the bus in the knitting-shop doorway. I want to go in the sweet shop next door to spend my penny, but I know it won't be allowed. I think about the marshmallow shrimps, white chocolate mice, and fruit salad chews. I'm so hungry my tummy can't stop rumbling.

'Is that you?' Mum says, after a really loud rumble.

'Yes,' I say.

She looks down at me. 'That was a stroppy voice, if ever I heard one. You're not sulking, are you?'

'No.'

'No, it doesn't sound like it.'

I turn my face into the wall, so my back's to her.

'Come on,' she says, pulling me against her. 'It's nothing to cry about. We'll put it behind us now and forget it happened.'

I lean into her.

'Just make sure you don't do anything like it again,' she warns.

'Are you going to tell Dad?'

'We'll see. If you're a good girl tonight, maybe not.'

I turn my face up to look at her.

She looks down at me and shakes her head.

'Do you like Gary better than me?' I ask.

She opens her eyes wide and laughs. 'What kind of question's that? Of course not. I like you both the same.' She pulls me inside her coat to keep me warmer. 'Come on bus,' she mutters. 'It's freezing standing here.'

'Tell me stories about when you were little,' I say.

'What, now?'

I nod. I always like hearing stories of when she was growing up in the war and her mum and dad used to snore all the way through the air raids, while Uncle Maurice, who was a fire warden, used to rush home to grab the little ones and take them out to the shelter. Or how they used to sell flowers from Grandad's allotment so they could buy meat for the stew. Or how they'd heat water in a kettle over the fire to have a bath on Friday nights. It was a big old tin bath that they used to keep outside, next to the toilet, and carry in on Fridays. They all used to get undressed in front of each other, and people even used to visit when they were in the bath. There are lots of funny stories about bath night, that always make me and Gary laugh.

'I know, tell me about when you used to steal apples,' I say. 'No. Tell me about how you and Auntie Jean hitch-hiked to the RAF camp to see Uncle Gordon one night and ended up sleeping in a field.'

'You've got too good a memory,' she tells me.

'What about when you all used to sleep three and four in a bed? How many brothers and sisters do you have?'

'You know the answer to that.'

'Twelve,' I say. 'And you make thirteen. No, Uncle Tom makes thirteen, because he's the youngest. And only Uncle Tom and Uncle Gord are your real brothers. The others are from Gran's first husband, so that makes them your half-brothers and sisters.'

'That's right. And then there's Aunty Kathleen and Uncle Maurice, who are my half-brother and half-sister, because they've got the same dad as me, but a different mum.'

'And Aunty Kathleen lives in London, and Uncle Maurice is in the RAF in New Zealand. Will we ever see him?'

'I hope so. He said in his last letter he was coming home soon. Gran's sending him a telegram tomorrow to wish him happy Christmas from us all, and to give him the number of the phone box at the bottom of Holly Hill so he can ring us next Friday at six, so you might be able to say hello if he calls. Ah, at last, here's the bus.'

We hold hands and run through the rain to the bus stop, getting there a long time before the bus. Uncle Bob's not driving, but Mum knows the conductor so we get away with paying only one fare. I keep hold of the yellow ticket in case the inspector gets on, and go to sit in the front seat, upstairs, while Mum has a cigarette and chats with someone she knows a few rows back. She knows everyone.

It's pitch dark by the time we get home. Tree lights are twinkling in all the windows along the lane and in our street. You can't see ours, because our kitchen's at the front, but Dad's put some lights round the pane of glass in the front door, which look lovely. Him and Gary are already home, so the fire's lit and it's all warm inside, with even more presents under the tree from Grampy and Aunty Beat. Gary and I are getting really excited now, because there's only one more day to go and it'll be Christmas. Tomorrow Dad's going to pluck the goose that's hanging in the shed, and Mum will try to get it in the oven. She thinks it might be too big.

All the next day we're really busy, taking last-minute presents to everyone, or going up Fine Fare to buy the vegetables, or tidying up and vacuuming to make sure it's nice for Father Christmas (who Gary still believes in). At four o'clock Dad and Gary go round the barbers to get their hair cut, while Mum's hairdresser comes to give her a wash and set. After she's put the rollers in, she puts a carrier bag over them, then sticks the hairdryer inside and tells Mum to hold it. It's my turn next for a trim, Mum already washed it last night. It's so long now I can nearly sit on it.

Aunty Doreen and Uncle Alf come, Dad's sister and her husband, then his other sister, Aunty Nance and Uncle Stan. They drink some sherry and put even more presents under the tree. None of them smoke, which is a relief for Mum, because she doesn't want to give them any and then run out over Christmas when the shops are closed. Uncle Bob and Aunty Flo are bringing Julie and Karen down tomorrow, and Gran will be here too, if Dad can get the car going to pick her up. It started earlier, so he's got his fingers crossed for the morning.

Gary and I don't mind going to bed early tonight, to make sure we're asleep before Father Christmas comes, so about six o'clock we pour some milk in a glass and put out a saucer of chocolate biscuits for him and the reindeer, then we hang our stockings over the fireplace and get a piggyback from Dad up the stairs. Mum's too busy icing the Christmas cake to come and tuck us in, so Dad does it for her and tells us no nonsense, or Father Christmas won't come.

It's very hard getting to sleep. Gary keeps calling out to ask if I'm asleep yet. He goes quiet for a while, so I call out to him. 'Are you still awake?'

'No,' he answers.

'Are you asleep?'

'Yes.'

'Me too.'

In the middle of the night, when I'm fast asleep, I wake up for a minute. I can hear someone in my room, so I open my eyes just a little bit, and I see a big man in red at the end of my bed. I go back to sleep then and don't wake up until half past five when Gary comes in.

'He's been,' he whispers, all excited. 'He's been.'

I sit up, all excited too.

'Look,' Gary says, pointing to the end of my bed.

In the dim light I can see something lying there. It's my stocking, all full up and bulging.

'I've got one too,' he says. 'Shall I get it?'

'Yes.'

He runs back to his own room, making so much noise I don't know why he bothers whispering when he comes back. 'Can I get in with you?' he says. 'It's cold out here.'

I make room for him and together we open our stockings. We've got apples and oranges, nuts, a selection box, sticks of liquorice, a yo-yo, a key ring and two Christmas crackers each. We pull one. Gary wins, and out tumbles a noughts and crosses game with a yellow paper hat and a joke we can't read because it's in Chinese. We pull again, Gary wins again, but he lets me have the little spinning top and the green paper hat.

'Shall we go and show Mum?' he says.

'They're still asleep.'

'I know, but I want to.'

'Then you go first.'

'What if she tells me off?'

'She won't. She never tells you off.'

'Yes she does.'

'No she doesn't. You're her favourite.'

'You are.'

'Shut up and go first.'

'No, you.'

'You're such a baby.'

95

'You are!' He gives me a thump.

I thump him back. 'If I go first, I'm going round Dad's side,' I tell him.

'All right.'

We put on our hats and pick up our stockings. At Mum and Dad's bedroom door we stop and listen.

'They're still asleep,' I whisper, starting to shiver.

'What shall we do?'

'I don't know.'

'I know, we can go downstairs and see if he's left anything there.'

I'm not sure about that. I don't think it's allowed until Mum and Dad are up too. 'Go and pull the chain,' I say. 'It might wake them up.'

'I can't reach it.'

We jump as Dad's voice says, 'Is that elves I can hear out there?'

Gary and I look at each other and grin.

'Yes, it's elves,' Gary answers.

'Are you good elves, or bad elves?'

'We're Christmas elves,' he says, which I think is a really good answer. 'Can we come in?'

'Do you know the password?'

'Umm?' Gary looks at me.

We whisper to each other, trying to guess what it is.

'Merry Christmas,' I say.

'Very good. Come on in.'

We burst in through the door to find Mum and Dad sitting up in bed in their pyjamas. 'Father Christmas has been!' Gary shouts. 'He's been. Look what we've got!'

He leaps onto the bed with his stocking and lands on Mum. Dad swings me up and plonks me next to him. We show them all our things, and pull the other crackers so they've got hats too. Dad wears his downstairs to light the fire. Gary and I wait at the top of the stairs.

'Has he been?' Gary shouts.

'Yes,' Dad shouts back.

Gary and I jump up and down and run back to Mum.

'He's been,' Gary tells her. 'Can we go down now?'

'All right, all right,' she laughs. 'Bring me my dressing gown, and you can go and put yours on too, the both of you.'

We rush off to do as we're told, still dragging our stockings and hanging onto our hats. Mum goes downstairs first. We follow her until we reach the dining-room door.

'Go on then,' she says, standing back for us to pass her.

We push open the door and have to blink, because we can hardly believe our eyes. 'Cor! Look at all that,' Gary cries, running over to a Beatles drum set and starting to thump. 'It's real drums. And look, a horse on springs. Can I get on?'

Dad scoops him up and settles him in the saddle. 'Gee up!' he shouts, bouncing up and down. He spots a cowboy suit laid out on Mum's chair and has to put it on straight away. There's a hat too, and a gun in a holster. He goes back to his drums and starts to sing 'Yeah, yeah, yeah.'

On my side of the room there's a real table and chairs, made of wood, that's big enough for Gary and me to sit at. Next to it is a twin doll's pram with real sheets and blankets and lacy pillows. I've got a Tressie doll, whose hair grows, some coloured chalks for my blackboard, a hula hoop, a pair of jumping jacks that are like roller skates, but they have springs instead of wheels; lots of different books and games, a lovely white Bible, a doctor's set and a tea set to use on my new table.

I throw my arms round Mum, then Dad, give them a big kiss and go back to my table and sit on one of the chairs. It's the best present I've ever had. 'Can I eat my breakfast here?' I ask.

'Oh, I think so,' Mum answers. 'What do you want? Cornflakes and toast?'

'Yep.'

'Yes please,' she corrects. 'Gary? The same for you?'

'Yes please. Can I sit at your table?' he asks me.

'Yes, but mind you don't make a mess.'

'Can we open our presents under the tree now?' he asks Dad.

'Go on then.'

There are so many it takes ages to unwrap them all and there's so much paper Dad can hardly pick it up before there's more. Mum's watching from the door, and keeping an eye on the toast. I have a silver bracelet with my name on, some record tokens, a compendium of games, a dressing-table set, some false nails, a pair of red and green stripey gloves with the fingers in, some pink flannelette pyjamas with flowers on, and lots and lots of other things. Gary has a bow and arrow, a fire engine with a driver and ladders, a pair of football boots and a football, a monster mask, a set of dominoes, and a transistor radio from Grampy and Aunty Beat that's a bit broken, but Dad says he can probably get it going.

This is turning into the best Christmas we've ever had . . .

Eddress

They have too much these kids. Spoiled rotten they are, when there's so many children starving in the world. It's not decent to see them with so much they don't even know what to play with first, but it don't half do your heart good to see their faces lighting up the way they do. We never had anything like it when we was kids. There was too many of us in our house to start with, and we was as poor as church mice. I'll always remember our mam keeping the wrapping paper from one year to the next so she could iron it out and use it again. She thought we were a bit daft, I reckon, because she used to nick toys off one of us to wrap up and give to another, and hope we never noticed. She got a bit mixed up one year and gave our Tom one of our Phyllis's cast-off blouses. Funniest part was, he liked it and wouldn't stop wearing it. After that we all thought he was going to turn out queer when he grew up, but he didn't.

Watching my two now I can't help thinking how lucky we are to have each other, and this house, and food on our table. I know we're a bit broke, and we have to scrimp at the end of the week to get us through to Fridays, and we don't always have everything we'd like, but thanks to the Co-op, and Green Shield stamps and the coupons from me fags, we have our little treats, and manage to get by a lot better than some. I mean, who else do you know's roasting a goose for Christmas? Eddie managed to stuff the great thing in the oven last night (it's out there cooking now, on a low light) – we never had anything like it when we was young, neither of us. Eddie's mam never liked to talk about it, but I know, when they was down in Wales, they had to go to the soup kitchens sometimes, or they'd have nothing to eat. I'm not saying we didn't, mind, because God knows, we had our share of handouts and the like, especially when the war was on. Bit of tripe or pork chitlings was about the best we got then. Chicken was a rare treat, but even if we managed to get one, scrawny bugger hardly had enough meat on it to go round three of us, never mind thirteen.

'All right, Mum, we've finished our breakfast, so you've got to open yours now,' Gary declares.

They look so funny sitting there at Susan's little table and chairs. Shame the camera doesn't work in the house, it would be nice to have a picture. Susan's busy clearing the dishes off her table and wiping it down. She's as proud as Punch of it, and twice as pleased because when she saw it in the club book we told her it was too dear so she couldn't have it.

I think funny thoughts sometimes, when I look at her. I wonder who she is inside, and what she's really thinking. She's such a mix of me and Eddie, it's hard to say who she's like most. I think she's got the bad bits of me and the good bits of him. She's got a strong will, I know that, and a stubborn streak the like of which isn't going to do her any good if we don't tame it. Our mam and Eddie are always going on at me that I'm too hard on her, but it's the only way she's ever going to learn. I want her to make something of herself, to have a good education and find herself a good job.

Of course I want her to get married too, but times are changing, women are becoming more independent these days, and if you ask me, it's no bad thing. Gary'll be all right, men always are. It's harder for a girl, no matter what she wants to be. In our Susan's case, I don't think it's going to be a ballerina, which is a shame, because that would have been nice. She's not exactly shining at the piano either, but we're going to keep it up. Ballet she can leave after Christmas. The elocution lessons didn't come to anything – the teacher gave up because there weren't enough people to make it worthwhile. Still, if we can get her into Red Maids School, over on the Downs, when she's eleven, she'll have all the elocution and piano she'll ever need, not to mention deportment, Latin, Greek and God knows what else. Next thing you know she'll be up at university, mixing with debutantes and the like, and flying off round the world. Won't want to know her common old mum and dad then. (She'll get the back of my hand if she ever gets too big for her boots with us, I'm telling you that now, I don't care how posh and successful she is.)

'I'm coming, I'm coming,' I call back, as they all start singing 'Why are we waiting'.

The fire's roaring up the chimney when I go into the room, the guard's around it but Gary's sitting too close. I make him move away, then go to sit in my chair where all my presents are lined up along the arms. We're all still in our dressing gowns, no-one's opened the curtains yet, and there are some Christmas carols on the telly. We're so lucky to have a telly. Not many round here do.

First I open a blue and yellow check headscarf from our mam (the one I gave her last year). Then there's a box of Dairy Milk from our Gord and his family; a fancy packet of shortbread biscuits from our Tom and his family; a tin of lily of the valley talcum powder from Eddie's sister Nance, some lavender bath salts from his other sister, Doreen; a nice pair of leather gloves from our Phil who's got more money than the rest of us, and a little clipboard to rest my bingo card on from Betty and her family next door. She'll laugh when she opens hers, because I've bought her the same thing.

'Open mine now,' Gary insists, pushing it at me. 'It's a surprise.'

It is too, because I've got no idea what he's been spending his little bit of pocket money on.

His eyes don't leave my fingers as I tear open the wrapping that he must have done himself, because the

101

sticky tape's all twisted and not where it should be. It's a bar of Cadum soap. 'Oh look!' I cry, holding it up so they can all see. 'It's exactly what I want. Thank you my love,' and for once he doesn't pull a face as I give him a smackeroo on the cheek.

'Mine now,' Susan says. 'I wrapped it myself, and I made the bow.'

'You've done it beautiful,' I tell her. And she has.

'Oooh, some Parma violet scent,' I declare, holding it up so I can smell it. Can't stand the stuff, but for some reason she seems to think I like it. 'I'll put some on now,' I say, and dab a drop on my neck. Lucky I haven't had a wash yet, it'll come off then. 'Thank you my love,' I say, and give her a great big smackeroo too.

'I wrapped this one too,' she informs me as she passes me another. 'It's from Dad.'

I've got no idea what this is going to be either; he wouldn't tell me what he was getting, and the shape and size of it isn't giving anything away. 'Do you know what it is?' I ask Susan.

'No. It's in a box and Dad wouldn't let me have a look in case I couldn't keep a secret – which I can,' she added, giving him a nudge.

It's a small flat white box with nothing written on the outside. I glance up at Eddie, who's smiling away, and looking as mysterious as . . . whoever he says, I've forgotten her name now. I open the top, lift it up, then pull back the tissue. 'Oh, Eddie,' I say, hardly able to believe me eyes. 'Oh, you daft thing. You shouldn't have spent all that money. Oh, look at it. It's lovely.'

'What is it Mum?' Susan cries. 'Can I see?'

'Go careful now,' I say, leaning down for her to have a look. 'It's a gold compact for my powder with my initials engraved on the front, see?'

'E.L.,' she reads. 'Eddress Lewis.'

102

I look up at Eddie who's grinning like the Cheshire cat now, and I wonder who's the most pleased, me or him. 'Thank you,' I say. 'I still say you shouldn't have, but it's very nice.'

'Now you Dad!' Gary shouts. 'It's your turn. Open mine first.'

'What about all the others?' I remind him. 'From Aunty Nance, and Aunty Doreen . . .'

'But they'll only be socks and hankies,' Susan pipes up. 'Can you open them last Dad, and open ours first?'

'As you like,' he laughs. 'Oh my goodness, what's this?' he cries as he pulls a massive copy of *War and Peace* out of its wrapping. 'How did you know I wanted this? Look, Mum. Look what they bought me. Isn't that perfect? *War and Peace*. I'll be able to read it to you both at bedtime.'

'Oh no!' Gary groans.

'He's teasing, silly,' Susan says. 'We got you something else as well,' she tells Eddie, which is a surprise to me, because I only got the book for them to give. 'Well, it was for Mum,' she explains, 'but she already had two presents, so we're giving this other one to you instead. I made it.'

'And me,' Gary says. 'I put the coat . . .'

Susan's hand goes over his mouth. 'Don't give it away, stupid.'

'All right, that's enough of that now,' I tell her.

'So what can this be?' Eddie says, peeling back the edges of the wrapping. He takes something out and holds it up. 'That is . . . It's smashing,' he says. 'Isn't that smashing, Mum? It's, it's . . .' He's turning it round in his hand, trying to work it out, and I want to laugh.

'It's the best peg bag in the world,' I declare, deciding to give him some help.

'And I made it,' Susan reminds us. 'I did it in needlework, and I embroidered the word PEGS on the front, only the "E" ended up looking a bit like an "I", but you can see it's an "E" really.'

'And I put the coat hanger in,' Gary chips in.

'It's the best present ever,' Eddie informs them, scooping them onto his lap for a kiss. 'I'll always keep my pegs in it.'

I'm trying not to laugh again. He might drive me mad at times, but there aren't many who can make me laugh the way he does.

'Now you've got to open the one from Mum,' Gary reminds him. 'I know what it is.'

'Don't tell him,' Susan snaps.

Eddie starts feeling it. 'It's a tie?' he guesses.

'No. It's too big to be a tie,' Gary scoffs. 'Shall I open it for you?'

'Here you are then.'

Gary tears at the paper, tosses it over his shoulder and hands his father the book. 'See, I told you, it's a book,' he declares.

'*The Ragged Trousered Philanthropists*,' Eddie reads aloud. He couldn't look more delighted if he tried.

'Thought you might like it,' I say. He lent his other copy to someone months ago who never gave it back, the robbing scoundrel – everyone knows how much he loves that book.

'Oh, I like it all right,' he says. 'It's just what I wanted.'

I wish I'd spent a bit more on him now he's got me the compact, but I didn't know he was going to do that, and it's all his money anyway, so I don't suppose it makes that much difference. It would have been nice if I had though. Still, he's got his birthday presents to come tomorrow, that'll help make up a bit.

'All right,' I say, getting up, 'time to get dressed. Is it light out yet?'

Susan drags back the curtains. 'Just,' she answers. 'And it's raining. We wanted snow.'

Rain or snow, it's still Christmas Day and there's a lot to do. After we're all washed and dressed and have tidied around a bit, Eddie goes up to fetch our mam who brings down more presents, then gives me a hand with the dinner, while Eddie plays with the kids and their toys. They don't half make a noise, the three of them in there, and our Susan doesn't sound a bit lady-like screaming out for someone to bash his stupid head in, but it's Christmas so I decide to turn a deaf ear for today.

'So how are you feeling now?' our mam says, as I turn down the gas under the cabbage.

'Me?' I say. 'I'm all right. Why wouldn't I be?'

'I was just wondering, that's all. No need to bite me head off.'

'I'm not. I just don't know why you're asking. Don't I look all right?'

'Course you do. I was just meaning . . . You know . . .' She nods towards my chest.

'Well it ain't grown back, if that's what you mean,' I tell her, and picking up a tea towel I open the oven door to check on the roasters. Fancy bringing that up now. I see her every bloody day and she never mentions it, but she has to go and bring it up right in the middle of cooking Christmas dinner.

'I'll go and lay the table,' she says.

'Use the best cutlery, in the sideboard,' I tell her, 'and you can get the best plates out too.'

The kitchen's all steamed up, so I open the back door to let some of it out, then get on with making the gravy. Eddie likes Bisto, Gary likes Oxo, so I make two, seeing as it's Christmas. Getting Susan to eat her carrots and greens isn't going to be easy, but she won't be leaving the table until she does, Christmas or not. Maybe I just won't give her as many today.

Eddie carves the goose and we start serving up. There's some church service going on on the telly now, and the room's got so warm we open a window to let in some air. There are toys everywhere, you can hardly move. I've made sure my compact is put away safe, though, it's upstairs in my handbag along with my lipstick and a couple of spare packets of fags. Which reminds me . . .

'How many coupons have you got now, Mam?' I ask her. 'I've got some left over, so I reckon between us we might have enough to get you a new kettle.'

'I don't know. Our Gord and our Tom bring 'em in. You'll have to count them when you come up.'

'I'll do it,' Susan offers.

'And me,' Gary chimes in. 'I'm a really fast counter.'

'All right, all right,' I say. 'That's enough, let's start our dinner now.'

Eddie says grace, and is the first, when he starts eating, to say, 'Delicious.'

'It's a bit tough,' I say.

'Tasty though,' Mam decides. 'I've never had goose before. Where did you get this'n from?'

'The farm, up Siston. They was only ten bob dearer than the turkeys, so I thought we'd splash out and give it a try. Not bad I s'pose. Don't know if I'd get one again.'

'It made a right mess of the shed,' Susan tells her. 'There are feathers everywhere. We're going to collect them and make a pillow for you, Gran.'

'That'll be nice. They're expensive, goose feathers. It's what all the rich people do have in their pillows.'

There's Christmas pudding, Christmas cake, Christmas log or mince pies for afters, but everyone's too full to have any straight away, so we clear the table and sit in front of the fire to let it all go down. Susan and Gary play tiddlywinks from her compendium, while Eddie has a leaf through his books and I have a fag. Our mam's already dozing, but we wake her up when it's time for the Queen's speech – she wouldn't want to miss that.

The Queen talks about all the important things that happened through the year, our new Labour government under Harold Wilson, and the first London elections, that Labour won too. She tells us how concerned she is by what's going on in Rhodesia, and Cyprus and various other parts of the world, and asks God to bless all the poor people who are suffering at this time. Then she mentions the two new additions to her family, her son Edward, and Princess Margaret's girl, Sarah. I wonder what sort of Christmas they're having, up there in Buck House, or wherever they are, with all those servants and nothing more to worry about than whether or not they'll catch the fox on their hunt tomorrow.

'Notice she didn't say anything about Brezhnev, or what's happening in the Soviet Union,' Eddie comments as the picture fades.

'What's that got to do with us or the Commonwealth?' I say, but before he can answer I add, 'No, don't let's get into your politics now. I'm going to get our mam's coat to give it a warm by the fire before you take her up our Gord's.'

'You still getting the *Soviet Weekly*?' our mam asks him.

'Yes. Do you want to take one with you, when you go?'

'Not me. I'm a Tory, me. Terrible, what they've done to Churchill. I can't get over that, voting him out, after all he did for this country.'

'The war ended nearly twenty years ago,' he reminds her. 'He was good then, but him and his party haven't done anything for us common people since. You wait

and see, things'll start improving no end now the Social-
ists are in.'

'Well, if they put my pension up, I might not think
'em so bad,' she says, taking his hand so he can pull her
up.

'Are you picking up Uncle Bob and Karen and Julie
on the way back?' Susan asks.

'Yes. Now give your gran a kiss before she goes.'

After Eddie's gone I make a start on the washing-up,
leaving the kids to go on playing. Normally I'd make
them help, but it's such a mess out here, they'll only get
in the way, and I wouldn't mind a quiet five minutes to
meself. At least out here I can hear meself think. I'm
feeling a bit bad now about snapping at our mam like
that earlier, but she'll know I didn't mean it. If she brings
it up again I'll say sorry, otherwise it's probably best left
alone. I hope she doesn't mention it to Eddie, while
they're in the car, but I can't imagine she would. They'll
talk about Churchill, or the war, knowing those two, or
the price of everything now.

When it's all done and put away I stick the kettle on
to make a nice pot of tea, and carry it in next to the fire,
where my fags are on the arm of my chair. Glad Eddie's
not around to give me one of his looks, I light up and
sit back to enjoy it. I'm only about halfway through
when the kids drag me into a game of ludo, which we're
still playing when Bob, Flo and their kids come back
with Eddie.

Flo and I go out to the kitchen to make a fresh pot,
leaving Eddie and Bob to the games. What a palaver.
The place is turning into bedlam. Hide-and-seek, blind
man's buff, musical chairs, you name it, Eddie, Bob and
the kids play it, while Flo and I take the tea in, then
sit and have a chat and do our knitting. Bob's as soft
as Eddie when it comes to his children, so like me, Flo

108

has to take a firm hand. Hers are still young though. Julie, her eldest, is Gary's age, and Karen's only two, so she doesn't have a strong-willed young madam to deal with yet, though watching the two of them now, as bright as buttons and twice as cute, the time doesn't seem too far off.

They're on to hunt the slipper now. The kids are all out in the kitchen, while Eddie and Bob find a place to hide it. They're like a pair of kids, honest they are. Where shall they put it? Somewhere not too obvious and not too high. Bob has an idea which makes me smile. He's as sharp as his brother, he is. Let's see what the kids make of this now.

'All right, you can come in,' Eddie shouts out.

They spill in from the kitchen ready to start searching, until they spot the slipper in the middle of the floor in front of them, right next to its mate.

'Which one is it?' Bob wants to know.

For a moment they all look a bit bewildered until they get the joke and start to laugh.

'That's cheating,' they cry. 'You can't do that.'

'Yes I can. Now come on, which one is it?'

The real joke is neither Eddie nor Bob can remember either, but they just make it up and let Karen be the winner. She gets a selection box from under the tree to go with the packet of Opal Fruits she won in pass the parcel.

It's time now for some home-made mince pies and custard, or cream, or both if you're Gary. Eddie and Bob have a big helping of Christmas pudding with real Cornish clotted cream, Flo has a slice of cake, and I'm still too full up after dinner, so I just have a cup-a-tea and a fag.

All in all it's turning out to be a lovely Christmas Day. The kids seem tickled pink with their presents, and God

knows they had enough; the goose wasn't bad, something a bit different, anyway; reckon our mam enjoyed
herself while she was here (she never says anything, but
you always know from how much she eats); and what
better way to end it than with Eddie rolling round on
the floor with his brother and the kids. What a pair they
are. Never saw a couple of brothers like it. And to think
I was scared out me wits when they whisked me into
that hospital a few months ago, that I might not be here
to see it. What a daft bugger I am. Good job I never said
anything to anyone then, I should feel proper soft now
if I had.

Chapter Six

Susan

It's March now, and I'm sitting here, at the back of the class, with my hands stuck on top my head, because I flicked ink over Kelvin Milton. He flicked it at me first, but it missed, so I'm clean and he has dark blue splodges in his sticky-out ear and on his frayed white collar. Good. Serve him right. Trouble is, now, every time I put my hand up to get the teacher's attention she just ignores me, or tells me to wait. But I can't wait. I have to meet Mum at the bus stop outside the park at twenty past ten, and if I don't leave now the bus will go without us.

I try putting up my hand again, but the teacher just waves it back down and goes on telling us all about the Romans and Christians and gladiators. It's a really good story, but I'm very worried now about what Mum'll have to say if we miss the bus. I've got to take a test today for the stuck-up school at Westbury-on-Trym. I don't want to go there, so I don't care if we're late, but Mum will. She'll play merry hell, because she doesn't want me going to any other school but the best.

It's quarter past already. I look up at the windows. They're too high for me to climb out of, and the teacher would spot me anyway. Also, I don't want to go without my coat because it's cold and windy outside, and Mum would be furious. I try saying a magic spell to make myself invisible so I can walk across the room, but when I look down I'm still there.

If I was sitting next to Sophie (who used to be my best friend until she went off with Carol Adams) I could whisper to her to put her hand up for me, but I'm stuck back here on my own, like a dunce. And I'm not a dunce, because I came sixth in the class at the end of last term, and I had a really good report that put Mum in a good mood with me for days. She still gets lots of bad moods, but she hasn't gone off with her other family again for ages, and anyway, they don't exist so she won't.

I'm getting a bit panicked now. I wonder what'll happen if I just stand up and walk out. The teacher wouldn't be able to stop me, would she? She might try though, and the next thing I know I'll be sent to Mr Dobbs and everyone'll be so angry with me I'll be like a Christian in a den full of lions. I wonder if Dad will be able to rescue me, it would be hard fighting a lion and I don't want him to be eaten.

Suddenly the door flies open and there's Mummy, looking even crosser than a lion.

'What are you doing back there?' she roars at me. 'What's she doing back there?' she roars at the teacher. 'I gave her a note this morning. She's supposed to leave here at ten past ten. Did she give it to you? Did you give it to her?' she asks me.

I nod.

'Oh, Mrs Lewis,' the teacher says, going all trembly and red in the face, 'I'm really sorry. I completely forgot. Yes, she gave me the note . . .'

'Go and get your coat,' Mummy commands me. 'And make it double quick. As for you,' she says to the teacher, 'when I give my daughter a note I don't expect you to forget and make me come in here to fetch her.

I'll be having words with the headmaster about you.'

I can hear the others sniggering as we leave. No-one ever dares to tell the teacher off, except my mum. She did it once before, when I fell over in the playground and landed on my head and nearly bashed all my brains out, and the teacher didn't send me to the doctor. Mummy came up here the next day and tore her off such a strip she was nearly crying by the time Mummy finished. I could have fractured my skull, Mummy told her, and what would have happened then? She deserved to be reported to the police, because it's criminal, not making sure a child gets the proper attention when she hits her head that hard. And it was hard. I kept throwing up when I got home, so Mum stopped Dr Tyldesley as he was coming out of Witchy Beryl's, to come and have a look at me. I wasn't going to die (it hurt so much I thought I might so I was already saying sorry to God for all the things I've done wrong so he'd let me into heaven), but I had a great big bump and she had to keep me home the next day. It was almost worth falling over for that.

As we get outside the bus is coming up the hill.

'Quick!' she cries, grabbing my hand. 'Run!'

We're closer to the bus stop than the bus, but it's going too fast. It catches up with us as we cross over Park Road, and there's no-one at the bus stop to make it stop anyway.

'Wait! Wait!' Mummy shouts as it draws alongside us.

Everyone listens to Mummy, even the bus, because it stops, right there next to us, just like she told it to.

'It's your Uncle Bob,' she laughs, spotting the driver. 'Lucky for us, or it might have gone straight past.'

We can't speak to him, because he's in his driver's cabin, but he waves out, and when we get to Bristol Centre, where the bus has to wait for ten minutes before going on to the Downs, he comes to sit on the top deck with us to have a chat.

'So where are you two going, all dressed up to the nines?' he asks.

It's true, I've got my best coat on today, and so has Mum. Mine's dark blue with silver buttons and a scarf for a collar, and Mum's is green with wooden buttons, great big pockets and a brown fur collar. She's got her smart A.G. Meek shoes on too, with pointed toes, high heels and slingbacks. I think her feet must be very freezing because the wind is bitter, and the gloves that match don't have any fur so her hands must be cold too. I know mine are.

Mum reminds Uncle Bob that I'm sitting my first test today for the Red Maids School. I start to feel a bit nervous. I don't like tests, and I have to pass this one or I won't be any daughter of Mum's.

'What sort of test is it?' Uncle Bob asks, giving me a wink.

'General knowledge and IQ, that sort of thing,' Mummy answers. 'It's a preliminary entrance exam. The big one comes when she's ten.'

'So you're going to be a lady,' he says to me.

'If I have anything to do with it she is,' Mummy tells him. 'She's going to pass that exam, or else, aren't you, my girl?'

I give her a salute which makes Uncle Bob laugh and Mum roll her eyes.

'I don't know where she gets it from, really I don't. It must be your side of the family.'

'Oh she's a Lewis all right,' Uncle Bob says. 'But I think she's got a bit of her old mum in her too, all that fiery red hair and plucky spirit.'

'Don't encourage her,' Mummy admonishes. (New word I learned at the weekend with Dad. We learn two a day, but I keep forgetting them.)

'I think it might be easier for me to pass if I'm not wearing my glasses,' I mention to Mum. 'I can't see properly with them on.'

Mummy looks at Uncle Bob. 'Now if that isn't crafty,' she says.

I grin cheerfully at Uncle Bob who gives me another wink. I nearly love him as much as Dad, especially when he says, 'She'll sail through, won't you, my angel? She's going to make us all proud.'

'She'd better,' Mummy replies, tidying up my hair after taking off my glasses.

'Gary still got his patch on?' Uncle Bob asks.

'It came off yesterday. Still too early to tell how much good it did, though. A right pair of wonky-eyed kids I've got myself. Must get that from your side of the family too.'

'No!' I cry. 'It's you who's got wonky eyes, not Dad.'

'They're not wonky, and mind who you're talking to in that tone of voice.'

'At least Gary didn't have to wear a patch on a pair of glasses,' I tell Uncle Bob. 'Not like me. Will he have to go in hospital again?' I ask Mum.

'Not that we know of.'

I wouldn't mind if he did, because Mum went with him in January and slept there, so it was just me and Dad at home, which meant I got to stay up late and do everything Mum never lets me do. I don't want her to go again though, and I missed Gary a lot, so really it's better when we're all together. We all made a great big fuss of him when he came home, which he really liked, because he had all his favourite food, and was allowed to stay up late to watch his favourite programmes.

'All right, better get this bus back on the road,' Uncle Bob says, looking at his pocket watch. 'Still in plenty of time, are you?'

'Oh yes,' Mummy assures him. 'Just make sure you don't break down going up Blackboy Hill.'

I know he won't, but I wish he would.

By the time we get off it's started to rain and Mum has to fight the March wind to keep her umbrella up. A car splashes us and makes her feet all wet. She shouts blue murder after him, waving her fist, but he doesn't care, he's in a car and she can't get him. (Lucky for him.) My feet are dry because I've got boots on.

We walk past lots of tall, posh houses with great big windows and driveways, and statues outside. They must be where dukes and duchesses live. There's no-one around. Apart from the traffic and wind there's no noise either, which makes it all seem very scary indeed.

After a while we reach some big gates that are open. Just inside, on the edge of the grass, is a sign saying 'Red Maids School for Girls, Westbury-on-Trym. Founded by John Whitson, 1634'.

Mummy treads on her cigarette end, tidies up her headscarf, and takes hold of my hand. 'All right?' she says.

I think I'd better say yes, so I do, but I'm not. It looks a horrible place, with a long winding drive that disappears into thick, dark trees like *The Lion, the Witch and the Wardrobe*. It's leading to an evil person's castle, I can tell, so I hold on tighter to Mummy's hand in case we have to run away. I don't want her to go without me.

It's not raining too much any more, but big fat blobs are falling down from the trees as we walk under them. The ground is covered in thick brown slimy leaves. There's no sign of anyone, but on a field one side of the drive I can see some goal nets and I think I can hear some singing coming from somewhere.

We go round the bend and there it is, the evil person's castle. It's the most frightening-looking house I've ever

116

seen in my whole life, with dark red walls, huge tall pointed windows and secret towers where people can be locked away and never seen again. I expect it's got a dungeon too, and a torture chamber and kitchens where I'll be whipped and beaten with brooms.

Mummy stops walking. I look up at her. 'Your father should have brought you,' she murmurs.

That really frightens me, because Mummy's usually never scared of anything. 'Let's go home,' I say.

She just ignores me and carries on up to the massive front door that's definitely the entrance to Satan's house.

'There's no knocker or bell,' she says. 'How are we supposed to get in?'

'I don't think we are,' I answer.

She ignores me again and takes off her glove. Her knocks don't seem to be very loud, even though she thumps the door really hard.

'Where is everyone?' Mummy says, standing back to look up at the place. 'We can't be the only ones taking the test today, so where're the others?' She checks the Timex watch Dad gave her for her birthday last September. 'We're not late.'

'I expect they've cancelled it,' I tell her.

'We know we're in the right place. It said, on the board by the gates.'

'Maybe they've moved and forgotten to take the sign down.'

She spots a rope hanging down one side of the door. 'What's this?' she says, and tugs it.

Somewhere, a long way off, deep inside, a bell clangs, and I shiver. What if she's woken up all the ghosts and vampires? They'll come swooping and screeching down through the halls and out through the windows to suck out all our blood and turn us into toads. I really want to run away now, and I think Mummy does too.

We wait.

'There's no-one in,' I say, but then the door starts to open. I'm so sure a witch is going to appear out of the darkness, that I'm a bit surprised when we see a fat woman who looks like Harry Worth, the comedian, in a nurse's uniform. I wonder if she stands sideways against a mirror and puts out an arm and leg the way Harry Worth does. I love it when he does that, it always makes us laugh, especially when Dad did it in C&A once.

'Can I help you?' the woman says.

'We're here to sit the test,' Mummy tells her. 'Susan Lewis.'

The woman frowns. 'I'm sorry?'

'The entrance exam.'

'Oh, I see. Mm, you'd better come in.'

We follow her into a dingy hall where paintings of people from olden times hang on the wooden walls, and a huge staircase leads up into dark shadows.

'Wait here,' she says, pointing to a couple of chairs.

'She looks like Harry Worth,' I whisper as she goes off down a corridor.

Mummy claps a hand over my mouth, but I can see she's trying not to laugh. 'Ssh,' she says sharply, and taking a hanky out of her A.G. Meek matching handbag she dabs it with her tongue and starts wiping my mouth, and rubbing the mud splashes off of her nylons.

I look around. The faces in the paintings are mostly round and red-cheeked. You can tell they're lords and ladies, or dukes and duchesses. I wonder if they used to live here, before it was a school. They probably get down from the paintings at night and haunt the place.

'It's ever so quiet,' I whisper. 'Where are all the girls?'

'In class I expect.'

'Do you think they have playtime here? I didn't see a playground.'

'It's probably round the back. Now, ssh.'

After a while we hear the sound of high heels coming our way. Mummy starts to get up, so I do too. A tall, skinny woman appears from a corridor, her hair all piled up on top of her head, like Dusty Springfield's, except hers is black, and her arms are full of books.

'Oh, hello,' she says, in a squeaky posh voice that sounds as though it's coming out of her nose. 'Are you being helped?'

'Yes. Thank you,' Mummy answers, turning red.

I wonder if we're supposed to curtsey.

'Very good,' Dusty Springfield says, and walks on across the hall into a room the other side.

'She's no better than she ought to be,' Mummy mutters after the door has closed.

'Let's go before anyone comes,' I say. 'They're all snobs . . .'

'Be quiet and sit down.'

A grandfather clock in the corner starts to chime. I count all twelve bongs and wait for something horrible to happen. Nothing does, so I swing my feet back and forth, until Mummy tells me to stop, then I have a rummage in her bag for some Embassy coupons to count.

'Don't do that,' she says, stuffing them back in. 'Now behave, someone's coming.'

This time the footsteps are coming down the stairs. The floorboards creak and so do the shoes. I see them first, they're brown lace-ups, a bit like Daddy wears.

Mummy and I stand up. We keep watching whoever it is descending from the shadows, first the shoes, then the thick stockings, then the black dress, then . . . my eyes nearly pop out of my head. It's a man! Wearing a dress! And stockings! Blimey. I don't know whether to be scared or not now.

'Hello, I'm Miss Diamond, the headmistress.' It's

119

definitely a man, I can tell by the voice. 'I'm afraid you've come to the wrong place for the preliminary exam. It's being held in a special hall, near the city centre. Didn't you get the letter?'

'Uh, no,' Mummy answers, turning red again. 'Hi thought we 'ad to come here.'

The headmistress smiles, which makes her look hungry, so I step back a bit behind Mum. 'I'm awfully sorry,' she says. 'Can you tell me your name?'

'I'm Mrs Lewis and this is my daughter, Susan. Uh, Lewis.'

The headmistress looks at the watch pinned to her chest. 'Mm, you're too late to sit the exam this morning now,' she informs us. 'But maybe they can squeeze you in this afternoon. Would it be convenient?'

'Oh yes,' Mummy assures her. 'Most. Yes. Thank you.'

'I'll see what I can do. Please wait here.'

She waits till we're sitting, then goes through a door the other side of the hall and closes it.

I turn to Mummy. 'Is she a man?' I ask.

'Ssh!' Mummy snaps.

'But is she?'

'No. Of course not.'

'I don't want to come here and grow up to be a man,' I tell her.

'I told you to be quiet.'

I lean forward and look up into her face.

'If you make me laugh, Susan Lewis, you'll go straight to bed when you get home.'

I start to giggle.

'I'm warning you.'

I put a hand over my mouth.

Next to me I feel Mummy starting to shake.

'You're laughing,' I accuse.

'I am not.'

'Yes you are.'

'Be quiet.'

A few minutes later the door opens and the head-mistress comes back, carrying a piece of paper. 'Yes, they can fit you in this afternoon,' she tells us. 'They start again at two. Here's a map of how to get there. It's just off College Green.'

'Thank you,' Mummy says. 'Thank you very . . .'

She stops so I look up to see why.

'Thank you very much,' she says.

She's trying not to laugh.

The headmistress goes to open the front door. 'Goodbye,' she says.

Mummy starts to say goodbye back, but it turns into a great big snorty snigger. 'I'm sorry,' she says, 'I'm very sorry,' but she's still laughing. She can't stop and now nor can I.

The headmistress closes the door behind us and Mummy leans against a statue to get her breath back. 'I bloody hope we haven't cocked this up,' she says, wiping her eyes with her gloves. 'You shouldn't have made me laugh in there. I've made a right charlie of meself now.'

'But it's not my fault she's a man,' I say.

'That's enough. Now let's get out of here before someone chucks us out.'

As we start to move off a bell rings and then lots of girls start spilling out of a terrapin hut that's round the side of the school. We stand back and watch them go past. They're all wearing dark red uniforms with white shirts and grey knee-length socks, and they all look older and posher than me. They definitely sound it too, because we can hear them talking like donkeys as they go by. Hee, haw! Hee haw!

I can tell by Mummy's face that she really likes the look of them. It's exactly how she wants me to be, all upper-class and better than everyone else. It's all right for them though, they're all lovely-looking and I expect their dads are really rich. I notice one who's as pretty as Elizabeth Taylor in *National Velvet*. She's laughing with her friends, but when she catches me watching her she gives me a look that makes me feel like a worm. I want to poke my tongue out, but I'm a bit afraid to.

'They're probably gypsies,' I hear someone say, and I realise they're talking about us.

I hope Mum didn't hear, because it'll make her really mad. 'I never want to go back there again, ever!' I say as we walk on down the drive. 'I hate it. It's horrible and creepy and I'm not going to pass the test.'

'You'll do as you're told,' Mummy responds. 'You're going up in the world, my girl, if it's the last thing you do.'

'Then *you* go and let me stay at home with Dad and Gary.'

'Don't talk ridiculous. And stop answering back.'

We catch the bus down to the centre and I cheer up a bit when Mum says we can have a Wimpy for dinner. She only has a cup of tea and a fag though, otherwise we won't have enough bus fare to get home. We find a ha'penny spare, which she lets me put in the fruit machine, but we don't win.

It only takes a few minutes to walk up round from the Wimpy Bar to College Green, which is next to the cathedral. In the summer people sit out on the grass to eat their sandwiches, but it's too cold today. Everyone's hurrying in and out of the council offices, which curve round one side of the green, glad to get out of the wind and rain. The place we're looking for is just round the corner, behind the offices, a large white building with black window frames and a black double front door. All the railings in the street have gold tops like spears, and outside some of the houses are shiny brass plaques with names on.

This time we're not the only ones arriving, there are quite a few others, girls with their mothers, and some dads are here too. Just inside the door a woman takes our names, ticking them off a list, and pointing us through to where we have to sit the exam. I eye the other girls warily, waiting for someone to be snotty so I can be snotty back, but they don't seem to be taking much notice of me. I think we're all about the same age, but most of them are prettier than me, even without my glasses. Some of their mums are nice-looking too, with smart clothes and hair. I wish my mum was as nice-looking as some of them.

After we've found the tables with our names on the parents have to leave, and when we're given the signal, we turn the exam papers over to begin. I'm shaking a bit, and can't read the first questions very well, but then I settle down and get on with it.

Some of it's easy-peasy, like how many wives did Henry VIII have? I know that, and I can even name them, but that would be showing off. I have to write out a poem I know, so I write two verses and the chorus of 'A Smuggler's Song' by Rudyard Kipling, because it's my absolute favourite. Then I have to fill half a page about a Shakespeare story, so I choose *The Taming of the Shrew*, which I like even better than *A Midsummer Night's Dream*. There's some arithmetic to do, which I get a bit stuck on, but then I work it out and turn over the page to answer some questions on Bristol, like who built the Clifton suspension bridge and Temple Meads station (Isumbard Kingdom Brewnell); what rare species of wild cat is in the Clifton zoo (white tigers); what's the name of the gorilla in the museum, Alfred; how many people live in Bristol (I don't know so I guess, more than a million). There are some questions on geography then, which are a bit harder, like how do you tell a position on the globe – I think it's something to do with longitude and latitude so I just put down those two words, hope they're spelt right and go on to the next. What is the capital of Australia? Sidney. (I go back after, cross it out and put Brisbun.) What was the name of the Turkish empire? I know that, because it's where Gran keeps her blankets, in the ottoman.

After an hour a bell rings and we all have to stop. I'm on the last question, so I quickly write 'the Queen' in answer to who's the head of the country, and put down my pen. I wonder if it's the prime minister. I think it is, but it's too late to change it now.

I can't find Mum when they let us out, and I start to panic in case she's gone off and left me. Maybe she's arranged for that evil man in a woman's frock to come and get me while I'm not looking, so he can lock me up in that haunted castle. I don't think she loves me very much really, so she might do that. Or she could have popped off to see her other family for an hour, and forgot to come back. How am I going to get home? Dad will be really worried, and I might get kidnapped off the fourteen bus and murdered down St Pauls. I don't want Mum to have gone and left me. I was trying to be good, and I did my best in the test. Then I spot her outside smoking a cigarette and talking to a lady in a long black coat with a white fur collar.

'Hello,' Mum says as she sees me coming. 'How did you get on? Did you answer them all?'

'Most of them,' I tell her. 'Some were really easy.'

'This is Mrs Cranfield,' she says, nodding towards the other lady. 'Her daughter Emily's been sitting the exam too.'

Mrs Cranfield's smile is the loveliest I've ever seen. 'Hello,' she says. 'What beautiful hair you have.'

I feel a bit shy, and pull a face.

Mum nudges me. 'Say thank you!'

'Thank you.'

'Oh, Emily, darling, there you are,' Mrs Cranfield says in a voice that's all happy and soft. 'How did you get on? Look at you, silly. No tears now, it's all over.'

'I didn't answer them all,' Emily wept.

'Oh, darling, that's all right,' her mother says, stooping down to her level and giving her a hug. 'I'm sure you did your best, and Daddy and I will be proud of you for that. Now won't we?'

Emily nods her pretty head, then buries her face in her mum's neck. I think I'd like to bury my face in Mrs Cranfield's neck too.

'Come on,' my mum says, 'time we were going. Bye Mrs Cranfield, nice to meet you.'

'And you Mrs Lewis. I hope Susan passes.'

As we walk off down the road Mum starts mimicking Mrs Cranfield, '"Oh darling, there you are,"' she says in a stuck up voice.

I glance up at her.

'What a load of old nonsense,' she laughs.

'Yeah, a load of nonsense,' I say and laugh too.

Eddress

I can tell you what the first words out of Eddie's mouth will be when he comes in from work, and I'm right. 'So how did my best girl get on with the test today? Did you answer all the questions?'

'Course she did,' I tell him, pouring the potatoes from the colander into a bowl ready to mash. 'She's an old clever clogs, aren't you?'

'No!' She's leaning against the living-room door with a face as long as a fiddle.

'Sulking because there's no-one to play with,' I tell Eddie. 'But she did very well today. Better than her old mother, who took her to the wrong place this morning. Made a right blooming chump of meself, I did.' I tell him what happened, and by the time I finish he's laughing too.

'I reckon that headmistress might be a man, mind you,' I say. 'She bloody well sounded like one. Then we met this lovely woman, down at the proper exam place. Really nicely spoken she was. Not a bit stuck up like the rest of them. That's how you're going to talk,' I inform Susan.

'No I'm not,' she retorts.

'Oh yes, you are. Once you start mixing with people like that.'

'I don't want to be like them. They're all snobs. And I'm not going to that bloody school.'

I stop what I'm doing. 'Did I just hear you swear?'

She stares at me, eyes as defiant as I've ever seen.

'Upstairs! Now! Swearing, and cheeking me back. Who do you think you are?'

'She's tired,' Eddie says.

'She'll do as she's told. Go on. Bed!'

'You're always picking on me,' she shouts, close to tears. 'And you only want me to go to that school so you can get rid of me.'

'I'm trying to do my bloody best for you, is what I'm trying to do, and this is the thanks I get. Now don't just stand there, bed!' I can see she's about to argue again so I raise my hand.

She flounces off in her high and mighty way, and stomps up the stairs like a bloody elephant. I start to shout after her, but Eddie says, 'All right. Leave her now.

It's been a long day for both of you, and we don't want it to end in tears.'

I shrug him off and go on mashing the spuds. 'You don't help bloody matters,' I tell him. 'Taking her side all the time. She's got to learn, Eddie, and she's never going to with you mollycoddling her all the time.'

'What can I do to help?' he says. 'Has anyone laid the table yet? Where's Gary?'

'He's staying up our mam's tonight. And he's in the bloody doghouse too, when he gets home. He's been crayoning on his wallpaper, he has.'

Eddie doesn't have anything to say about that, he just takes the cutlery in to the table and wipes over the place mats, while I carry the plates through, corned beef, mashed potatoes and beans.

'I'll go and get her,' he says.

I notice that he's only set places for me and him, Susan's is on her own little table that she had for Christmas. Her and Gary always sit there now, so I suppose it was worth the money, even though we're still paying it off.

'Come on,' I say, as she walks in with Eddie. 'If you eat all that you can have someone in to play for ten minutes after.'

'I don't want to.'

I look at Eddie. 'What do I do with her?' I demand.

'Eat your tea,' he tells her. 'I'll play a game with you after, if you like.'

We all sit down and no-one says anything for a while. Eddie pours us out a cup of tea, I make myself a corned-beef-mash sandwich and Susan just mucks about with hers.

'If you don't start eating that properly you'll be straight back up to bed with nothing,' I tell her.

'I don't want anything,' she answers stroppily.

'Right, that's it . . .'

'Yes, you do,' Eddie jumps in. 'You like corned beef, so don't be daft now. Eat it up like a good girl.'

'I can't if she's going to shout at me.'

'*She?*' I repeat. 'Who's *she*? The cat's mother?'

She puts her head down and I see two tears drop into her food.

'What are you crying for?' I shout. 'It's me who should be bloody crying, having a daughter who can't ever do as she's told.'

'Eddress, you're making her cry for no reason.'

'No reason? You call her attitude no reason? All right. All right. Have it your way. I can see nothing I say matters around here, so you just do it your way, and I'll leave you to it.'

'No, Mum, no,' Susan cries as I march down the hall and start putting on my coat. 'Don't go. Please. I promise I'll be good. I'll eat all my tea. *Mum,*' she screams, as I walk out the front door. '*I promise I'll be good.*'

I'm about to slam the door and take myself off up our mam's for an hour, but the panic in her voice makes me turn back. She's really frightened. She's sobbing so hard that her little body is jerking around all over the place. I sit on the bottom of the stairs and pull her onto my lap. 'It's all right,' I tell her. 'I'm still here. Come on now, pull yourself together, there's a good girl. There's nothing to get yourself so worked up about.'

She still can't speak, and she's clinging to me like she thinks she's going to fall off a cliff. I look up at Eddie.

'There you are,' he says, kneeling down next to us. 'Mummy's still here. Everything's all right.'

'I-I don't want you to go,' she finally manages to say.

'I'm not,' I tell her. 'I'm right here.' I smooth back her hair, and kiss her forehead. 'There, is that better?'

She nods. 'I don't want to go to that school, Mum. Please don't make me.'

'Ssh,' I say. 'We won't talk about it now. Let's just go back and eat our tea, shall we?'

Later, when Eddie's upstairs reading her a story, I finish the washing-up and sit down in front of the fire to smoke a fag. *Take Your Pick*'s on the telly, but I'm not paying much attention. I'm thinking back over the day, and what happened at tea-time. It's niggling me, the way she's being about that school, and how frightened she got when she thought I was leaving. Such a lot of fuss to make about nothing, but it's not the first time it's happened. Still kids are kids, they get themselves into a state about all sorts of things, and the next thing you know it's all forgotten. So I decide to put it down to a long day with a lot of things happening, and a bit of over-tiredness at the end.

'Is she all right?' I ask Eddie when he comes down.

'Fast asleep,' he answers. He's already got his coat on and is warming his hands in front of the fire before putting on his gloves. 'I should be back about nine,' he says. 'Shall I get some coal in before I go?'

'No, there's enough there. Where are you going?'

'Up the Union.'

'You can bring me back some fags, if you like.'

He shakes his head. 'I'm not buying them for you.'

'Don't be so bloody po-faced,' I tell him. 'There's a ten-bob note behind the clock, take that.'

'I've got half a crown for the Union, that's all I need.'

'Eddie, I can't go and get any myself while Susan's in bed.'

'Then you'll have to do without, won't you?'

I feel like landing one on him. 'If you don't get me any fags, then you better find somewhere else to spend the night.'

'Cheerio,' he says, pulling on his gloves and taking a cap out of his pocket.

'Eddie!' I shout after him.

The bloody sod just ignores me. Well let him wait till he gets home, if he doesn't have a packet of fags he's going to be bloody sorry.

It's ten past nine when I hear the back door open and his feet wiping on the mat. He goes to hang his coat on the bottom of the stairs then comes into the living room. I can feel the cold around him as he goes to stoop down in front of the fire.

'Did you get them?' I say.

He reaches in his pocket and tosses twenty Embassy into my lap. Just as well, because I've only got one left in the other packet and I need more than that to last me till morning.

'I only did it because I don't want any more rows,' he tells me.

'Then we won't be having one, will we?'

He stands up. 'Why don't you make more of an effort to give up?' he asks. 'You don't even try.'

'What's the point? The damage has been done, hasn't it? So it's a bit late now to think about giving up.'

'You want it to come back, is that it? You're not satisfied with what's already been done to you . . .'

'Honest to God, you talk a load of old bunkum sometimes. They got rid of it, didn't they? It's gone. They cut me up, fried me with radium . . .'

'I know what they did. I'm just saying, you were told to give up the fags and you haven't even tried.'

'Well that's my business, innit? I'll do what I want, without you interfering, thank you very much.'

'Then don't come to me if you get it again, because it'll be your own damned fault.'

'I won't, don't worry. Now, do you want a cup of tea,

or are you just going to keep standing there getting on at me?'

'I'm going in the front room to do some homework for night school.'

'It's too bloody cold in there. You'll freeze to death.'

'I'll take the paraffin heater in. Have you checked on Susan?'

'About half an hour ago. She's all right.'

He goes off into the next room, leaving me to light up without his accusing eyes watching my every move. He makes it bloody hard for a person to enjoy a simple fag when he goes on like that, honest he does. Gets right on my bloody nerves, nagging and moaning, lecturing me like I'm some bleeding imbecile who can't do anything right. God knows, we don't get many pleasures in life, so it's a bit much, if you ask me, begrudging me a fag now and then.

I decide to make a cup of tea and take him one in, whether he wants it or not. He'll be cold in there, so it might warm him up a bit.

I find him with his overcoat and cap on, sitting at our best table trying to do something with a slide rule. The paraffin heater's warmed the room up a bit, but we can still see our breath and there's a little dewdrop on the end of his nose.

'You're a big 'a'p'orth sometimes,' I tell him, putting his cup down and taking a hanky out of my pinny pocket. 'Shutting yourself up in here in the middle of winter with no fire to keep you warm. Why didn't you say something, I'd have got one going for you while you was out.'

'It's all right, I'm not going to do much tonight. Thank you.'

'Like a big kid, you are,' I say, tucking the hanky up his sleeve. 'Don't know what you'd do without me to take care of you.'

'Nor do I,' he says.

I wasn't being serious, but from the tone of his voice I know he is. That's the trouble with Eddie, he never knows when something's meant to be a joke. 'I'm going back in the warm,' I tell him. 'Don't stay in here too long, or I might have to come and chip the ice off you.'

I reckon there's time to have one more fag before he finishes his homework, but I'm only halfway through when I hear the front-room door open and him coming down the passage. I quickly chuck the rest of the fag on the fire and pick up my knitting. I don't normally let him boss me around like this, and I'm not very happy about wasting half a fag like that either, but I'm feeling a bit tired after all the fuss today so I'm in no mood for a row. But if he starts, I'll give him one all right and he's the one who'll end up sorry.

'Hungry?' I say, as he sits down in his chair. 'We've got some luncheon meat if you want a sandwich.'

He shakes his head. 'Still full up from tea,' he says. 'What's that you're knitting?'

'A cardigan for our Gary.' I hold it up so he can see.

'Why don't you teach me how to knit?' he says.

'You?' I laugh. 'Men don't knit. Men get out there on the garden and clear away all the muck that's built up over the winter.'

'I'll do it at the weekend,' he promises. 'I want to knit now, though.'

'Eddie, you're a soft old bugger sometimes,' I tell him. 'It's no wonder they used to call you a nancy boy and a poof, with your art and your poems and all the reading you do. And now you want to knit. Whatever next, I ask myself. You'll be putting on my clothes and going down the bingo.'

He laughs. 'It'd get the neighbours going if I did.'

'Anything gets them going, bunch of nosy-parkering

132

old gossips they are. Not that I don't enjoy a nice chat and a cup of tea myself, when I've got time . . . What are you laughing at now?'

'You.'

'Why? What did I say?'

'Nothing. Come here and give us a kiss.'

'Oh now, don't you start that . . . Eddie, I'll lose my stitches,' I say as he starts to pull me out of the chair.

'Put the bloody knitting down and come over here. Come on, on my knee.'

'I'll squash you flat, you silly bugger.'

'Do as you're told for once, will you?'

I sit on his lap and put my arms round his neck. 'What a pair of blinking chumps we look, sitting here like this,' I say.

'There's no-one to see us, so stop moaning and give us a kiss now.'

'I'm sitting awkward, your arm's . . .'

'Eddress.'

'What?'

He gets hold of my face and plants a kiss right on my lips.

'There,' he says.

'You're a soft old sod,' I tell him.

'Bit soft on my wife, it's true.'

I settle down and rest my head on his shoulder. 'So what's brought all this on then?' I ask after a while.

'I just thought it would be nice to have a bit of a cuddle.'

He's right, it is nice, so that's what we do, sit there in front of the fire, with the telly and the lights off, having a cuddle, while he tells me poems from Longfellow and Shelley and Keats. That's my Eddie for you, not like anyone else I know. I wouldn't want him to be, either. I just wish he was rich enough for us to pay for Susan

133

and Gary to go to good schools, in case they don't pass the exams. But we'll get by, all of us. No, we'll do more than that, we'll go right to the bloody top, that's what we'll do, and the next thing you know we won't just be hobnobbing with the Mrs Cranfields of the world, we'll be living right next door to them.

Chapter Seven

Eddress

Sometimes I wonder where the weeks go, honest I do. One minute it's Christmas, the next we've got Easter coming up on us, then before we know it it'll be Whitsun and we'll be thinking about our summer holidays again. I think we'll go back to Dawlish this year, in a chalet. It worked out all right last time, apart from when Gary decided to go missing and we had the police out looking for him. What a to-do. Had the whole bloody campsite upside down, hiked people out the showers, off the lavs even, until we found him playing with a little boy seven chalets down, happy as Larry and twice as daft. Little perisher, going off like that. Gave us the fright of our lives.

I've been doing a bit of baking today ready for Easter, a dozen biscuits, a fruit cake for our mam, gingerbread men for the kids and some shortbread for Eddie. I'll do the hot cross buns on Thursday night, I think, then warm them up in the oven on Good Friday morning. It's lovely when the kitchen's all warm and full of mouth-watering smells like this, and the wireless is on. I was listening to a programme just now about what's supposed to be in, and what's out. Didn't half give us a laugh when Betty and June from over the road dropped in for a cup of tea and a chat after. Bloody Peregrine for a boy's name's supposed to be in. I ask you. Poor little bugger, fancy having to grow up with a moniker like that. Annabel's all right for a girl, I suppose, quite nice really, wish I'd thought of it when our Susan was born. I gave Eddie his way over that. I wanted to call her Diane, but he liked Susan Heywood, so Susan it was. Gary was my choice, bloody sight better than Peregrine! Thanks to Eddie he's ended up with Nakita too. Gary Maurice Nakita.

They even did what was in and out for things like cigarettes (Gauloise are in – none of us have ever even heard of them, Consulate are out, good job too); women's shoes (Fortnum and Mason are in – I thought they sold food to the Queen; Freeman, Hardy and Willis are out – just as well because none of us can afford the place); clothes designers (Mary Quant and Jaeger are in, Hartnell and Tinling are out – we've only ever heard of Mary Quant and Hartnell and none of us is skinny enough to wear one, or rich enough to be out of fashion with the other). On and on it went, Donovan in, the Bachelors out, Jack Russells in, corgis out, Habitat in, Harrods out – never heard such a load of old bunkum, but it don't half make you wonder about how the other half live, especially when they got into which artists you should have hanging on your walls, or how it's not the done thing any more to have sanitary towels for your dogs! There's a whole other world out there, in't there, and I bet they don't know anything about us lot either. I can tell them this much though, we've never bought sanitary towels for our bloody dogs.

June's gone now, but Betty's still here, upstairs checking on the kids. They were playing mothers and fathers earlier with Susan and Geoffrey as the grown-ups, and Gary and Nigel having to do as they're told. It went quiet for a bit, which is never a good sign, so I'm just dusting down Eddie's shortbread with some sugar, while Betty goes to find out if they're up to no good.

'Gary and Nigel are fast asleep,' she says, coming back in the kitchen and picking up a tea towel to dry a few dishes, 'and Susan and Geoffrey are playing ludo.'

'I wouldn't mind having a bit of a doze myself,' I remark, clearing the sugar away. 'This weather always makes me feel tired, don't it you?'

'A bit, yeah. Where do you keep this mixing bowl?'

'In the cupboard next to the back door. I'll put the kettle on again, shall I?'

'I'll have to go and get some more fags, I can't keep borrowing off you.'

'That's all right, you can let me have them back later on. The packet's there, on the window sill, if you want one now.'

She lights two, passes me one, and leaves hers in the corner of her mouth as she rinses out the teapot.

'How much longer's Don on nights?' I ask her,

'A couple more weeks. We should have enough saved up to get a car soon. He's got his eye on an old Wolseley he saw down Two Mile Hill.'

'I wouldn't be in too much of a hurry,' I warn. 'Ours is always breaking down and if Eddie can't repair it, it just sits out there getting on my nerves.'

'What's the matter with it now?'

'God knows.' I yawn, loudly, and rest my fag on the window sill so my hands are free to put the biscuits and cake on a shelf in the pantry. 'I'm bloody tired today, I know that,' I grumble. 'It's hard work having the kids home from school when it's raining, always under your feet, moaning they're bored or fighting fit to kill each other. I can't believe they've been good for this long.'

'How did you get on up the doctor's the other day? Did he give you anything for your cold?'

'Ssh,' I say, going to close the hall door. 'I don't want old big ears, Susan, hearing I went up the doctor's, or

137

she'll start asking questions. You know what she's like, wants to be told the ins and outs of everything, and with an imagination like hers, the less she knows the better. We haven't even told her she passed the test for Red Maids yet, or she'll just start getting herself in a state again. Honest to God, you'd think we were sending her to Transylvania the way she carries on, bloody witches, vampires and ghosts. I keep telling her, she's not even going to be a boarder, like some of them. She's only going as a day girl, so she can get the number eight bus all the way there every morning, and all the way home again every night. But try telling her that. She thinks we're wicked and mean and we don't want her any more. Honest, kids, who'd have 'em?'

I cover the pot with a cosy and carry it through to put next to the fire, while Betty spoons sugar into a couple of cups and pours in a drop of milk.

'So what did the doctor say?' she asks, keeping her voice down as she comes into the living room behind me.

'Oh, he just gave me a prescription, but I'm not going to bother getting it. I'm all right now, just a bit of a cough.'

'Anything about your check-up? Have you heard when it is yet?'

'No.' My answer comes out a bit snappy, but I don't like people mentioning anything about what I had done.

'It's over six months now though, innit? I thought they wanted you back . . .'

'Maybe they don't any more. They haven't been in touch, and I'm definitely not going to go chasing them. Eddie thinks I should, but he would. Do you know, he actually accused me of hiding the appointment letter the other night. Bloody fool, as if I'd do that.'

'You didn't, did you?'

'Don't you bloody start. No, course I didn't. Where would it get me if I did? I have to let them make sure it's still all clear, I know that. But if there was something wrong I'd know, and there's not. Now, let's have a cup of tea and then I've got something to show you.'

There's an advert for kids' coats that I cut out of the paper. They've got fur linings and hoods, they're waterproof and half the price you'd pay down Millets or somewhere like that. The reason they're so cheap is you have to send away to China for them, where everything's a lot cheaper than here, but they're nice, good-quality-looking coats, so I think we should get some.

'How do we pay?' Betty asks.

'It says here we can send the money by postal order or cheque. Well, seeing as neither of us has got a bank account, I can sort it out when I go to the post office tomorrow to pick up the family allowance. Do you want to get two for Geoffrey and Nigel?'

'I don't know if I've got a fiver to spare this week,' she answers. 'I'll ask Don when he gets up. See what he says. Have you told Eddie?'

'It was him what spotted the advert in the first place. You know him, anything to do with Russia or China.' I finish off my tea, then put the strainer on the cup to pour myself another. 'Blimey, listen to that rain. It sounds like it's going to come straight through the bloody windows.'

'Never get the washing dry in this weather,' Betty grumbles.

We stare down at the fire as the coals shift and settle again. My eyes are feeling heavy, I reckon I could drop off right where I'm sitting. 'I've promised to take the kids up the zoo next week,' I say, 'so I hope it clears up by then.'

'That'll be nice. Up the zoo. Our Geoffrey likes the

reptile house. Gives me the bleeding creeps, all those sodding snakes and toads, but he has to go in. Thought I might take 'em to the pictures instead this holiday.'

We go on chatting about this and that, what's happening on *Coronation Street*, whether they'll really ban cigarette advertising on the telly the way they're saying, about Molly Carson, over in the next street, whose husband just ran off with some floozy from St George leaving her with four kids to bring up, until it's time for me to start putting Eddie's tea on. Betty's got to go and wake Don up too, but her kids stay to watch children's hour, even though they've got their own telly next door now.

When Eddie comes home his food's ready to go on the table – fish pie made with a nice piece of cod, chips and peas. Susan and Gary have fish fingers sitting at her little table, then Eddie's back out the door again, off to night school. Before he goes he puts the paraffin heater in the bathroom to warm it up a bit, so after Susan helps me wash up I send her up to have a bath while I play a game with Gary. When she's finished I boil a kettle to warm up the bathwater, then I plop Gary in while I go to give Susan a brisk rub-down to try and stop her from shivering. I'm always too rough, she tells me, with her teeth chattering together, she can do it herself. So I let go of the towel and take her pyjamas out of the airing cupboard. They're nice and warm, which puts a smile on her face when I pull the top over her head.

As usual her record player goes on, 'Bobby Shaftoe's gone to sea', so I leave her to brush her own hair while I scoop my boy out of the bath and carry him into his bedroom. Eddie decorated it a couple of weeks ago with some wallpaper we found in the club book that's all pictures of the Beatles. So there we are, me and Gary, shivering, rubbing and laughing in his tiny little boxroom being watched over by John, Paul, George and Ringo, who's Gary's favourite. Susan prefers George and has dreams about him, she tells me.

Before getting into bed in his Beatles pyjamas Gary has to have a quick bang on his drums, so I make sure Susan's all tucked up, go through the usual 'you're horrible for making me go to bed early' business, then I turn off their lights and take meself back downstairs. I wait in the kitchen doorway, and sure enough, as soon as the little devils think I can't hear them they start calling out to one another.

'If you come in here I'll tell you a story,' Susan offers.

Seconds later I hear Gary's door creak open and his little feet pad across Susan's room, followed by a few grunts and slaps when he obviously manages to step on her as he climbs into her bed. It's no wonder he has nightmares with the horror stories she tells him, but he can never seem to get enough of them, so it's his silly fault if he keeps listening. (I won't be saying that when he comes waking me up in the middle of the night, I'll want to clout her one then.)

There's a good film on tonight with Rod Cameron and Yvonne de Carlo. It doesn't start for another half an hour though, so plenty of time to get some more coal in and make a nice cup of tea before I sit down to write to our Maurice in New Zealand. Funny Rod Cameron and Yvonne de Carlo should be on telly tonight, when our Maurice only mentioned them in his last letter. He said Rod Cameron was starring in a programme over there now called *State Trooper*, and Yvonne de Carlo's husband got injured, apparently, so she's come out of retirement to work as a strip artist to make some money. Fancy that!

The wind's still howling away outside as I rummage in the sideboard drawer for one of the flimsy blue airmail letters I use. Poor Eddie having to be out in this. I'll make

141

him a nice bit of supper when he comes home, Cheddar cheese and bread with some Branston pickle. Meanwhile I sit down at the dining table to write. I always wait till Eddie's out of the way to do it, because I think he gets a bit jealous, even if I offer to let him read it. He never does. He won't read the ones Maurice sends either, says they're none of his business. God knows what he thinks are in them, but if he wants to be like that, then let him.

It don't take me long to fill Maurice in on the news about our mam and the others, and to reassure him that I can use my arm, no trouble at all now. I remind him of his promise when he rang at Christmas that he'd come home for the next one, then I go on a bit about the plans they've got to change things up Kingswood, though I might already have told him how they've turned the picture house into a bowling alley. Then there was the fire at the pickle factory, and there's been some talk of them closing down Jones's. He'll remember that place only too well, because he got accused of shoplifting there once when he was a teenager. It was all false and they never pressed charges, but he's never had any fondness for the shop since. I think about the other things I could write, but I don't. There's not much space left and most of it's not things I want to bring up again. It's in the past now, so it won't do any good remembering.

I lick the edges, seal them down then pop it in my handbag ready to post in the morning. All's quiet upstairs, it seems, but I creep into the hall to make sure they're not somewhere they shouldn't be. Not a peep. That's good. Eddie won't be back for at least another hour, so I'm safe to have a bit of a look at my other bosom in front of the fire without someone coming in. Not that I think there's anything wrong, it's just been on my mind a bit lately, what with everyone asking when the check-up's supposed to be. I reckon the doctors have decided I don't need one, that's why I haven't heard, and I don't think I do either, but I might as well have a quick look myself, just in case Eddie decides to get in touch with the hospital to remind them. This way, if there's no lumps, I can tell him we don't need to do anything, and if he insists he can even examine me himself. Dr Eddie Kildare.

The curtains are drawn, and the door's closed, so I pull up me jumper and tuck my petticoat and brassiere cup under Cyclops, as I call the one I've got left. It don't look any different to normal, a few freckles on it, and a nipple that wouldn't let me feed either of me kids. I stand back a bit so I can see it in the mirror. It still looks all right, though I'll have to hope Eddie never gets injured, because I don't suppose I'd get a job as a stripper these days. I prod it about a bit. Everything feels as it should. No lumps or bumps, or aches or pains. I knew there was nothing to worry about, but I don't mind admitting I'll be able to enjoy my cup of tea and the film a bit better now. I might even, if the check-up letter does ever come, put it on the back of the fire and forget it. I mean, what's the point in messing about with things that have got nothing wrong with them in the first place?

Susan

'Ow! Ow! OOOOWWW! You're hurting me. Stop it!'

'Sit still, will you?' Mummy snaps and grabs on tighter to my ponytail.

'Ooowww!'

'For heaven's sake, anyone would think I was torturing you.'

'You are!'

She doesn't care though, because she just tugs the brush even harder right through the knots, like she's trying to tear off my scalp. She gets it caught and it hurts so much when she tries to pull it out that I jump up from the arm of the chair, before she can wrench my whole head off.

'I don't want you to do it,' I cry. 'You're cruel and you – you should be reported to the police.'

She drops her arms to her sides and sighs. 'What do you do with her, Mam?' she says to Granny. 'She's such a baby, isn't she? Can't even have her hair brushed without making a fuss.'

'I am not a baby.'

'You've got to have your hair brushed, my old love,' Granny says.

'I don't want to. I hate having it brushed. I want it cut right up to here.' I chop my hand against the side of my head.

'Go on speaking to your grandmother like that and you'll get the back of my hand,' Mummy warns, resting her cigarette in an ashtray. 'Now come here and let me finish.'

'No.'

'Then you won't be able to come to the zoo.'

'I don't want to go to the zoo.'

'Yes you do.'

'No I don't.'

I do, but I don't want to have my hair brushed any more, not by her. 'Let Gran do it,' I say. Gran never hurts the way Mummy does.

Mummy hands the brush over, and goes to get the milk in off the doorstep, and shouts upstairs to Gary to make sure he's cleaning his teeth. I know he's not, but the little fibber says he is.

'Are you going to help me make some sandwiches to take with us?' Gran says as she smooths the brush gently over my hair.

'We've already done them,' I tell her. 'You and Mum have got salmon and cucumber, I've got luncheon meat and Gary's got jam. We've made a flask of tea too and a bottle of orange squash. Dad gave us some money to buy nuts for the monkeys. I've got one and six now that I've saved up.'

'Then you're richer than me,' Gran chuckles.

I let my head drop back and grin up at her. She's got a lovely wrinkly, whiskery face with watery blue eyes and funny white fluffy hair. 'Are you sleeping here again tonight?' I ask.

'I expect so,' she answers.

'You can sleep in my bed, if you like.'

'You're a lovely girl, but there's not enough room in there for the two of us.'

'I can sleep with Mum and Dad, the way Gary did last night.'

'All right, we'll see.' I can tell she's not really listening now, because she's turned her head towards the door. 'Who's that your mother's chatting to out there?' she says.

'Probably the milkman, or Mrs Lear,' I answer.

The front door closes and Mum comes back along the hall into the room. 'Haven't you finished doing her hair yet?' she snaps at Gran.

'Nearly there,' Gran says and starts twisting an elastic band round my ponytail. 'Who were you chatting to?'

'No-one,' Mum answers.

Gran doesn't say anything, but I can tell she wants to. I turn to look at Mum, but she's got her back to me as she puts something in the sideboard. I don't know what it is, but I expect if I ask she'll tell me to mind my own business.

145

She does, but when she turns round again she looks a bit strange, like she's put too much powder on.

'Is that what I think it is?' Gran says to Mummy.

Mum gives me a quick look and says, 'Not now, Mam. It's time to go. Susan, go and tell that brother of yours to hurry up or we'll miss the bus. Ah, here he is. Did you wash behind your ears?'

'Mummy it's working again!' he shouts up at her. 'I got it working. Listen.' He's holding up the old transistor radio Grampy gave him for Christmas, and somewhere inside all the hissing and crackling there's the faint sound of a man's voice. 'Listen!' he cries again.

Mummy takes the radio and puts it up to her ear. The voice comes clearer, so we can hear the man reading the news, talking about all the people who were killed in an earthquake in Chile. (That's in South America and the capital is . . . I've forgotten. And anyway I don't care what Mum's hidden in the sideboard, so there.)

'Poor blighters,' Mummy says, giving the radio back to Gary. 'See, you two children don't know where you're well off. All those bad things happening out there and here you are with more than either of you deserve. Now, where's my handbag? Has anyone seen it?'

Finding it on the table, she lights another cigarette and lets it dangle from the corner of her mouth as she carries the cold teapot and milk jug out to the kitchen. Gran takes Gary into the hall to help him put on his coat, so I'm on my own in here now, but I'm too afraid to go and find out what Mum put in the sideboard, in case she comes back and catches me.

We catch the number eight bus outside the Tennis Court pub to take us all the way to Clifton. It's the same bus as the one Mummy and I caught to go to the wicked, horrible, haunted school that turns girls into men, but I don't say anything in case it reminds Mummy, and I don't

146

want to do that or she might start saying I have to go there again. I sit downstairs with Gran, because she can't get up on top, but Mummy has to go up there, because that's where you're allowed to smoke. Gary climbs up with her and we can hear him all the way downstairs, pretending to be a driver. I wish he was, because he sounds as though his bus is going a lot faster than ours.

When we get to the zoo there's a queue right along the road to go in. Lucky we brought our umbrellas and plastic macs, because it starts to rain as we wait, which makes all the mums grumble and moan.

'Bloody weather,' they say. 'It started out nice this morning, now look at it.'

It doesn't last very long though, and by the time we go through the turnstile the sun's out again making it all shiny and warm. The first thing we do is go to buy some peanuts for the monkeys. There's another queue there, but we don't mind waiting because there's a clown doing tricks with our money, making it disappear then come back again. I don't think I'll give him mine just in case his magic runs out.

Mum and Gran are standing behind us, chatting. There's lots of noise going on, with all the children shouting and playing and the mums and dads telling them to be quiet, so I can't hear everything Mum's saying, but I do hear some.

'No, I didn't open it,' she says. 'Not yet.'

'So how do you know who it's from?'

'It's written on the front of the envelope. When I saw Dr Tyldesley last week he said it should have come before, around Christmas. This one'll probably be the second reminder.'

'So you didn't get the first one?'

'No. If I had I'd already know when I have to go, wouldn't I?'

'It must be soon now then.'

'I expect so.'

'Is it with Michaels again?'

'I don't know till I open it, do I?'

A baby next to me starts screaming so I don't hear what they say after that, until the baby gets a dummy stuck in its mouth, and Gran says, '. . . it's hard for Eddie to cope on his own.'

I suddenly feel all funny. I don't like them talking about doctors and Daddy being on his own, because I don't understand what it all means. I just know I don't like it. I decide not to listen any more in case they start talking about Mummy's other family, where she goes when she's not with us.

I buy my peanuts and walk with Gary over to the monkey temple. There are hundreds of people there, all trying to get to the front to throw in their peanuts. The monkeys are funny and playful with big yellow teeth and gleaming red bottoms. They're lots of fun to watch, but it's hard to see with so many people around. I wish Daddy was here so we could climb on his shoulders. I wish he was here to stop Mum having secrets too. She can't hide things from him because he's her husband. If she does go off to her other family it'll be my fault, because I'm always getting on her nerves. I don't mean to, I just do.

'What's the matter with you?' Mummy says as I look up at her. 'You're not crying, are you?'

'No,' I say.

'Yes you are,' Gary jeers.

'No I am not.'

'Enough! Don't start arguing,' Mummy barks. 'Let's see if we can get through to the front.'

It's easy for Mummy to push her way through because she's tall and strong, and if anyone complains she just tells them to shut up or they'll be sorry. Next thing we're up on the wall and we can see everything that's going on.

We stay there until our peanuts run out, then we move on to see the lions and cheetahs and leopards. The white tigers are very special, but I tell Mum we don't really want to see them in case it reminds her of the test I did for the scary school.

The elephants are having a bath when we get there which is very funny, because they suck the water up in their trunks and squirt it out at the crowd. If you're at the front you get soaked, so we keep well back and nearly get knocked over as everyone tries to duck. The keeper has to keep ducking too, as he scrubs away with his sweeping brush and bottle of Vim. At least I think it's Vim, but it might not be. A space opens up and Gran gets drenched. Mum laughs so much that tears run down her cheeks.

We have to find a toilet then to get some paper towels to dry Gran's hair. We lose Gary for a few minutes, then find him all on his own queuing up to go and see the snakes.

Mummy and I wait outside because we hate snakes. We find a bench to sit down on and Mum opens a packet of salt and vinegar crisps for us to share. Eventually Gary and Gran come out, and we have to shout so they find us. Mum has an open packet of cheese and onion waiting for them, which Gary immediately starts scoffing. He's such a pig, because there are hardly any left for Gran. Then he keeps on and on that he wants to go back in the reptile house, so I give him a thump to shut him up.

He thumps me back, so I thump him again.

He kicks me, so I kick him, then he grabs hold of my hair, so I grab hold of his.

149

Mummy tears us apart, smacks our legs and tells us she'll leave us here if we start again.

After we've stopped crying Mum takes us both by the hand and walks us over to the bear pit. It's got huge high railings around it to stop anyone falling in, and the bears walking about the bottom are massive and cuddly and don't look frightening at all. I like the baby ones the best, and wish I could hold one. The mother – or it might be the father – stands up on two legs and reaches up towards the people. Everyone gasps and takes a step back – except Gary, because his head's stuck in the railings.

'How the bloody hell did you manage this?' Mummy grumbles as she tries to get him out.

'I didn't. It's not my fault,' he shouts.

'Hold still now. You're making it worse.'

It's the funniest thing I've ever seen and I can't stop laughing.

'Shut up, Susan, or I'll bash you,' he shouts.

'Be quiet,' Mummy tells him. 'And you,' she snaps at me. 'It's not funny, he's stuck and I can't get him out.'

Gary's going all red in the face and starts screaming blue murder. I look round and see that we've got more people watching us than are watching the bears.

'Mam, you'll have to go and get some help,' Mummy says. 'We might even have to call the fire brigade. Oh, you stupid boy, what did you go and stick your head in there for?'

'I didn't!' he cries.

'Oh what, it just opened up and grabbed you, did it?'

I still think it's funny, but I'm getting a bit worried now, in case one of the bears manages to climb up and bite off his head. A man is helping Mummy to try and bend open the bars, but they can't. Then Gran comes back with a zookeeper who tries to bend the bars too, but he can't either.

'The only answer is to chop off your ears,' he tells Gary, giving me a wink.

'No!' Gary screams. 'I don't want my ears chopped off.'

'He's only joking,' Mummy says, but she doesn't seem to find it any funnier than Gary. 'So what are you going to do?' she asks the zookeeper.

'I've got some tools in the workshop,' he answers, 'something in there should get him out.'

It ends up taking ages, and by the time he's free Gary's quite famous, because everyone in the zoo has come to have a look. He's acting as though he's some sort of hero now, instead of a great big idiot, but at least he won't be giving a bear a bellyache tonight with his stupid great big head.

'Just wait till I tell your father,' Mummy says when we're on the bus going home. 'You old nincompoop you! I dread to think what you'll get up to next.'

Daddy laughs and laughs when Mum tells him what happened, and swoops Gary up in his arms to give him a bear hug. Get it? (Dad's jokes aren't always very funny, but we laugh anyway to keep him happy.)

After tea Gran goes and sits by the fire to watch the telly, while Gary and I stay at my little table to draw some pictures for Dad of the animals we saw at the zoo. (I draw Gary with his head stuck in the bars. Gary draws a camel that looks like a dog, and a lizard that's really good.)

Mum and Dad are out in the kitchen washing up, then Mum comes in and takes the thing she hid earlier out of the sideboard. She catches me watching and taps the side of her nose with her finger.

I go on drawing, sea lions and elephants and giant tortoises, then I play noughts and crosses with Gary and let him win. It's only fair because he's little and I can win any time I like.

Suddenly the door swings open and Mum is saying in an angry voice, 'All right you two, up to bed now.'

'But it's not time yet,' I wail. 'It's only half . . .'

'Do as you're told and stop arguing.'

'But we haven't done anything wrong . . .'

'Susan.'

I look at Dad who's come in the room behind her.

'Eddress, it's not their fault . . .'

'You want to discuss it in front of them?' she shouts. 'Is that what you want? Well I don't want to discuss it at all, so just sod off . . .'

'Let's go in the other room,' he says.

'Leave me alone!' she snaps, shrugging him off. 'I don't want to talk to you. If you can't listen to what I'm saying . . .'

'I am listening, but you can't just not go, Ed . . .'

'I can do what I bloody well like, thank you very much. Now, you heard what I said, you two, up to bed.'

I'm still looking at Dad, but I can see he's not going to stick up for us again. I wish he would, because if they're going to have a row I want to be here to stop them. 'Come on, I'll give you a piggyback,' he says.

Mummy's face shows that she won't put up with any more arguing, so I get up from my table and go over to kiss Gran goodnight. It's not fair. I always have to go to bed earlier than everyone else anyway, and now I have to go to bed even earlier than me.

'Dad,' I say.

'Susan, you heard your mother. Now off you go.'

I want to cry and hit him, because he was on my side just now. 'You said you'd give us a piggyback.'

'That was before you started answering back.'

'I'm not answering back.'

'You're doing it now.'

'I'm not putting up with any more of this,' Mummy

152

suddenly shouts, and grabbing my arm she drags me out of the room and throws me down the passage. 'Up those stairs now and make sure you're in bed by the time I come up to tuck you in. And that goes for you too, Gary Lewis. Bed and no answering back.'

I can see he's about to cry, so I take hold of his hand and walk up the stairs with him. I want to cry too, but I'm the oldest so I can't. 'It's all right,' I tell him when we reach his bedroom door. 'You can sleep in with me tonight, after they've been up to turn off the lights.'

'It's not fair, we didn't do anything,' he says.

'I know. They're just wicked and anyway, they're not our real mum and dad. They stole us from kind people when we were born.'

'No they didn't.'

'Yes they did.' He's starting to look a bit worried so I say, 'Why don't we run away and find our real mum and dad?'

'I don't want to run away.'

'Don't be such a baby. We're going to see if we can get on a boat and go to an island where no grown-ups are allowed. I read about it in one of my books.'

'I don't want to go on a boat without Daddy.'

'Then don't come. I don't want you to anyway.'

I walk off into my bedroom, leaving him on the landing. It's not long before he follows me in though. 'You're not going to run away, are you?' he says.

'I might.'

He goes on standing there, watching as I play with my dolls. 'I'm going to tell Mum,' he says.

'If you do I'll smash your brains in.'

'I'll smash yours in.'

I snuggle my dolls down in their pram and button on the cover.

'I'm going to put my pyjamas on,' he says.

'Go on then, goody-two-shoes.'

'You'll be in trouble if you don't put yours on too.'

'See if I care.'

By the time Mum comes up I'm under the covers and facing the wall. She goes in to Gary first and I can hear them chatting, but can't make out what they're saying. I bet he's telling her I'm going to run away.

His light goes off, his door closes then she comes in to me. 'I hope you're not sulking,' she says.

I don't answer.

'Yes, I think she's sulking. Well I'll give her a kiss goodnight anyway.' She kisses the back of my head. 'God bless, sweet dreams,' she says.

I still don't answer.

'You're a proper little madam and you can stay up an extra half an hour tomorrow night,' she says. 'Will that make you happy?'

I nod.

'So do I get a kiss now?'

I turn over and put my arms round her neck. I feel like I want to cry, but I don't because there's nothing to cry about now. When she's gone I don't go and listen over the banister. I'm not sure why, I just don't.

Chapter Eight

Eddress

The kids is back at school after the Easter holidays, and now here I am at the hospital, me backside going numb as the wood it's parked on, I've been waiting so bleeding long. I'm telling you, me patience is getting as thin as the new nets I put up in the front room yesterday. Nearly fell off the ladder while I was doing it, I did, would have ended up crashing right through the bloody window, and that would have been a fine state of affairs, wouldn't it? I'd have been through that bloody door there a lot quicker than I'm getting through now, that's for sure. Come to think of it, I'd rather be in here for that.

Eddie's with me. He's looking a bit smaller than normal for some reason, maybe because the doctors are all so grand and he's so humble and respectful. I told him we can't afford for him to keep taking time off work, but he wouldn't listen. I think he's making sure I come, that's why he's here. Don't know what bloody odds it makes to him whether I turn up or not, but that's his business, not mine. It'll be mine when we haven't got enough to see us through till the end of next week though, won't it? It'll be me who has to make the pennies stretch to Friday so we've got food on the table and coins for the meter. It all comes down to me in the end, which is how it should be, I'm the wife, it's my job to run the home, I'm just saying, that's all.

When we got here they had me straight in for X-rays, but that was three hours ago now. Ever since we've just sat here, watching everyone come and go, reading the paper or having a little chat now and then. I have to pop outside to have a fag, because they don't allow it in here. Bloody nuisance, but I have to have one, because it's got me all on edge waiting about like this. I hate hospitals, always have. The smell's enough to put you off, and all that creeping about and talking in whispers gives me the bleeding willies.

A nurse comes through the swing doors into the waiting room, but it turns out she's not here for us. The old woman who's hardly breathing over by the fish tank goes in next with what must be her grandson. Everyone else looks as fed up as I feel as they settle down to wait again.

Last night I let Eddie examine the Cyclops, which he didn't seem to mind a bit. He was more thorough than I was when I did it, but he didn't find anything either, so we know there's nothing to worry about there. The scar on the other side's almost healed up completely now, and I feel as fit as a fiddle, so there's nothing to be getting worked up about. Nothing at all.

To get me mind on other things I ask Eddie how his dad was when he went up there yesterday. The old man's all right, he says, but he wishes Eddie's two sisters would speak to Beat, his new wife. Harmless little soul she is, Beat, gentle as a lamb and never wants to do anything but please. Course, they was devoted to their mam, those sisters, and don't want to see anyone take her place. I think Eddie was a bit upset when his dad married again too, but him and Bob still go to see their dad, which is only right. And think how those sisters are going to feel when he goes, knowing how they've turned their backs on him now.

I think about asking Eddie if he'd ever get married again, should anything happen to me, but it might upset him so I don't. He's worried enough, I can tell, even though there's nothing to worry about. It's all this bloody waiting around what does it. It gives you too much time to think, too much time to scare yourself to death.

I reckon I'd get married again if something happened to him, but there again, there's no-one else in the world like Eddie and I wouldn't want anyone who's not like him. We're not all soppy and romantic like some couples, but it don't mean we're not close, because we are. Course, we have our differences, and I know I'm not always that easy to get on with, but let me tell you, nor is he. When he's got his dander up about some Union thing, or some injustice in the world, like the blackie, Nelson Mandela, being sent to prison (you should have seen him then, I thought he was going to go and storm Downing Street all on his own – as it turned out thousands of others went with him), or if he thinks I'm being too hard on the kids, he's down on me like a ton of bricks. But no-one ever sees that, except me. He's got good principles and a soft heart, has my Eddie, so it makes me bloody mad to think he's got to sit here now, waiting and worrying, because some bleeding stuck-up doctor thinks his time is more important than ours.

'Tell me a poem,' I say. He'll like doing that. It'll take his mind off where we are, stop him worrying about things that don't need worrying about.

'Which one would you like?' he asks.

'Something by Robbie Burns.'

He thinks about it for a minute, then starts on one of the ones I love best. He keeps his voice low and leans his head into mine so only I can hear.

157

O, my love is like a red, red rose
That's newly sprung in June
O, my love is like the melody
That's sweetly played in tune

As fair art thou, my bonnie lass
So deep in love am I
And I will love thee still, my dear
Till all the seas gang dry

It's lovely listening to him, and marvellous how he remembers all the words. He even does the Scotch accent. Soft bleeding 'a'p'orth I am, got tears in me eyes now. Fine bloody spectacle I'll make of meself, won't I, blubbering in the hospital waiting room when I haven't even had the check-up yet.

The nurse comes in again and this time it's my turn. I stay sitting where I am, so Eddie stands up.

'Are you Mr Lewis?' the nurse asks him.

'Yes.'

'If you could wait here for the moment, thank you,' she says. 'We won't be long.'

'I'm not going in there without him,' I tell her. 'He's got to come too.'

'It's all right,' he whispers. 'I'll be here.'

'There's nothing to worry about, Mrs Lewis,' the nurse assures me. 'It's just a routine check-up. It won't take long.'

So Eddie stays in the waiting room while I follow the nurse through the double doors to a cubicle with a curtain across the front. She leaves me to take off all my clothes and put on a gown that opens down the back. There doesn't seem to me to be any point in taking my skirt and knicks off, when it's my upper regions he needs to look at, so I just remove my cardigan, jumper, brassiere and falsie and cover meself up with the gown.

Can you believe the bloody waiting starts all over again? I just sit there, on the edge of a trolley bed, staring at pictures of the human anatomy, or reading posters on different kinds of health care, while nurses' shoes squeak up and down the corridor and the odd siren wails in from outside as an ambulance rushes some poor bugger into the emergency ward.

When Dr Michaels, who did my operation, finally turns up the nurse is right, it don't take long. He just prods and pokes me around a bit, sticks the heartbeat listener, as our Susan calls it, in his ears to listen to my chest and asks me a few questions like how I'm feeling, and if there's any discomfort where my other bosom used to be. I can put his mind at rest on everything, except when he asks if I'm experiencing any 'undue tiredness' or 'loss of appetite'. My appetite's all right, but I do seem to get a bit tired now and then, in the day. I don't tell him that though, I just say everything's normal, otherwise he'll end up finding something else that's wrong with me and before I know it I'll be back on the bloody operating table having more bits removed in another experiment for the NHS.

'Right, you can get dressed again now,' he says with a pleasant little smile. 'Is your husband with you?'

'Yes, he's in the waiting room.'

'Good. Then perhaps you'd both like to come through to my office when you're ready and we'll have a little chat.'

No, we wouldn't like, I feel like shouting after him. Talk about scaring the living daylights out of a person. What's there to chat about? He's done the check-up, I've told him there's nothing wrong, so why can't we just go home now? All this bleeding fuss. Honest to God, if it weren't for Eddie, I'd tell *Doctor* bloody Michaels where he can stick his little chat.

By the time I'm dressed Eddie's waiting in the corridor outside the cubicle. He's looking a bit pale and as worried as I am that we're being called in.

'It's all right,' I say, giving him a wink. 'He just wants to tell us when the next check-up is, I expect. Probably won't be for another year.'

'That's what I thought,' he says.

'Ah, Mr and Mrs Lewis, you're ready,' a nurse calls from along the corridor. 'This way please.'

I keep thinking now about the blood Dr Tyldesley took a couple of weeks ago, that I never told Eddie anything about. I was only there for one of me regular check-ups, so I'm not sure why he took it, he just said he was sending it off to some laboratory, and at the time I didn't think any more of it. I can't get it out of my bloody mind now though. What if they've found something? I should never have let him take it. I won't next time.

Dr Michaels is wearing his nice pleasant smile again as he asks us to sit down on the chairs in front of his desk. The nurse leaves, closing the door behind her. Eddie's holding his cap in one hand and my best black handbag in the other. Silly sod, looks a right bloody fairy.

Michaels is reading a file in front of him, his half-glasses perched on the end of his nose. Eddie and I just sit there, waiting. Michaels picks up some X-rays and goes to hang them on the wall. I can't make head nor tail of them myself, but he looks at them with his hands on his hips, as though he's reading them like words.

'Mm,' he says.

My heart's thudding like a bleeding drum now. What the bloody hell's that supposed to mean?

Michaels walks back to his desk, sits down and starts reading his file again. 'You say you're feeling fine, Mrs Lewis?' he says to me. 'No unusual loss of energy or appetite that you've noticed?'

I shake my head.

'What about bathroom functions? Everything all right there?'

'Yes.'

'Breathing? Do you find yourself short of breath at all?'

'Only when I've been running,' I joke.

He smiles and gives one of those doctorly nods. 'Still smoking?' he asks.

If it weren't for Eddie I'd say no, but I can't with him sitting there, can I, so I just nod.

'How many a day?'

'About twenty.'

It's more and Eddie knows it, but he doesn't give me away.

'Have you tried to give up?'

If I have to come again, I'm going to come on my own. 'Not really,' I answer.

'Then you should. It's extremely bad for you, and though we can't actually say that it caused the problem in your breast, it most certainly will have aggravated it.'

I shift a bit in my chair.

'Will smoking make it come back?' Eddie asks.

'Let's put it this way, it most certainly won't make it go away.'

'Does that mean it's still there then?'

'Not necessarily. The area around the right breast, where we performed the mastectomy, and removed several lymph nodes, appears to be clear. However, there are some irregularities in the results of your blood test that I'd like to investigate further.'

I knew it! I bloody well knew it!

'What does that mean?' Eddie asks.

'It's all routine,' Michaels answers. 'I'm sure it's nothing to worry about, but we would like to be on the safe side, make sure it hasn't got into any other parts of the body.'

I start going all hot and cold. *What other part of the body?* 'How can it do that if you took it all out?' I demand. My voice is shrill and I feel like punching him. After all I've been through and now he's telling me it might be somewhere else.

'I'm going to be in touch with your GP,' he tells me, 'to let him know when we can admit you. It should be in the next couple of weeks.'

'What do you mean, admit me?' I cry.

'I'd like to have you in for a few days, so we can run all the tests at once. As I say, it's all routine. I'm sure everything's all right, so please don't worry. This often happens, a little side complication that can be sorted out in no time at all.'

A little side complication that might just mean . . . I don't know what it might mean, but I don't want to bloody well find out either. 'I've got two children,' I tell him. 'I can't go in hospital just like that, who's going to take care of them?'

'It's all right, we'll manage,' Eddie says.

I feel like hitting him now, but then I see how worried he is so I don't say anything else.

The doctor stands up, so we do too.

'Thank you for coming,' he says, holding out a hand to shake. 'If you make an appointment to see your GP some time next week he should have heard from us by then.'

Some time next week? Why so fast? I feel sick and dizzy. I want to run away, but where would I go, without the bleeding thing coming with me?

'Thank you, doctor,' Eddie says politely.

'Thank you,' I echo.

When we get outside I link my arm through Eddie's

and we walk out of the hospital grounds to the bus stop. Bloody car let us down again this morning. Hardly any point having the damned thing, if you ask me. Eddie's going back to work now, until six, to try to make up for some of the hours he lost today. I'm going to our mam's to pick up Gary.

We have to wait for buses on opposite sides of the road, because Eddie's going one way and I'm going the other. We look at each other across the street. It gives me a strange feeling that I don't like at all. I give him a little wave because I know it'll cheer him up. He waves back.

His bus comes first. I watch him get on, and look out the window at me as it pulls away. As soon as he's out of sight I light up a fag. I have to wait another ten minutes for my bus to turn up, bloody thing, lucky it's not too cold, or raining, today.

Course, the first thing our mam asks when I walk in her door is how I got on. I tell her everything's all right, just a couple more tests. I don't mention anything about going in hospital yet. I'll wait till I find out from Tyldesley when it's supposed to be.

She goes on asking me exactly what they did and what was said, so I tell her,

'It was just a normal check-up. Everything's all right, so let's change the subject.'

'What's a check-up?' Gary asks.

I didn't think he was listening, sitting down there on the mat wheeling his cars around. 'It's nothing,' I tell him. 'Come on, where's your coat? We have to be getting home, or Susan'll be wondering where we are.'

As he goes off to the hall I light a cigarette and throw the match in the grate.

'I don't like the sound of this,' our mam says.

'Well, nor do I,' I snap, 'but there's not a lot we can

do about it, is there? If they say I have to have more tests then I have to have them, and you keeping on about it isn't making it any better, so just bloody shut up about it, will you?'

'I was only asking, that's allowed, isn't it?'

'No. It's not. It's none of your business . . .'

'I'm your bloody mother . . .'

'It's no-one's business except mine.'

'Why are you shouting at Gran?' Gary asks.

'I'm not,' I answer. 'I'm just trying to make her understand something. Your coat's on inside out, so take it off, and put it on properly.'

Thankfully we don't have to wait too long for the bus, so we get down to the bottom of New Cheltenham in plenty of time to call in Bridges. I'm still feeling bad about shouting at our mam like that, because it's only natural she'd be worried, but it's too late now. I'll say sorry when I next see her, because she's a dear old soul really, who's only trying to show she cares.

There's a halfpenny off the Swiss rolls, so we get one for afters, they all like a nice piece of Swiss roll. I don't feel all that hungry meself, which scares me a bit after the doctor asked about any loss of appetite. This is the first time I've noticed it though, but it'll be more to do with nerves at having to go back in hospital, than with anything else.

The tiredness is worrying me a bit. I wonder if I should have told him the truth about that.

The minute we walk in the street Susan's on her way out of Betty's to come and meet us.

'Are you all right?' I say, as she reaches us.

'Yes. I've been playing hide-and-seek with Geoffrey and Nigel. They couldn't find me for ages.'

'Where did you hide?' Gary asks.

'I'm not telling you, or you'll know where to look.'

'You've got Brownies tonight,' I remind her.

'Oh, do I have to go?'

'Now don't start. Yes, you do. I'll walk up with you after tea and your father'll come to meet you.'

'What have we got for tea?' Gary asks.

'Beefburgers. Pick up the milk, Susan and bring it in. Then you can do ten minutes on the piano.'

'Oooooh,' she groans and stamps her foot.

'What am I going to do?' Gary says.

'You can practise your reading.'

'I can't on my own. Can I go out to play?'

'All right, but stay in the street where I can see you.'

'That's not fair, you never let me go out to play,' Susan grumbles.

'He's younger than you, but you can go out for ten minutes when you've finished the piano.'

There hadn't been time to wash the kitchen floor before I left this morning, so I give it a quick wipe over with a mop for now – I can get down and give it a good scrub in the morning. All the brass needs polishing too, and the carpets could do with a vac. It'll be all right till tomorrow though. Susan sounds as though she's coming along well with 'Für Elise' in there on the piano, just a few clangers here and there. I shouldn't mock, because neither Eddie nor I can play a note. She's a good girl. They both are. They'll go far, my two.

'Can I go out now?' Susan says.

She makes me jump, because I was miles away, staring out the window watching Gary play football with his friends in the street.

'Can I?' she says.

I want to say no, but that's daft. I said earlier that she could when she'd finished the piano, and what do I want her in here for, getting under my feet?

After she's gone I peel some spuds for tea, put them

on the gas, then go up to get her uniform ready for Brownies. There's some post on the mat inside the front door. Something for Eddie from the college, a postcard from our Kath, who lives up in London, and a brown envelope for me.

I tear it open and pull out a photo. The face is familiar, but I can't think who it is. Then I remember: he's someone me and Betty saw on the telly, ages ago now, in a play, and for a laugh we wrote him a bit of a saucy letter, asking for a picture we could hang next to our beds. I'd forgotten all about it, and to be honest, I didn't think we'd ever hear back from him anyway, but here's the photo, and he's signed it too. *To Eddress with love from Michael.* I wonder if Betty's got one as well. Funny, but it seems like a lifetime ago that we wrote that letter. It wouldn't have mattered if he'd forgotten, because I don't know what the bloody hell to do with it now.

I'm not really thinking about it any more as I go back in the kitchen, open a drawer and slide the photo inside my cook book. I'm trying to remember what I was doing when I went down the passage . . . That's right, I was on my way to sort out Susan's Brownie uniform.

It's hanging up in her wardrobe, clean and pressed, so I lie it down on the bed and start to look for her shoes and test card. Gary'll be off to Cubs soon. He's growing up fast. He starts school in September. Little rascal can't wait. I'm going to miss him, being at home here on me own all day. I might find meself a little job, cleaning an office somewhere, or helping with the old people along The Chase. The extra money'll come in handy, I know that. Eddie won't have to do as much overtime either, give him a chance to do some writing, because he hasn't done any in ages now. We're always so busy, what with one thing and another, but it's important for him to keep that up, it's what he loves, and he's good at it too. He

166

says I'm the only one who thinks so, but that won't always be the case.

Someone knocks on the front door, so I go back down to answer. It's Mrs Weiner from up round the corner, the one with the German husband.

'Hello Mrs Lewis,' she says. 'I just came to see if you'd like me to walk Susan to Brownies tonight. I've got to take Wendy, so to save you going too . . .'

'It's all right, I can take her,' I answer. I can see right through this woman, the nosy old cow. Somehow she's got wind of me going for a check-up today and now she's trying to find out what happened. Well, she can go and stick her nose in someone else's business.

'Perhaps we can walk up together then,' she says. 'It'll be nice to have the company.'

Nice for her, maybe, but not for me. I just don't know how to get rid of her though, without seeming rude. Normally I wouldn't care, but Eddie likes the woman, so if I upset her, it'll upset him. 'I'll give you a knock as we pass,' I tell her.

She looks so pleased that I might have warmed to her were it not for the fact that she's a district nurse who's only after all the gossip on me so she can pass it round to her patients (in other words, my bloody neighbours). Course she'll be an authority on everything to do with it all, won't she? Being a nurse she'll be a bloody expert. Oh, I know what her game is all right, she tried it last time when I came out of hospital, pretending to want to help out when what she really wanted was to get in my house and have a look round, but I can't for the life of me remember how I got rid of her then.

After she's gone I realise I can't walk up the road with her in case she says something in front of Susan. Nor can I warn her not to without admitting I had a check-up today. If she doesn't already know about it she'll be all bloody ears to find out more, and if she does she'll still be poking her nose in. So, when the time comes to leave I pop Eddie's tea under the grill to keep warm, leave him a note to tell him where I am, then after sending Gary in to Betty, I walk Susan round the long way so we don't have to pass the Weiners' house. I don't particularly care about hurting the old cow's feelings, after all she married a bleeding German, didn't she, so what does she expect? I'm going to feel a bit awkward if I bump into her up the church though, which I probably will.

Luckily, I spot Grace Shepherd and a couple of other mothers I know, so we all walk together, up past the school and along the main road to Holy Trinity. Brown Owl's waiting at the door to see her little troupe in, and the vicar's having a chat with someone over by the cemetery gate. He spots me and waves. I wave back, feeling guilty that I never go to church with Eddie and the kids. Some bloody Commie, my husband is. One week he's up here, at Holy Trinity, the next he's marching the kids off down the Sally Army, then they're over Whitfield Tabernacle. I got a job to keep up with it all, I can tell you. I might start going with them now though, if I can find the time. Might put God in a better frame of mind towards me.

As the doors close behind the girls, us mothers are just walking back out of the churchyard when Mrs Weiner comes hurrying up with her Wendy, the perfect child. I know they're late because they waited for me, but I pretend not to see them. They've seen me though, but Mrs Weiner doesn't say anything as she passes, which is a good job, because I'm not in the mood for a row. When she comes to pick Wendy up later she'll see Eddie. That'll keep her happy. Just as long as she stays away from me.

168

'I walked back from Brownies with Mrs Weiner,' Eddie says as we're getting ready for bed.

'Did you?'

'Yes. Says she saw us at the hospital today.'

'I knew it! I bloody knew it!'

'She wants to know if there's anything she can do . . .'

'She can mind her own bloody business, that's what she can do.'

'Ed, she's only trying to be helpful.'

'Well let her try with someone else, because I don't want her round here, sticking her nose in where it's not wanted.'

He sighs and pulls on his pyjamas. So I sigh and pull on mine too.

We get into bed and he sits up reading for a bit, while I just lie there trying to get off to sleep. There I was earlier, tired enough to conk out for a week, and now I can't go off at all.

Eddie turns out the light and snuggles down under the blankets.

'Goodnight,' he says.

'Goodnight.'

It's a long time before either of us goes off to sleep.

Susan

The trouble with Gary is he's never any good at playing shops. He always wants to buy things he can eat straight away, like biscuits or jam tarts, but that's not how you play. He's supposed to buy things I can put in a carrier bag for him, like tins of beans and jars of fish paste, but what I really want him to buy is some flour or sugar, so I can weigh them on Mum's weighing scales.

'But I don't want any flour,' he tells me angrily.

'Yes you do.'

'No I don't. Flour's stupid.'

I've got the bag in my hands, ready to tip into the scales. 'Just buy some flour,' I say, 'and then I'll sell you a Wagon Wheel.'

'But I haven't got enough money for some flour as well.'

'I'll let you buy it for a penny.'

'I've only got tuppence and just now you said a Wagon Wheel was tuppence.'

'Well it's gone down now, sir. Wagon Wheels are only a penny today.'

'Then I want two Wagon Wheels.'

I tip up the bag and start filling the scales. 'That's four ounces of flour, sir. Will there be anything else?'

'I said I don't want any,' he shouts.

'You have to!'

'No! I'm not playing any more.'

His fists are clenched ready to thump me, so I pick up the scales and empty the flour over his head. 'There, that's what you get for not playing properly,' I tell him.

'Mum! Mum!' he chokes, flour going everywhere. 'Mum! I can't see.'

'It serves you right,' I say, starting to giggle, because he looks really funny, like one of the Black and White Minstrels, but the other way round.

'What on earth's going on out here?' Mum says, coming into the kitchen. 'Can't you two play nicely for . . . Oh my Lord! Gary, come here!'

She grabs him and starts thumping his back. He's still choking and I can't stop laughing.

'Breathe!' she tells him. 'Breathe.'

'I am,' he coughs.

She gets some water and makes him drink it. He

170

splutters a bit, then stops choking, but he's crying now because he still can't see, so Mum sits him up on the draining board and washes the flour out of his eyes. 'Look at you,' she says. 'You're covered. It's all in your hair, your ears, and just look at your clothes . . .'

'Susan did it,' he wails. 'She threw it over me because I wouldn't buy it.'

'I'll be dealing with her as soon as we've got these clothes off.'

She strips him down to his pants and I creep back into the pantry to hide behind the potato sack in a very dark corner. She knows where I am though, because the next thing I know I'm being hauled out by the arm.

'You naughty girl,' she cries, smacking my legs. Smack! Smack! Smack! Smack! It really hurts and I'm screaming.

'What's the matter with you?' she says. 'He could have choked, and you're old enough to know better.'

Smack! Smack! Smack!

'I'm sorry, I'm sorry,' I cry. 'I didn't mean to . . .'

'Look at the bloody mess you've made. Now you can damned well clear it up, and I don't want to see a single speck left anywhere by the time I come back down again. Gary, up those stairs so I can wash your hair.'

My legs are all red and stinging and I'm sobbing really hard as I go to get the brush and start sweeping up. I'm Cinderella with a wicked stepmother and I wish my fairy godmother would come and save me, because nobody loves me, not even Dad any more, because he's too busy to read me a story or play any games, the way he used to. He hasn't read me anything since Mum went into hospital again, and that was three weeks ago. She wasn't in there for long, only two nights, but then she was in bed when she came home and we had to be quiet so we didn't disturb her.

She said she was having some tests, but I don't know if she's passed or not yet. I don't think they were tests like we do at school, I'm not sure though. No-one ever tells me anything, and anyway I don't want to know, so there!

I fetch the dustpan and brush to scoop up the flour, but even when I finish it's still all over the floor. It's gone all down the front of the drawers too, and over the doormat. If I don't clean it up I'll be beaten by my wicked stepmother again, so I have to do it. Then I've got mending and darning to do, and sticks to bring in for the fire. I could wear my new lemon dress to the ball if my fairy godmother comes to turn some carrots into horses and my table into a coach – and Gary into a frog.

I get one of my wooden chairs to stand on and put the dishcloth under the tap. As I start wiping the counter top and fronts of the drawers the flour turns all gooey and clings to the cloth. This is a very hard job, but I must finish or my wicked stepmother will be very angry indeed. My wicked stepsisters are Janet and Sarah who live across the road, because they won't let me play with them today. I don't care, I don't want to play with them anyway. Dad's working all day even though it's Saturday. I wonder if he'll go in the library and bring me home a book. I asked him for *What Katy Did*, so I hope he doesn't forget.

I pull open a drawer because some flour's gone inside. There's some on Mum's best cookery book which I take out and start reading, because I have to make everyone's tea tonight, then do all the washing-up and scrub the floors and clean the windows. It's a big, heavy book with lots of recipes for disgusting things like brains on toast and pig's trotters in . . . (a word a I can't read), and for delicious cakes and pies. I've got some flour on my glasses, so I take them off and put them in the drawer.

Then I drop the book on my foot, which really hurts, but I don't say anything because no-one cares. A picture has fallen out, so I pick it up. It's a photo of a man. There are some words written on it, *To Eddress with love from Michael.*

I feel all funny all of a sudden and I don't know what to do. I remember Mummy saying something to Mrs Williams about having to see someone called Michael. This is Michael. *To Eddress with love* . . . I feel a bit sick now and I still don't know what to do. He's handsome and horrible and ugly and I want to tear him up into small little pieces – so I do. Now Daddy will never find him. I don't want Daddy to know, because he's the only one Mummy should love. It would make Daddy very unhappy if he saw the picture, so it's a good job I tore it up. Now I'm going to put it in the bin, then this nasty person called Michael will be all gone and Mummy won't be able to look at his picture any more, or go off and be with him when she should be with us.

I'm still trying to clean up when she comes back downstairs. I think it's a worse mess than before, because the flour's gone all globby, but luckily she doesn't smack me again, she just says, 'Come on, let me do it,' and takes the cloth.

I stand there watching her. She's down on her hands and knees and the flour's coming up really easy for her. I wish I knew what to do to make her love me and Dad and Gary more than anyone else in the world.

'What's all this, you daft thing,' she laughs, as I go to put my arms around her and bury my face in her neck.

'I don't want you to go away again,' I say.

'Sssh, ssh,' she says, smoothing my hair and giving me a kiss on the head. 'I'm not going anywhere, so there's nothing to get upset about. Come on now. It's all right. I'm here.'

I'm doing those stupid sobs so I can't talk properly. 'I didn't mean to be naughty,' I say, all jerky. 'I tried to wipe up the flour.'

'I know, I know. And you did a good job, and you've learned now that you mustn't do it again. Haven't you?'

I nod.

'You're a silly sausage sometimes,' she says, 'throwing flour over your brother, getting yourself all worked up like this. What am I going to do with you? Eh?'

'I don't know.'

'I think I might have to eat you all up, that's what I'll have to do,' she decides, and she pretends to start biting me which makes me laugh.

'Can I play?' Gary cries, charging down the passage.

'Oh no! Look out!' Mum warns, 'he's going to land on us.'

He throws himself right on top of me and we all tip over onto the floor. Mum's laughing and laughing and so are we. We tickle her and make her laugh some more. Then she tickles us and chases us upstairs where we hide in the bathroom, but she manages to push open the door and then she gets us.

We scream and try to run past her, but she's got hold of us and makes us walk into her bedroom where we have to do three bounces each on her bed, which she doesn't normally allow us to do.

After that she gives us a Wagon Wheel and glass of milk each, and because the rain's stopped she lets us go out to play. Gary takes his football up to the green where some of his friends are, and I play hopscotch on my own, on the pavement outside our house. Mum's in the kitchen window watching me, then Dad comes home and he's remembered my book. I don't want to read it straight away though, because Janet and Sarah are my friends again now, so we're playing French skipping.

Louise and Caroline want to join in so we let them, then we play The Big Ship Sails through the Alley-Alley-oh, up against the lamppost outside Louise's house, until Sarah starts being silly, so we won't let her play any more and now I'm Janet's best friend.

Dad comes to call us in for tea. I don't want to go in case Janet makes friends with Sarah again, but I have to. Mum's laid my and Gary's places at the big table, but we want to eat at my little one, the way we always do. We have sausage, egg, beans and chips with a glass of Tizer, which we're only allowed at weekends. After tea Mum and Dad have a talk and decide that tonight we'll all go up the Horseshoe for a drink, instead of just Dad and Gary while me and Mum go to bingo.

'Oh no, we don't want them coming with us,' Gary cries.

'What's the matter with you?' Mummy says to me. 'You don't look very happy. Don't you want to go for a drink?'

I shrug.

'Well, what would you rather do?'

'Nothing.'

Mum rolls her eyes. 'Talk to her, Eddie,' she says, 'because I don't understand her.'

'What is it, my love?' Dad says. 'Why don't you want to go for a drink?'

'I want to do what we usually do,' I tell him.

Mum and Dad look at each other and I'm afraid I might be in for it, until Mum says, 'Then bingo it is, and you'd better win something tonight, my girl, or there'll be trouble.'

I really love my mum. She's the best mum in all of the world. And my dad's the best dad. And my brother's the best brother, but I still want my fairy godmother to turn him into a frog. Wouldn't it be funny if I kissed him and he turned into a prince? I wouldn't be able to marry him though, because he's my brother. He'd just have to stay as a frog.

Chapter Nine

Eddress

'I'm afraid the news isn't good, Mrs Lewis.'

His voice is like the toll of doom and my head's the belfry. I can feel everything inside of me going tight and hot, and like a blooming baby I want to start bawling.

I've been dreading this day ever since me last check-up. Three weeks of bloody hell it's been, trying to keep normal for the kids, making sure Eddie's not worrying too much. He pretends not to, but I know he is. I kept telling meself it would be all right, but it's not, is it? That's what Michaels is saying, it's not all right. The news isn't good, which means . . . I don't want him to tell me what it means, I just want it all to stop now before it gets any worse.

Michaels is looking at me. I don't know if he's waiting for me to say something, but if he is, I can't. I look at Eddie to see if he's got something to say, but it doesn't seem like he has either.

'It appears that the cancer has spread,' Michaels says, 'but there's a chance, if we start treatment right away, that we should be able to arrest it, and maybe even reverse it.'

'You mean you've got to operate again?' I say.

'Not at this stage. Hopefully, if you respond to treatment, not at all.'

'So more radium is what you're saying?'

'Yes. And a course of medication that is likely to have some side effects.'

I look away, around his office, trying to take it all in.

'What kind of side effects?' Eddie asks.

'Lethargy, nausea, weight gain . . . Of course your wife might not experience them all, it would be unusual if she did . . .'

'I thought you said, when we came in before, that the last operation was a success,' I remind him.

'It was, for that area of your body. Unfortunately, we weren't in time to stop it developing elsewhere.'

'So where else is it?'

His eyes go down to the page in front of him, and I go cold. He can't be looking it up, because he's bound to know already, and if he can't look me in the eye . . . *Oh please God please help me.*

'It's recurring in the liver,' he says.

The liver. I don't know much about the human body, but I know enough to understand that, unlike a right bosom, a liver is something you can't function without. I'm starting to feel a bit light-headed now, and I'm afraid I might be sick. Shall I ask to go to the lav? There's a bloody great lump in my throat so I'm not sure I can speak.

Eddie's saying something to the doctor. I watch his lips moving and then the doctor's, but I'm not taking it in. It's like I'm going numb all over, but then I turn restless and want to leave. They're still talking though, so I stare out the window and ask God why He's doing this. Course, He doesn't answer, He never does, does He?

It's not up to Him though is it, because He don't exist, and if you ask me, this proves it. So there's no point getting into an argy-bargy with someone who's not there, or thinking He's got some kind of power to make this all go away, when He's just something that's been made up by rich people, in the church, to scare us poor people into giving them money to save our souls. So they get richer and we get poorer which means they're the ones with all the power, not God. I wish Eddie could see that, but he can't. He might change his mind now though, we'll see. What shall I make for his tea tonight? I don't know. Chops? A nice piece of cod?

'Mrs Lewis?'

It's the doctor. He's looking at me as though he's waiting for an answer, but I don't know what he asked me.

'Have you got any questions?' Eddie prompts me.

I shake my head. No, no questions. I feel sorry for the doctor. I don't expect it's easy giving people news like this, but once we're gone he'll move on to the next, and we'll be forgotten until it's time for me to come in again. So really it's all right for him, isn't it, because it's not him, or his wife, who's sitting this side of the desk. It's me, Eddie's wife, the mother of our kids, that's who's sitting on the wrong side of the desk. I wonder how I got here, because I've never been ill in me life before, so I don't understand why this is happening now. If anyone mentions the cigarettes I'll thump them, because thousands, millions of people smoke twice as much as I do every day, and they're all right, aren't they? Eighty or ninety years old some of them, and still going strong. So I don't want to hear any more baloney about the fags, because that's all it is, baloney, put about by doctors who can't come up with the real reason for this happening, so they have to blame something.

Michaels walks round his desk and opens the door for us to leave. He shakes my hand first, then Eddie's and tells us not to worry, he's sure we've caught it in plenty of time. I'm sure we have too, it's just been a bit of a shock, that's all, but I'm pulling meself together now. I'll get on this treatment he mentioned and before we know it, this'll all seem like a bad dream.

'Let's go to the cafeteria and have a cup of tea, shall we?' Eddie suggests.

To tell the truth he looks like he needs one as much as me, so we roll back the iron gate on the lift and take it up to the top floor.

'I think you're in good hands with Michaels,' Eddie says when we're sitting down at a table by the window. There aren't many people around, so it's all right to talk, though I wouldn't be surprised if that Cissy bleeding Weiner doesn't have her beady eye out somewhere, and her radar lugs.

I nod. 'Yeah, he seems to be good. Got rid of it last time, anyway. Let's hope he can do it again.'

'He sounded confident he could. Lucky you don't have to go in again.'

There doesn't seem to be any more to say, so we stare out the window and drink our tea. It's a nice day out there. Sun's shining and it's warm enough not to need our coats, but we've brought them anyway. It said on the forecast that it might go off a bit chilly later, so just as well I made Susan take her anorak this morning, even though she didn't want to. I don't know, everything's a battle with that girl.

'Well, I suppose I'd better be getting on then,' Eddie says, finishing his tea and pushing his empty cup and saucer across the table.

Yes, he better, heaven knows we don't want him losing any more money for taking time off.

'Are you all right?' he asks.

'Course I am,' I answer. 'Right as rain. So what do you want for your tea?'

'Oh, I don't mind. Anything.'

'Steak and kidney pie? I can call in the butchers on the way home.'

'Steak and kidney pie. That'll be nice.'

We walk outside, and the birds are singing. The gardens are very well kept here at Cossham. A lot better than at that dreary place where I had the operation, the General. Everything looked as though it was about to die down there, including the people. I've always liked Cossham. I mean if you have to like a hospital, this one's very nice.

'Are you going to call in to see Tyldesley?' Eddie says, as we reach his bus stop.

'What for? I think one doctor in a day is enough, don't you?'

'Well, Michaels said you should, and you're going past.'

I don't remember Michaels saying that, but I expect he said a lot I don't remember at the minute.

'Are you seeing your Bob later?' I ask him.

'I'd forgotten about that.'

'Take the kids up. Susan always likes seeing Julie and Karen. There's some bingo on tonight. I'll go with Betty.'

'Here's the bus,' he says. 'Are you going to be all right?'

'Course I am. You just make sure you're not late home if I'm making steak and kidney pie.'

'Oh, I'll never be late for that,' he says, grinning. 'You make the best steak and kidney pie this side of the Severn tunnel.'

'Go on,' I say, giving him a gentle thump on the arm. 'Get on that bus and go and earn us some money so we can go on holiday this summer. Dawlish again? Let's invite your Bob and Flo to come with us, shall we?'

'All right. I'll ask him tonight.'

The bus is alongside us now. We both know the driver,

so we give him a wave, and Eddie jumps on. He stands on the platform watching me as the bus pulls away. I wave then turn to cross the road. I don't want to watch him until the bus goes out of sight, because it's soppy, with everyone looking on. Anyway, there's no point wasting time, I've got to go up Kingswood now to find a new pair of shoes for Susan to wear with her new lemon dress up the Whitsun parade, and a nice shirt for Gary so he'll look smart on the back of the Sally Army lorry too. Only a few weeks to go now. Me, Eddie and our mam'll stand outside Woolworth's to watch them go past, I think, or a bit further down towards the park. I'd better make up me mind, because the kids will want to know where to look out for us. We can follow the lorry back then, if we can get through the crowds, and take them down the Shant, the same as we do every year. We always have a good laugh down the Shant. I'll get our Phyllis to go early to make sure we get a table in the garden, if it's not raining. It never rains on Whit Monday though, or not that I can ever remember.

By the time Eddie comes home from work both kids have been sent to bed, though I can't for the life of me remember what they've done wrong. I expect they were just getting on my nerves, screaming and yelling about the place, and getting under my feet. I'm not in the mood for it today. I'm just not.

'How long have they been up there?' Eddie asks.

To tell the truth, I can't remember that either. 'About ten minutes,' I say.

'I'll go up to them now then, and get them to come down and say sorry.'

'All right. Tea's ready in about five minutes.'

'Steak and kidney pie?'

'Lamb chops.'

He goes to hang up his coat then I hear him trudging

up the stairs, putting on the monster's voice that thrills them to bits. I don't expect they'd mind it too much if it was just him and them, they love him so much. Now there's a bloody daft thing to think, of course they'd bloody mind. I'm their mother, for God's sake.

I pull out the grill to check on the chops, then spoon some Bisto into a jug to make the gravy. The cabbage is done, so I carry the steaming saucepan over to the sink, tip it into a colander and catch the water in a bowl underneath. Eddie likes to drink the cabbage water, and believe it or not, so does Susan. I have the dickens of a time making her eat the stuff though. She don't like carrots much either, or boiled potatoes, so she's not going to be very happy with her tea tonight.

Here they come, thundering down the stairs.

'Sorry Mum,' Susan says, coming into the kitchen.

'Sorry Mum,' Gary echoes.

I wonder if they know what they're saying sorry for, because I'm blowed if I do. 'All right. Go and lay the table now then, your tea's nearly ready. Snowballs for afters.'

I thought that might raise a cheer, and it does, a typically noisy one. We're all partial to a snowball in our house, a cream-filled chocolate ball covered in coconut flakes. I make them meself sometimes, but I bought these in a box up Fine Fare today.

'Did you call in to see Tyldesley?' Eddie asks when we're sitting down at the table.

I glance over to make sure the children can't hear, but they're busy arguing about who's best, Cliff Richard or the Beatles. 'No,' I answer. 'I'll go tomorrow.'

'Want me to come with you?'

'Don't be daft. You've taken enough time off already. We'll end up broke if we go on like this.'

He doesn't argue, because he knows I'm right.

Anyway, I don't want him to come with me. I just want to get it over with now, with the minimum of fuss.

'Have you thought about what to tell the kids for the days you have radium?' he asks.

'Not yet,' I say, irritably. 'Probably the same as last time, that I've got a little night job.'

'What about telling them the truth?'

'Don't be ridiculous. They're much too young to understand.'

'I don't mean about everything, I just mean about the hospital. We can say you're having a course of treatment to make you feel better, because you've been a bit tired lately. Something simple like that.'

I don't suppose it's a bad idea, but I'll have to think about it, because I don't want them going blabbing round the street that their mum's not well, and knowing my kids they will.

I put down my knife and fork and pick up my cup of tea. 'Want that other lamb chop?' I say to Eddie.

'Mm, if you're not going to eat it,' he says, and lifts the one I've left from my plate onto his.

'Are you eating your cabbage over there, you two?'

'Yes Mummy.'

'Yes Mummy.'

'It doesn't look much like it to me. Come on, eat those greens and the carrots, they'll help you see in the dark.'

'Why do we have to see in the dark?' Susan says. 'Why can't we just put the light on?'

'Eat them, Miss Clever Clogs. No snowballs until you do.'

'Are you coming up Uncle Bob's with us?' Gary asks.

'No. I'm going to bingo.'

When the washing-up's done and all put away, Eddie takes them off and I go and knock for Betty. She doesn't know I went up to get the results today, so I don't say

184

anything. Course, I'll have to tell her some time, because I'll need her help with the kids, but she's as good as gold, never gossips behind my back and never goes making a fuss when there's no need to.

Can you believe it, I go round the bingo with only a shilling in me pocket and I come back with thirty-five quid. I've never had such a big win. It perks me up no end, it does. Thirty-five bloody quid. Wait till I tell Eddie.

'I think you should get something nice for yourself,' he tells me. 'A new suit to wear up the Whitsun parade, or a nice string of pearls. You always wanted one. We can go up Zaringers on Saturday and have a look if you like.'

'I'm not going to spend it all on me,' I laugh. 'I want to get something for you lot too. What about a nice new suit for *you* to wear up the Whitsun parade? You haven't had one since we got married.'

'I don't need one. That's a smart suit, that is.'

He's right, it is, with its waistcoat and pinstripes, and he looks handsome in it too. 'You could do with some new shoes though,' I remind him.

'Get something for yourself first, then we'll see what's left over.'

'It'll pay for our holiday. Let's use it for that. Did you ask Bob and Flo if they want to come?'

'They're going to think about it, see if they can afford it. They've got a surprise for you though. One of Bob's regulars gave him three tickets for *My Fair Lady* down the Odeon. I said why don't you go with them and I'll look after the kids.'

'Well, why don't we buy another ticket so you can come too, and we'll ask your Nance to babysit? We've got the money now.'

He's laughing and so am I.

'We're rich!' I cry.

'We're rich,' he echoes.

The children are up getting ready for bed, so it's all right to have a bit of a cuddle. We might do a bit more than that after he's read them a story.

We'll see.

Chapter Ten

Susan

I love Whitsun. It's the day that everyone who lives in Kingswood goes up to the main road to watch the parade. We all wear our best clothes and wave different sorts of flags, like Union Jacks, or St George and the dragon, or those made from coloured streamers that you can buy on the side of the road. The lampposts are decorated with bunting and flowers, and garlands are strung across the street like frilly washing on the line.

Gary and I are in the parade, riding on the Salvation Army lorry. He's over the other side with the boys, so I can't see him. I'm sitting with the girls and we're playing our tambourines as we go slowly through the crowds who are all cheering and pushing forward trying to get a better look. The Salvation Army band is leading our lorry, playing 'Onward Christian Soldiers', which we're playing too, shaking our tambourines, and hitting them against our shoulders, elbows, wrists and even the tops of our heads, all in time with one another. It looks lovely the way all our ribbons ripple through the air like flying rainbows.

The Brownies from Holy Trinity are behind us (I could have gone with them, but then I wouldn't have been able to play the tambourine), and behind them are the Guides and the Scouts. There are lots of other Brownie and Scout groups marching, from Hanham, Two Mile

187

Hill, and Warmley, and people from all the churches in the area, singing hymns and playing in their bands. There are cheerleaders and clowns, pantomime horses and even real horses that the police are riding. Whenever I go past a policeman I pull a face so he won't recognise me. I don't want to be arrested, you see.

When we get outside Fine Fare I spot Aunty Doreen and Aunty Nance, Dad's sisters, so I give them a wave, and a bit further on I see Uncle Bob and Aunty Flo with Julie and Karen, who look very pretty in their new dresses. (We're going to their house for tea later, after we've been up the Shant.) There are lots of people I know, from school, or who live near us. I expect they all recognise me, but I can't wave to everyone or I'll lose my place and go out of time.

Mum, Dad and Gran are outside Kingswood Park, where the parade turns around and goes back the way it came. Mum looks lovely in her navy blue dress with big white dots and Dad's very smart in his pinstriped suit. He's got a red flower in his lapel that matches the one pinned to Mum's big white collar. Gran's wearing a hat with a veil and the cream-coloured Crimplene suit that she bought in Littlewoods down town and always keeps for best. Mr and Mrs Williams are with them, and my Aunty Jean and Uncle Gord with some of their children.

As we go back up through Kingswood we pass Grampy who's outside the British Legion with a pint in his hand and a top hat on his head (every year his picture's in the paper wearing his top hat). It's easy to wave to him, because we're having a pause in playing. He waves back and topples into the people behind, who catch him and stand him up again. He's very funny, my Grampy.

I love riding on the lorry so everyone can see me, I just wish Mum would have let me leave my glasses off for once, but she wouldn't, and I didn't argue because she hasn't been very well lately. Of course she's always well enough to tell me off and make me do things I don't want to do, but I don't want to make her headaches worse by getting on her nerves, so my glasses are on, and so is the patch.

When it's all over we walk all the way down Soundwell Road, eating candyfloss and holding Gran's hands. Mum and Dad are walking in front. Mum's got her white high heels on, and a white handbag over one arm. With the other arm she's holding onto Dad, who walks very upright, like a soldier. I tried to walk with them just now, but they told me to go away in case I get candyfloss all over them. Gran doesn't mind if we get it on her, it all comes out in the wash, she says.

When we reach the waterworks, which is just after Dr Tyldesley's surgery, we turn right into Crown Road, where Mummy was born, at number five. The funny thing is, Daddy's mummy was born in the same house, but a long time before. (That's called a coincidence.) The Shant is at the end of Crown Road, a big white pub that's really called the Crown, but everyone calls it the Shant. I don't know why. They just do.

Aunty Phil and Aunty Ivy are already there, baggsing some tables out in the garden. We need quite a few with all our family. Dad and Uncle Gord go inside to get the drinks. Gary and I have shandy, Mum has a port and lemon, and Dad has a pint of best. There are lots of bags of crisps and peanuts to share, and some toffee apples that our cousins Geoffrey and Deborah brought with them.

Mum sits with the women, chatting and laughing. Her headache seems better today, though I just heard her telling Aunty Phil that the way Dad keeps on at her makes her bloody head throb. I don't know what he keeps on about, because I've never heard him, but I saw her let go of his arm before we got here, and she gave him a really dirty look just now. I'm not going to take any notice though, because they get on my nerves, always rowing. And he shouldn't be mean to her, because she has to go to hospital every week to have some treatment for her bad head. I don't think it's doing much good though, because she's in bed all the next day with the curtains drawn. She lets me go in and lie down with her, but only for five minutes, because I can't keep still, and Gary's even worse.

Dad's over by the pub door with the men. Gary's on his shoulders dropping crisps in his hair.

'Do you want to see how good I am at cartwheels and handstands?' I ask Gran and Aunty Phil.

'Stop showing off,' Mummy says.

'Let her be,' Gran admonishes. 'Go on my love.'

As I go up my dress tumbles all the way down over my face. It's all right because I've got my vest and knickers on, but Mum says it's not, so I can't do any more.

'Will you come on the swings with me?' Gary says. 'Dad won't let me go on on my own.'

'All right. I'll give you a push. You'll have to go in the baby swing though, in case you fall off.'

We take it in turns pushing each other, then we jump on the roundabout with some other children and whizz round so fast that everything goes blurry. There's a queue for the slider, so we wait, then come whishing down together, Gary sitting between my legs. He goes up again, on his own, and comes down head first, which is really brave, but the next thing I know I'm getting a smack from Mummy for letting him do it.

It's not fair, it's always my fault, and now she's gone and shown me up in front of everyone.

I don't want to be here any more, not with her, so I

go over to Dad who's sitting at a table with Uncle Gord and climb up on his lap. They're talking about the miners who were killed down Wales last week. Dad used to be a miner, so did Grampy and Uncle Bob.

'It's not as bad as when all those people died in Pakistan though,' I say. 'I saw it on the news. Nearly sixteen thousand people might have died then.'

'She's her father's daughter,' Uncle Gord comments.

'It's true, sixteen thousand is a lot more than thirty-one,' Dad agrees. 'But anyone dying is a tragedy for their family, no matter who or where they are.'

'Do we know anyone who's dead?' I ask.

'Well, Granny Lewis is dead, but she died before you were born, so you didn't actually know her but she's still your grandmother.'

'People don't die until they're very old, do they?'

'Not usually, no.'

'Unless something bad happens, like in the mines, or in Pakistan?'

'That's right.'

'Dad?'

'Yes?'

'Can we have a dog?'

'Not today, my love.'

I lean my head back against his shoulder and just listen as him and Uncle Gordon go on chatting. It's a bit boring though, about the Union and a man called Tony Benn who came to give a talk in Kingswood that they went to. Then Uncle Gord says, 'So how's our Ed coping?'

'Oh, all right, you know,' Dad answers.

'Yeah, yeah,' Uncle Gord says, nodding. 'That's good then.' He finishes his beer. 'Do you want another?'

'I'll just have half,' Dad says. 'Susan, go and ask your mother if she wants a lemonade.'

I do as I'm told and come back and say, 'No, she wants another port and lemon.'

Dad goes into the pub and comes out with lemonades for all of us, including Mum.

She doesn't say anything, but I can tell by the look she gives him that she's really cross.

'And you can put that out too,' he says, pointing at her cigarette.

'Don't you bloody talk to me like that,' she snaps.

'If you won't listen to me at home, then maybe you'll listen in front of your family,' he says, sounding really angry. 'Now put that bloody cigarette out.'

Dad swore!

'I'll put it out on you if you don't shut up.'

Dad leans forward, grabs the cigarette from her and stubs it out in the ashtray.

Everyone goes very quiet.

'If you light up another, I'll do the same again,' he warns.

'You do that again and you'll be sorry,' she tells him.

He stands staring at her. I've never seen him this cross before. She stares back. I think they're going to have a fight. I wish Gran would stop them. Or Uncle Gord. Please God, don't let them have a fight.

Mummy opens her handbag and takes out her cigarettes.

'No, Mum, don't,' I cry.

'You'd better listen to her, Ed,' Daddy says.

'Don't you use my kids against me,' she says through gritted teeth. 'If I want a cigarette I'll have one, and no one, not even she, is going to stop me.'

'If you light that cigarette you're going to regret it,' he tells her.

I feel Gary's hand go into mine. I stand in close to protect him and look at Mummy. The cigarette's in her mouth, her lighter's in her hand. She's staring at Daddy as though she hates him. She snaps open the lighter and rolls the little wheel. A flame pops up. She brings it to the end of her cigarette and sucks in.

For what seems like ages no-one moves, then Daddy turns round and says to me and Gary, 'Come on, we're going.' He takes us both by the hand and starts walking away.

'Don't you dare take my kids,' Mummy shouts after us.

Daddy ignores her and just keeps on walking, across the garden and off down the road. His face is very white. Mummy's shouting things after us, but Daddy won't stop.

'Where are we going?' Gary says.

'To your Uncle Bob's.'

'What about Mummy? Is she coming too?'

'I don't know.'

'I want to go back with Mummy,' Gary says.

'No you don't,' I tell him.

'Yes I do.'

'Then you won't be able to play bus conductors with Uncle Bob.'

When we get to Uncle Bob's, which is in Northend Avenue, Aunty Flo puts the kettle on and sends me and Gary out the back to play cricket with Julie and Karen. Dad and Uncle Bob go in the front room and close the door.

Usually I love being at Uncle Bob's. Julie and Karen are my favourite cousins and it's lots of fun when Dad and Uncle Bob play with us, which they normally do. But they aren't playing today, they just stay shut up in the room and we're not allowed to go in.

'They've got some private talking to do,' Aunty Flo tells us and comes out to play with us instead.

The others are all too young to understand what's going on, but I'm not. I know something is, and I'm getting upset. I want my dad. I want my mum too, but lots of time goes by and she still doesn't come and knock on the door.

When Dad and Uncle Bob come out of the front room they're smiling and joking the way they usually do. I don't think Dad should be happy when we don't know where Mum is. She might leave us and go and be with Michael and her other family. I want to go and find her, but Aunty Flo's just serving up some tea, so it would be rude to ask Dad if we can leave now.

I keep looking at him as we sit at the table. I wish I knew why he got so angry about Mum having a cigarette. She always smokes, so why did he do that up the Shant, in front of everyone? It was wrong of him to act like that, and he should say sorry. I want him to find Mum and say sorry.

Julie and Karen are sitting either side of me at the table and keep asking me if I'll sleep at their house tonight. I want to, but I can't. I have to find Mum. We eat lemon jelly and blancmange, some chocolate marshmallows and raspberry trifle. Karen offers me her chocolate marshmallow, because I haven't eaten mine, but I don't want it. I just want to go home.

I'm nearly crying so I ask to leave the table. When I get to the stairs I'm just going up when Uncle Bob comes out and closes the door behind him. I turn my face into the wall so he can't see me.

'Come on, my darling,' he says, picking me up and sitting down with me on his lap. 'It'll be all right. Mums and dads have arguments sometimes. It's nothing to worry about.'

'I want to go home,' I tell him.

'I know you do. But why don't you stay here tonight,

with Julie and Karen, and I'll take you home in the morning?'

I shake my head. 'I want to go now,' I say. 'I want my mum.'

He puts my head on his shoulder and gives me a kiss. 'I know,' he says.

'I wish Mum and Dad would be like you and Aunty Flo,' I say. 'You never have rows.'

'Oh, we do,' he laughs. 'Everyone does. That's why it's nothing to worry about. We always make up after.'

I rest my head on his shoulder and wonder if I should tell him about Michael and Mum's other family. He'd understand then that I have to go home to make sure she's there.

The door opens again and Dad comes out.

'She wants to go home,' Uncle Bob tells him.

Dad nods. 'I thought she might.'

When Gary finds out I'm going with Dad he wants to come too. I wish Uncle Bob would come with us, because if Mum is there he'll make sure her and Dad don't row.

The sun's gone in now so it's quite chilly as we walk down New Cheltenham Road, past the post office and the infants' school where Gary's going in September. It's where I went until I was seven.

By the time we arrive at Greenways it's starting to rain, so we run down the street because we don't have any coats. I'm the first in the back door and there's Mum, coming down the passage into the kitchen.

'Dad!' I cry excitedly. 'She's here.'

Dad comes in behind me, but he doesn't say anything.

Mum doesn't either, except to me. 'Go and change out of your best clothes,' she says. 'Then you can put your pyjamas on. That goes for you too, Gary.'

'Can we come back down after?' he asks.

'Just go and do as you're told,' she answers.

195

Dad comes up with us and changes out of his suit into his old working trousers and a grey woolly jumper. I can hear Mum doing things downstairs, then the telly goes on and Gary comes into my room with his slippers on the wrong feet.

'Shall we go down?' he whispers.

'I don't know. Where's Dad?'

'In the bathroom. Do you think they're going to have another row?'

'No,' I answer, because I can see he's scared. I put my arm round him and sit down on the bed with him while I decide what we should do.

The flush goes and Dad comes out of the bathroom. We hear the landing curtains swish across the rail as he pulls them, then the sound of him going downstairs.

Gary looks up at me. 'Do you think they've forgotten about us?' he asks.

I nod. 'I think so.' I get up and go to the door. 'Wait here,' I tell him, 'I'm going to see if I can hear what they're saying.'

I creep across the landing, and get almost halfway down the stairs when I realise he's behind me. 'Ssh,' I say, putting a finger over my lips. 'You mustn't let them hear you.'

We stand very still and listen, but there's only the sound of the telly coming from the living room. Then the front-room door opens and Dad comes out.

It's too late to run so we stand there, staring down at him and knowing we're in for it the second he spots us.

Just as he does the living-room door opens and Mum comes out.

She doesn't see us. She doesn't see Dad either. She only goes over to the kitchen sink and fills up the kettle.

'Come on,' Dad says to us, 'back up to bed. I'll read you a story.'

'Can I sleep in with Susan tonight?' Gary asks.

Dad doesn't answer, so Gary comes in with me anyway.

The rain is making so much noise on the windows outside that Dad says, 'Sounds like it's turned to hail.'

'Will it snow?' Gary asks.

'No. Not in May.'

He doesn't ask us which story we want, he just picks up *Lamb's Tales from Shakespeare*, sits down on my dressing-table stool and starts to read *The Merchant of Venice*. After that he reads *As You Like It*. Gary's fast asleep by the time he finishes that, but I'm not so he opens the book again to *The Taming of the Shrew*.

I don't know what time it is now, but it's dark and Daddy's not here any more. I was asleep until something woke me up, but I'm not sure what it was. It might be the telly.

'Gary?' I whisper.

He doesn't answer, so I push back the blankets and get out of bed. If there are any witches under it they don't come and get me as I tiptoe across the room and open my bedroom door. Maybe they know what the noise was and are too afraid to come out.

I take one step at a time on the landing, trying not to make the floorboards creak, then I jump out of my skin as something goes bang downstairs. Someone might be breaking in. I have to go and wake up Mum and Dad, but then I hear someone shouting and I think it's Mum.

I go to the top of the stairs and look down at the passage. It's too dark to see very much, but I can hear Dad shouting now. My heart's beating hard. I don't know what to do. I think they're having a fight. Or maybe they're chasing off robbers.

The living-room door swings open and I quickly hide behind the banister.

'I'll do what I bloody well like,' Mum shouts, 'so just shut your bloody mouth . . .'

'The trouble is you can't give them up, can you?' Dad yells. 'So why don't you just admit it?'

'I can give them up any time I like. I just don't want to, all right.'

'Then they'll be the bloody death of you.'

'Just shut up,' she screams. 'I've had enough, do you hear me? I'm sick to death of you going on all the time, and I'm sick to death of this house.'

'Then bloody go. No-one's stopping you,' Dad shouts back. 'And take those filthy things with you.'

'Don't worry, I'm going.'

'The trouble with you is, you never listen. How many times have you got to be told . . .'

'Shut up!' she screams and there's a loud crash. Then another crash.

'That's right, smash the bloody house up, why don't you?'

'I'll smash you up,' she yells.

'Come on then! Right here!'

I can hear them fighting, punching one another and making horrible noises. I want to shout at them to stop, but then there's another crash and Dad comes out into the kitchen. Mum comes after him. I can see their reflections in the mirror. They're wrestling with each other and shouting and swearing.

Dad breaks away and starts walking down the passage. A bottle of milk comes flying after him. It smashes on the wall and the milk goes everywhere. Then another one comes and that smashes too. Next comes Gary's tractor, then the kitchen stool. Dad yells that she ought to be locked up.

She goes on throwing things. I can't tell what everything is, but it's all smashing to pieces, and Mum's shouting, calling him names and telling him she hates him. He's shouting too and I can't stand it. I put my hands over my ears and sob and sob. But I can still hear them.

'No! No!' I shout, but they just won't stop.

'They all think you're a saint,' Mum cries, 'well they should see you now. Look at you. Just bloody look at you.'

'Shut up, Eddress, or so help me God I'll throw you out that bloody door.'

'Just you try it!'

He goes towards her.

She punches him in the face, then picks something up and bangs it over his head. It's one of my little chairs, broken in pieces now.

Dad grabs the other and I think he's going to hit her with it, but he breaks it against the wall.

Mum snatches up the table. He ducks and it goes crashing down the passage.

I run down the stairs, screaming for them to stop, but they don't listen. Dad's got her hands behind her back, and is trying to push her into the room, but she flings him off and punches him again. There's blood all over his face.

'Dad! Dad!' I cry.

He doesn't hear me.

Mum runs into the dining room. The clock comes flying out and smashes behind Dad's head. He goes in after her and picks up the telly.

'Just you dare!' she shouts.

'Oh, I will.'

'Come on then. Throw it. I'm right here. Let's see if you've got the guts.'

'No, Dad, no,' I scream, running towards him. 'Don't throw it. Please don't throw it.'

'Don't go near him,' Mum shouts. 'He's mad. You're mad, do you know that?'

Dad's looking at me, but I don't think he can see me.

'I'm not staying in this house with you,' Mum cries. 'You're not safe to be around. Come on Susan, get your coat. We're going.'

I look up at her.

'I said get your coat!'

I'm shaking and shivering and afraid of them both.

'Susan, up to bed,' Daddy says sharply.

I don't want to be here any more, so I run back along the passage and up the stairs. When I get to the top I nearly can't breathe. I want my gran to come and stop them. Or Uncle Bob. I put my hands together and say some prayers.

'. . . and don't think I'll be back,' I hear Mummy shout as she comes down the passage.

She goes on shouting as she takes her coat off the hook and puts on her boots. Then she ties a scarf round her hair and slams out of the front door.

I run into Gary's room and look out the window. It's dark, but the lampposts are on so I can see her walking down the path and out of the gate. She crosses the street and goes along the lane, splashing in the puddles as she lights a fag.

'Susan.'

I jump.

'Come on,' Dad says, 'into bed.'

'I don't want to. I want Mum to come back.'

'Come on now,' he says firmly.

'Where's she going?'

'Up your gran's I expect.'

'Is she leaving us. I don't want her to leave us,' and I start to cry. 'Go after her, Dad, please. Make her come back.'

'Not tonight, my love.'

I put my arms round his neck and hold on tight. 'Can I sleep with you?' I ask.

'All right. Where's Gary?'

'He's in my bed.'

'Let's go and see if he's awake.'

He's not, he's still fast asleep, so Dad tucks the blankets up around him and carries me into his room.

'I'll go and warm you up some milk,' he says as I slide down under the covers.

I'm still sobbing and shaking, so he gives me a cuddle.

'Why are you and Mum so angry with each other?' I ask.

'Oh, we're a couple of silly things,' he answers. 'We're not really angry, we're just . . . Well, we're just silly.'

'She will come back though, won't she?'

'Yes.' He gives me a squeeze.

I know Dad doesn't tell lies, so I think she might come back, but I don't want to stay up here on my own while he goes downstairs, in case he goes too.

We walk down together, holding hands. The lights still aren't on in the passage, but I can see the mess. All our toys are broken in bits and floating in milk, my table and chairs, puzzles, paint sets, fuzzy felts, the tractor, building blocks, a saucepan, books, my Tressie doll . . .

'Are your feet all right?' Dad says. 'You didn't cut them on the glass, did you?'

I lift up one, then the other, for him to check.

'Well, let's be thankful for that,' he sighs when he sees there are no cuts. There's still blood on his face, and a gash on his lip.

He looks around at the mess and shakes his head. 'I think you might have to have orange squash,' he says with one of his funny little smiles.

'Yes, I think so,' I say.

When I get up in the morning, just like magic, all the toys are mended and all the milk's cleared up, but Mum's not back.

'Can we go and look for her?' I ask Dad.

'No,' he answers. 'She'll come back when she's ready and not before.'

All day goes by and all the next night and she still doesn't come home. Good job Dad's off work this week, or we wouldn't have anyone to look after us. We play cricket in the garden and help Dad make the tea. I wish he'd go and look for her, but he keeps saying no. He's still angry with her, I can tell, so maybe it's better for her not to come in case they have another fight. I wonder if he knows where her other family lives. I hate them, whoever they are. If it weren't for them she'd come home, I know she would.

It's the second day now. Dad's out digging the garden and Gary and I are in my bedroom studying the map we've made of the streets leading from our house to Gran's. I've told him I think that's where Mummy is – it wouldn't be fair to tell him about her other family or he'd get upset. I'm not even sure I should let him come and find her with me, but he's in on it now, so I have to or he'll just run straight to Dad the minute I've gone.

'Go and make sure Dad's still on the garden,' I tell him.

He jumps up and goes to the window. 'Yes, he's still there,' he whispers.

'All right, then let's go. Are you ready?'

His face looks a bit worried, but he nods and follows me out of the room.

We creep down the stairs, clutching our map. It's warm out, so we don't need our coats. I think we should take some crisps though, in case we get hungry, so we tiptoe into the kitchen and take two packets out of the bread bin.

It's best to go out the front door, because Dad's round the back, so that's what we do. There are lots of children in the street who ask if we're coming out to play, but we say no and walk on up to the green. Then we turn right to go along the top lane to Holly Hill where I make Gary hold my hand, because we're on a main road now.

We walk down past the phone box then stop on the kerb to look right, then left, then right again and when it's all clear we cross New Cheltenham Road.

We're just starting up Pound Road, which is a very steep hill, when I realise we should have left Dad a note, or he'll worry. I stop and look back.

'What's the matter?' Gary asks.

'Nothing,' I say. We can't go back in case Dad's already come in from the garden.

We walk on, still holding hands, up past lots of red-brick houses and others made of white wood. I keep thinking that Mum might be in one of them with her other family, but I don't know which one, so I can't knock on the door.

By the time we get to the top of the hill we're all puffed out. There are some shops where we could get a bottle of lemonade, but we don't have any money.

'I want to go home now,' Gary says.

I do too, but we've got to find Mum. 'Gran's isn't far now,' I tell him.

We walk and walk, taking care when we cross roads and holding tighter to each other's hands when a lorry roars past. I think we're going the right way, but I'm not really sure. Our map only has the streets we know, and now we're in a street I haven't seen before.

'Are we lost?' Gary asks.

I think we are, but I mustn't tell him that or he'll cry.
I wish Dad would come along in his car and find us
now, or that we could turn a corner and see Gran's house.
I hate Mummy for running away, because if she hadn't
we wouldn't have had to come and look for her.

'Let's eat our crisps,' I say. 'Have you got them?'

'No. You had them.'

'No I didn't, you did.'

'No I didn't, you did.'

We go on like that until he punches me and I start to
cry.

'I'm sorry,' he says, putting an arm round me. 'I didn't
mean it.'

I can't stop crying though, because we're lost and I
don't know which way to go.

'Shall we see if we can find a policeman?' Gary says.
'He might know where Gran lives.'

'No! He might arrest us for running away.'

'Then what shall we do?'

'I don't know. I want to go home.'

'So do I,' he says and starts to cry too.

I put my arms round him, then quickly turn him away
from the road as a car pulls up next to us. 'Don't get in,'
I tell him. 'You mustn't get in.'

'All right. No, I won't get in.'

'Hello you two, what are you doing all the way up
here?' a voice says from inside the car.

'Don't answer,' I whisper. 'Don't look either. He'll go
away.'

'Susan! Are you all right, my love?'

He knows my name. I turn round. It's Mr Williams
from next door in his new car.

'Are you all right?' he says again. 'What are you doing
all the way up here?'

'We're looking for Mum,' I tell him.

'Oh, I see. Well, you're a couple of chumps aren't you, because she's at home, and she's very worried about you.'

'Mummy's at home?' I say.

'She was the last time I saw her, which was about ten minutes ago. Your father's out looking for you, along with half the street. So come on, you pair of scallywags, hop in and let's get you back.'

He's got one of those cars with a long front seat and a gearstick on the steering wheel, so we climb in next to him and sit forward to look out the window as he drives us home.

Mum's out by the front door when we get there, looking very worried. I'm so glad to see her that I leap out of the car and run straight over to her.

'Oh here you are, here you are,' she cries, catching me. 'Where on earth have you been? You've had us all worried sick. And my boy. Look at you, are you all right? Come here, let me give you a kiss.'

She scoops Gary into the hug and we all hug together.

'Where did you find them?' she asks Mr Williams as he comes up the path.

'They wasn't all that far from Staple Hill school,' he says.

'Oh my Lord. What on earth were you doing all the way up there?'

'We were trying to find Gran's to see if you were there,' I tell her. 'We wanted you to come home.'

'Oh you silly billies,' she laughs. 'You didn't think I'd gone and left you, did you?'

'I didn't,' Gary says. 'It was Susan.'

'It was not,' I say, hitting him.

'I'm hungry,' he says. 'Can I have something to eat now?'

'That's my boy,' Mum says. 'What do you want?'

'Beans on toast.'

We go inside and she's just putting the bread under the grill when Dad drives down the street. 'Go on out and meet him,' she tells us. 'Let him know you're home safe.'

Gary dashes out the back door.

Mum looks down at me. 'What about you?' she says.

'You aren't going to have a row with him, are you?' I say.

Her eyes seem very big and brown as she looks into mine. 'No,' she answers.

'Will you be nice to him now?'

She wipes her hands on her pinny and comes down to my level. 'Always sticking up for your Dad, aren't you?' she says.

I nod.

She just looks at me and doesn't say anything, until she says, 'Sometimes grown-ups have got a lot on their minds, and they end up getting angry with each other, but it doesn't mean they're going to leave each other, or leave you. Now I want you to promise me that you won't go running off like that again?'

'All right, I promise,' I say. 'But you haven't got to hit Dad again, or smash up my toys.'

'I'm sorry about that,' she says. 'It was wrong of me, and I won't do it again.'

I look past her as Dad comes in the door. He's holding out his arms so I run into them and get swung up into a great big hug. 'I've been up your gran's, your Uncle Bob's, your Aunty Nance's . . . I didn't know where the dickens you were,' he laughs.

'Mr Williams found us,' Gary tells him. 'We were miles and miles away, weren't we Susan?'

'We had a map,' I say, 'but we've lost it now. We didn't speak to any strangers though, and we always looked both ways before we crossed the road.'

'You still shouldn't have gone,' he answers sternly.

'Can we go out to play now?' Gary says.

'I thought you were hungry,' Mum reminds him.

'Oh yes. After?'

'I suppose so.'

Dad puts me down and I go off to lay my table. We can use it now, because the glue is dry where he repaired it. I'm about to go and tell Mum that, when I decide not to. I just want to forget all about the other night now, so I sit down with Gary to wait for our beans on toast, and feel glad that we're back home and not lost any more.

Chapter Eleven

Eddress

It's a shame Eddie's not here to watch this film, because it's blooming luvverly, as Audrey Hepburn would say. She's a beautiful woman, she is. I've always liked her, ever since we saw her in *Roman Holiday*, in London, while we was on our honeymoon. Had a luvverly time we did, going all round Trafalgar Square and Buckingham Palace. Had a bloody big row on our first night though, when we got to Paddington and I found out the silly bugger hadn't booked us in a hotel. I'd have been on the next train back to our mam's if he hadn't walked off out of the station with our tickets and all the money.

'We'll find somewhere,' he said, 'don't worry.'

The middle of bleeding November, half past nine at night, howling a gale and we've never been to London before in our lives, but we'll find somewhere, he says. And where do we end up spending our first night, in a house of bloody ill repute, that's where. I thought there was a lot of coming and going in the night, and I find out why when we get up in the morning, and some bloke offers me two and six for a quick how's-yer-father. I nearly knocked his bloody block off, cheeky sod.

The picture house is full, no spare seats anywhere. Bob and Flo are over the other side somewhere. We didn't realise till we got here that our seats weren't together. Doesn't matter though. You can't have a chat while the film's on, can you, and I'll meet them outside after to get the bus home.

It isn't half a treat coming out tonight, though right up to this morning I was afraid I wouldn't be able to, because I haven't been feeling at all well after my treatments this time. Bloody exhausted I am by the time they've finished, and I reckon the tablets they're giving me aren't helping much either. I'm not getting the ambulance this time. I'm all right to get the bus up Cossham, and Eddie usually manages to pick me up on his way home from work.

It doesn't hurt, or anything, what they do to me, but if you ask me, that's why it came back, because we all know what radium does to you, don't we? It's in the bloody papers all the time, what'll happen to us all if Russia drops their bomb, so I'm damned if I know why they use the same stuff to try and cure you. I should never have let them do it. If I hadn't I swear this wouldn't be happening. Anyway, no point going on about it, is there? It's there and that's that. We just have to get rid of it now.

The bloke next to me is lighting up, so I think I will too. Just put one out, but never mind, Eddie's not here to get on at me, is he? Thank God we haven't had any more humdingers over it like the one we had at Whitsun. That was terrible, that. I don't even like thinking about it now, the way we carried on, yelling and screaming, brawling like heathens. He's never hit me before in his life, but he did that night. Clobbered me right round the bloody earhole he did, though I can't say I didn't deserve it for all I did to him. Honest to God, I could have murdered him that night, but he was bloody asking for it, stubbing my fag out like that up the Shant, in front of everyone, then walking out with my kids. Showed me up good and proper he did.

209

Then it all erupted again later, after the kids went to bed. He came in the room while I was having a smoke, took one look at my fag and started doing his bloody nut. So there we was one minute not speaking, and the next we're going at it hammer and bleeding tongs.

Fancy breaking up the kids' toys, the way we did. There was no need of that, and I'll be the first to admit I felt ashamed of meself after. But at the time we was beyond caring. To be honest, if our Susan hadn't come in when she did I dread to think what we'd have done. I reckon he'd have thrown that telly. He was mad enough, I could see that, and I was ready to go for the poker to beat his bloody brains in. What a pair. What a bloody pair.

Our poor Susan. She should never have had to see anything like that. Must have frightened her to death. Well, I could see that it had, but I was too bloody angry to stop. The only way to end it was for me to walk out, so I did, but I should have taken her with me. She'd have known then that I was up our mam's, and she wouldn't have led our Gary on a wild goose chase all over Staple Hill looking for me. Course, she wouldn't have wanted to stay up our mam's without knowing what her precious father was up to, so I wouldn't have had the time to calm down that I needed. I don't like admitting this, but there was moments during those couple of days when I considered never going back. I don't know what good it would have done, running away, but I didn't half feel like it, because let me tell you, it's bloody hard having to cope with them all while I'm going through this. Not that I'm feeling sorry for meself, you understand. It's them I feel sorry for, because I'm scared out me wits half the time, and that don't do any of them any good, does it? And I can't tell them I'm scared or it'll frighten them too.

Anyway, enough about all that. That's why I'm out tonight, to forget all about it and have a good time. I had a choc ice during the interval and a little chat with the woman in front who works as a cleaner here, she said. I wonder how much she gets an hour. Wouldn't be worth me applying though, by the time I pulled out for the bus fares, there wouldn't be anything left. I'm still of a mind to get meself a part-time job though, when all this is over and Gary starts school.

The film's just finishing now and I'm blowed if I don't fancy Rex Harrison, who I've never been all that partial to before. Bloody lovely ending it is, her turning into a proper lady like that. Let's hope we have the same success with our Susan.

You can hear all the seats thumping up as the audience starts making their way into the aisles. You can tell we've all enjoyed it, because we've got soppy great smiles all over our faces. Not for long though, because trying to get out of this place is turning into a right bloody fiasco. You've never seen so many people in your life, and we're moving like bloody snails. Someone should shout fire, that'd put a bit of vim in their step. Ouch! Some stupid swine has just trod on my foot, now someone else is jostling me about while he tries to put on his coat, the silly sod.

'Can't you wait till you get outside?' I say.

'Sorry Mrs,' he answers and puts his coat back over his arm. Good bloody job.

As we go out the doors into the foyer I'm being squeezed within an inch of me life. Then everyone comes to a stop and we're jammed up against each other like sodding sardines. I can see Bob and Flo across the other side. Flo waves, so I give her a wink and shout at the top of me best Audrey Hepburn voice, 'Come on, move your bloomin' arses.'

Everyone laughs and would you believe, it starts us moving again, spilling out onto Union Street where the Saturday night rush is turning the place into Piccadilly bloody Circus.

I go back to Bob and Flo's where Eddie's been looking after the kids. They're all in bed now, so we have a nice glass of port and a chat, before Eddie and I get in the car to go home. We'll come back tomorrow to pick up the kids, rather than wake them up now. I don't like leaving them really, but they'll be all right with Flo. She's as good as gold, she is. Always liked her, ever since Bob first brought her home. Another Taffy, like the rest of them, but I wouldn't hold that against her.

No rows tonight, I hope. At least Eddie didn't say anything about me having a glass of port. I don't know why he should, because the doctor never said I couldn't have a drink. I suppose with all the pills I'm taking, I probably shouldn't, but what harm's the odd one or two going to do? Bloody pills, if I had a pound for every one I took I'd be rich by now. Instead I'm blowing up like a sodding balloon, and it's not as though I was ever a skinny minnie before. It's the steroids they say. That's what happens. You get all built up like a bloody wrestler, then they give you radium to turn you weak as a jelly. Don't make any sense, do it? Or it don't to me.

No sooner do I get into bed than I'm fast asleep. Course I didn't know that till this morning, did I, when I woke up. Can't believe I went out like that. It's not as though I was feeling tired before, or not that I realised. But here it is, twenty past seven in the morning and Eddie's lying flat on his back, still in dreamland. Might as well go downstairs and make us a nice cup of tea before he gets up. I can have a quick fag too.

Eddie went to see Tyldesley last week about the

stomach aches he's been getting. I didn't know anything about them until he told me he was going to be late home that night, because he was calling in the doctor's. Silly sod kept it from me because he didn't want me to worry. Well, I'm hardly going to worry about an upset stomach, am I? Just as long as that's all it is, which apparently it is. A good dose of Milk of Magnesia or a Beecham's powder will soon sort him out, the doctor told him, so he's been taking one or the other all week.

It's the Beecham's powder that he got wrong. It's not for stomach ache, is it, it's for colds and flu, so that's how I know there's nothing wrong with him, and now I reckon he went to see Tyldesley to talk about me. I can't help wondering what Tyldesley said, but even if I asked I bet Eddie wouldn't tell me, and anyway, I don't want to know. I don't ask Michaels about anything either. What's the point? They never tell you anything anyway, and if you start reading about it in books you'll have yourself dead, buried and doing seven rounds of purgatory before you get past A for Acne. I should know, I tried it with one of the books Eddie brought home from the library. It didn't take much more than an hour before I was ready to be carted off to the loony bin. I played merry hell with him after, I did, bringing that sort of morbid stuff into the house.

'There's no point trying to work it out ourselves,' I told him. 'We don't know anything, so we have to let Michaels do his job and get on with our lives the way we always have.'

'But if you learn a bit about it,' he said, 'it might help you to fight it.'

'I'm fighting it well enough, thank you very much,' I told him. 'And I don't need any books to help me.'

And that was that. He took the book away and I haven't seen another one on the subject since. No, the less you know, the less you've got to worry about, is what I say.

Our holiday in Dawlish is all booked up now. Bob and Flo aren't coming, which is a shame, because we had a good laugh with them in Cornwall, a few years back. Our mam's coming though, and Alwyn, our Gordon's girl. Being the oldest of seven I expect it'll be nice for her to have a few less children to put up with for a week. She'll be fourteen in August, same month as our Susan's nine and Gary's five. God, the time flies, don't it? It don't seem five minutes since Gary was born, and now here he is, on the verge of starting school already.

I've had a letter back from our Maurice. He says he's definitely coming this Christmas, so I better break it to Eddie, just in case Maurice wants to stay with us. We don't have a lot of room, but he can always have Gary's bed, which is a bit bigger than Susan's, and Gary can sleep in with us. Our Jacqueline, my niece, stayed with us for a couple of nights last week. She's nineteen going on twenty, and married to a right bleeding sod of a bloke who's been hitting her around and carrying on with some trollop behind her back. Poor cow. She's in a terrible state. She's staying with our mam now, her own mam, our Ivy, can't have her, because the bloke Ivy's married to isn't Jacqueline's father and he don't want her there. If you want to know what I think, I think Jacqueline'll end up going back to the swine she's married to. If it was me I'd just wring his bloody neck and be done with it, but that's me.

Fat as a bloody house I'm getting now. Look at me there in the mirror, face all bloated, arms and legs looking like overstuffed sausages. I don't know how many different corsets I've tried, to help me get into me clothes, but I've still got me waistbands held together with safety pins and buttons popping off me blouse. I've had to start wearing Eddie's shirts just to be decent, and I'm borrowing some jumpers off our mam till I can wear me own again. That day can't dawn soon enough for me. Still, at least me lopsidedness don't show any more. It's all hidden by big baggy clothes. What I wouldn't give though, to be sliding into those Mary Quant dresses all the models are wearing, poker straight, halfway up their thighs and lovely long white boots. I've never been thin enough for any of it really, and if you ask me it's not strictly decent to have your hemline halfway up to your ass. They've only got to tilt over an inch and you can see next week's washing. Disgusting it is, really, but they look nice in the magazines. Our Susan's on all the time about having a mini dress, but I don't think I should let her, not at her age. She's too young to be getting into all that fashion malarkey. Time enough when she's older.

Eddie's gone up Bob's to fetch them now, while I sit here on the back doorstep, smoking a fag. I'll go in and finish the breakfast dishes in a minute, I was just feeling like a bit of a sit-down. I should get out there later and polish up that front step. Haven't done it all week and it's starting to look a bit dingy. Time the council painted it, if you ask me. I'll tell the rent man when he comes next Monday. Time it was all done round here, the windows, doors, bars and garden gates. I swear, if I didn't keep on, it'd never get done.

I hope no-one's looking, because I've just lit one fag off another. Well, what's the harm? I can smoke it now, or ten minutes from now, it all goes down the same way, don't it? Our Susan told me off the other day. I could hardly believe me ears, uppity little madam that she is.

'Mum, you shouldn't smoke, it's bad for you,' she said, and if that's not her father speaking, I don't know who it is.

Funny, because it's usually me she sounds like in spite of how close she is to Eddie. That's the strangest part of being a mother, looking at this little human being and seeing bits of yourself. Not that I'm always proud of what I see, mind you, far from it sometimes, because she's got some lip on her that's too much like me own for me to feel comfortable hearing it, but there are other times when I swear I can be thinking a thought one minute, and hearing it coming out of her mouth the next. It makes Eddie laugh, because he always seems to know when it's happened. He says that's part of why he loves her so much, that she's her mother's daughter. He's a soppy sod, he is.

Here she comes, skipping up the garden path, hair in plaits, socks round her ankles and not a pair of glasses in sight. Can't blame her for leaving them off, though, they look awful, and if they're making her see any better then we've yet to find any sign of it. Two years she's been wearing them, and no improvement to that left eye of hers yet. Perfect vision in the right, all fuzzed up in the left. Just like me.

'What are you doing sitting here, Mum?' she says, skipping across the grass towards me.

I wish I could think of an answer, but I don't rightly know what I'm doing here when I've still got the washing-up to finish, and plenty of housework waiting to be done.

'What about your school report?' I ask her.

That's taken the skip out of her step. I didn't say anything yesterday when she brought it home, because we were taking her up Bob's, but if she was hoping I'd forgotten, she had another think coming.

'You were sixth in the class at the end of last term,' I say. 'This term you're twenty-sixth.'

Her head goes down.

'It says you're not paying attention in class, and you could try harder. It makes me ashamed of you to read things like that. What kind of example's it going to set for Gary when he starts school in September?'

'I don't know,' she mumbles.

'Yes you do.'

'Not very good,' she says.

'Not very good at all. Now, we were going to take you up Kingswood this afternoon to buy a new swimming costume to take on holiday, but it's only people who do well at school that get new swimming costumes so you can't have one now, can you?'

'No,' she says in a whisper.

I know she's got her heart set on one with a little white pleated skirt attached, but she has to learn. Hard work gets its own rewards. So if she doesn't work, she won't get what she wants.

'What's going on here?' Eddie says, coming round the corner of the house with Gary.

'I'm just having a word with madam, about her school report,' I tell him.

'Ah, yes,' he says. 'Not what we expected of you, my love. You can do better than that, now can't you?'

She nods.

'Not paying attention in class isn't going to get you very far.'

'I told her she can't have a new swimming costume now,' I say. 'Only girls with good reports can have new swimming costumes.'

'Can I have one?' Gary pipes up.

'If you're a good boy.'

'I'm a good boy.'

'That's what you think. Now come on in and give me a hand with the washing-up, the pair of you.'

To be honest, I've never felt less like doing it in my

life. Given half a chance I'd go straight back to bed, but that would just be giving in and I'm not going to do that. No bloody way am I going to do that.

Susan

We're on holiday now, in Dawlish, Devon, England, Europe, The World, The Universe. We've rented a chalet on a site that's not too far from the sea, with a very nice clubhouse and lots of swings and sliders and things. It's my birthday today. I'm nine. Mum and Dad gave me a swimming costume with a little white pleated skirt stitched onto it, but I can't wear it yet, because it's raining. I've had other things too, a packet of Spangles from Gary that he bought with his own money, some play lipstick and a mirror from Gran and a join-the-dots book from my cousin Alwyn. It's her birthday next week. She'll be fourteen, and she's going out with the pop singer Billy J. Kramer. She's got a picture of him that he gave her, of him sitting on his motorbike. She's even been on it, she told me, but her mum and dad don't know so I have to keep it a secret.

Our chalet's the same as the one we had last year, all made of wood with a nice little balcony in front that's a part of it, and a long pot of flowers hanging from the railings. There are two bedrooms inside, at the back, one with a big double bed where me and Alwyn sleep, and a little bed along the bottom for Gary, and another room where Mum and Dad sleep. Gran sleeps on the bed-settee in the living room, which is where the kitchen is too. The toilets and showers aren't very far away, and the water tap is just outside the next chalet so it's easy carrying it back. Some of the chalets have water in their taps, but we haven't got one of those.

I put my birthday cards up this morning, and I'm wearing my badge that says 'I am 9.' We're going over to the clubhouse later where Jim, who's in charge of the games, says we'll do something special to celebrate. (I wonder if they'll give me the bumps – if they do, I hope they don't slam me on the ground like some of the children did at school and it wasn't even my birthday.)

Us kids are playing old maid with Gran at the moment, while Mum has a lie-down and Dad goes over the shop to get us something for dinner. It's good that Mum's headaches are getting better, so she doesn't have to go to the hospital this week, but she's got a bit of one this morning, which is why she's not playing cards. She shouted at Dad earlier and he shouted back, then Gran shouted at them and I told them all off.

'It's my birthday, you mustn't quarrel,' I said, and that made them shut up. Honestly, grown-ups, sometimes they're worse than children.

It's being cooped up in here, thanks to the bloody weather, that makes us so irritable. It's better when we can go to the beach, or play on the swings, but we like playing cards. I've got the old maid at the moment, so I've poked it up a bit to try and make Gran take it when she has to choose one from me. She's not very good at cards, Gran, she always loses.

Here comes Dad, all wet through with his plastic mac and cap on. I can see him through the window.

'I think it's going off a bit,' he says, wiping his feet on the mat as he comes in the door. 'The woman at the shop said the forecast's supposed to be good for tomorrow.'

'Then let's hope she's right,' Gran answers. 'These kids could do with a bit of air, and I don't think it'd do our Eddress any harm either.'

'How is she?'

'Still asleep, as far as I know.'

'I'll go and have a look.'

'What have we got for dinner?' Gary says.

'Ham.'

'Yuk! I hate ham.'

'No you don't,' I tell him.

'I thought I did.'

'No, it's tongue you don't like.'

'Tongue! Oh, yuk, yuk, yuk, yuk. No-one eats tongue.'

'Gran does,' Alwyn says. 'Don't you Gran?'

'Course I do. Nothing like a nice bit of tongue.'

'But that's like French kissing a cow,' I tell her.

Her eyes go all big as she looks at me. 'What kind of talk's that for a young lady?' she demands.

I don't know, because I don't know what it means. I just heard Alwyn say it the other day, but I can't tell Gran that or, by the look of her, I'll get Alwyn in trouble.

'Just don't let your mother hear you,' Gran warns, 'or you'll be catching what for.'

I look at Alwyn. She's gone all red and is trying to hide behind her hair, which is the same colour as mine, but she's allowed to wear hers down. As usual mine's in plaits, which is how I always wear it when Mum can't be bothered to go through all the fuss I make when she puts it up in a ponytail.

'Let's play snakes and ladders,' Gary says. 'I'll go first.'

'We haven't finished playing old maid yet,' I remind him.

'Oh yeah. Whose turn is it?'

'Gran's.' I hold up my cards. She eyes them carefully and goes to take one from the end. 'No, take that one,' I tell her, showing her the one that's sticking up.

'Oh no,' she cries when she sees what it is, 'I'm not stuck with that old bitch again, am I?'

'Mam!' Mum snaps.

We all look up.

'Do you have to use language like that in front of the children?' Mum says.

'Like what?' Gran asks.

'You know.'

Gran shrugs. 'I can see a nap hasn't done much to improve your temper,' she comments.

'Don't start,' Mum warns her. 'Now, what do you all want for dinner?'

'I'll do it,' Dad says, coming out of the bedroom. 'You go and sit down over there, and I'll make us all a nice cup of tea.'

'Have we got enough water?' she asks.

'I'll see,' Gary cries, and he shoots out of his chair to go and check the big urn under the sink. 'I think we should get some more,' he tells Dad. 'This one's nearly empty.'

'No it's not,' Dad says. 'It's just you, wanting to go and fill it up all the time. So, ham sandwiches for everyone, and a packet of crisps?'

'Yes,' we all cheer.

Mum comes and sits down next to me and pulls a face as Gary climbs onto her lap. Then we all start laughing, because Dad's just put his pinny on, and the cook's hat that we found yesterday for a halfpenny in the second-hand shop.

'He's a daft old thing, isn't he?' Mum says. 'Makes you wonder what he's going to do next.'

'I've entered us in the ballroom dancing competition, up the clubhouse,' he tells her. 'It's the first round tonight, so we better do some practice.'

'Oh, I haven't got the energy for that,' she says.

'Oh, yes Mum, yes,' me and Gary cry. 'Please do it.'

'I can't, my old loves,' she says.

'Yes you can. You're a good dancer.'

She gives a big sigh. 'All right, we'll see after dinner. Gary, you'll have to get down, you're like an octopus.'

We all eat our dinners and keep looking at the window to see if the rain's gone off. When we've finished me and Alwyn help Dad clear away (with Gran's legs she can't stand for very long) then Dad puts on the wireless and finds a station that plays music him and Mum can dance to.

'Come on,' he says, taking hold of her hand.

'No,' she answers. 'Show our Susan how to do it.'

'Let's both show her. Come on.'

In the end she gets up and they start doing the waltz. (I think it's the waltz, but it might be a foxtrot or a tango, I don't really know the difference.) There's not much room, but they're really good, and Mum's cheeks are going all pink.

'There, that wasn't so bad, was it?' Dad says when the music ends. 'Do you think we'll win, you lot?'

'Yes,' we cheer.

Some more music comes on so Dad tries to teach me and Alwyn to dance, and Gary plays snakes and ladders with Gran. Mum watches us all, with her head resting on the window sill behind her.

Later on the rain is nearly gone, so we all put on our coats and wellingtons and walk down to the beach. Gary and I have brought our buckets and spades, but Dad won't let us bury him today. The tide's out and no-one else is around. It's like a black and white day because all the colours have gone, the sky's a dirty sort of grey, the sea's a darker shade of that, and the sand is a sludgy mix of the two. The wind's a bit cold, but we're wrapped up quite warm and Mum's brought some extra blankets in case we need them.

'Where are the donkeys?' Gary asks.

'They're sensible. They don't come out in this weather,' Mum answers.

'Let's go for a walk along to those rocks,' Dad says.

'Yes, we can find crabs,' Gary cries.

'I meant me and your mother.'

'Oh.'

'Take them,' Mum says. 'I'm going back. It's too cold out here for me.'

'Who'd ever think it was the middle of bleeding August,' Gran moans.

'Look! There's a ship,' Gary shouts, pointing towards the horizon. 'Can you see it?'

We all peer through the mist, and we're so busy looking that I don't realise straight away that Mum and Dad are having a row. I don't want to hear it, so I link Alwyn's arm and start walking off down the beach. At least Mum can't go off to her other family while we're in Dawlish.

'Can I come?' Gary says, running up behind us.

'No!' I say.

'Please.'

'I said no!'

He stops where he is and when I look back he's still standing there, staring at us, and nearly crying. I want to hit him now, because I want him to go away, but he's making me feel mean. 'Come on then,' I say angrily, 'but you're not to speak. All right? I don't want to hear a peep out of you.'

'All right. I promise.'

By the time we get over to the rocks Dad has caught us up and I suppose Mum and Gran have gone back to the chalet. I don't ask, because I don't care. Mum's always spoiling things. She never wants to do anything, and she's always shouting at me and Dad and Gary, and today's my birthday, so she shouldn't be like that. If I ever have any children I'm going to let them do whatever they want on their birthdays, and I'll be nice to them all day long.

Jim's there when we go over to the clubhouse at six. There's no rain at all now, but it's still a bit damp and we've brought our umbrellas just in case. Lots of other families are turning up, but it's no-one else's birthday today, except mine. Yesterday it was three people's, so they had to share the special cake and games.

Me, Alwyn, Gary and Dad all sit down at a table (Mum and Gran didn't come and I don't care), and then a drum rolls and Jim says, 'Would Miss Susan Lewis who's nine today please come up on the stage.'

Dad winks at me, and Gary gives me a thump as I squeeze past them and walk in my best ladylike way over to Jim. My glasses are a bit steamed up, so I can't see very well, but it's all right, I don't trip over.

There's a cake on the stage with nine candles, all lit. First of all though, Jim gets everyone to sing happy birthday, then they all clap as I blow out every single candle in one go. I'm allowed to make a wish then, but I can't tell anyone what it is, or it won't come true.

'Now Susan,' Jim says, 'because it's your birthday we've got a very special treat for you. Do you know what it is?'

I shake my head.

'Then I'll tell you. You're going to be the helper for Mervyn the Magician tonight. So how does that sound?'

I turn to Dad, all excited. He's laughing and clapping. I wish Mum was here to see me.

The first trick Mervyn does is with cards, and it's really clever. Then he makes my glasses disappear, which is even cleverer (I wish I could do it). He finds them under a hat on the table behind him, worse luck.

Next he gets me to lie on a table with my head and

feet sticking out of a box. He's going to saw me in half, he tells the audience, and they all go, 'Ooooooh.'

I'm a bit frightened now, because I don't want to be sawn in half. And I don't think it's very nice that Dad's laughing, because what if Mervyn can't put me back together again?

'Are you ready?' Mervyn asks.

I want to say no, but that wouldn't be polite, so I say, 'Yes.'

'Then prepare for the saw. Ah! Ah!' he growls to the audience, like a wicked pirate.

I squeeze my eyes tightly closed and try not to be afraid. I wonder if it's going to hurt. I feel really sorry for me, because I'm a poor, unhappy little girl, whose parents don't want her so they've given her to the wicked wizard to saw into bits. After they'll take me into the woods and bury me next to a stream, that turns into a river and carries me away to an enchanted castle where I'll become a beautiful princess and rule all the land. Billy J. Kramer will be my boyfriend then.

Everyone's clapping and Mervyn's bowing. I look down and there are my feet, a long way away, sticking out of the other end of the box. I'm in half, and it didn't hurt at all, but I wish he'd put me back together now in case his magic runs out and they have to take me to hospital to have an operation. That'll make Mum's headaches worse; it might give Dad one too when she tells him off for letting them cut me in half.

At the end of the trick Mervyn opens the box and I'm all in one piece. Everyone gasps. How did that happen? It was really cool. (That's one of Alwyn's words. She also says groovy and fab, which I'm going to say too as soon as I can.)

'Take a bow, Susan,' Mervyn tells me. 'You've been the best magician's assistant I've ever had.'

The best! Oh I wish Mum was here now. Fancy me being the best! I bow and bow as everyone claps and cheers, then I look up and there's Mum, sitting with Dad. I'm beaming all over my face as I go back to the table, and slide in next to her to get a kiss on the head.

'Well done, my love,' she says. 'You were very brave and I'm very proud of you.'

I'm still beaming.

'Can I saw her in half too?' Gary says. 'I could use your saw, Dad.'

Everyone around us laughs, which baffles Gary because he means it.

They're bringing my cake round now, a slice for everyone, and a paper cup of lemonade. Then there are games of blind man's buff and pass the parcel, before the ballroom dancing competition starts.

Mum and Dad don't go in for it though. Mum doesn't want to, and Dad says it's all right, she doesn't have to. I wish they would, because they're really groovy when they dance so I'm sure they'd win and that would be fab. But it doesn't matter, because she's got her head on his shoulder and they're not cross with each other about it, they're just enjoying watching everyone else.

Chapter Twelve

Eddress

Someone's knocking on the door. It's gone midnight, and someone's down there, banging on the bleeding front door as though the house was on fire.

Eddie's already awake and getting out of bed.

'Who is it?' I say, starting to get up too. 'If they go on like that they're going to wake up the kids.'

'Stay there,' he says. 'I'll go and find out.'

Normally I'd have gone with him, but I was up the hospital a couple of days ago so I'm still not all that steady on me feet again yet. Not too weak to know that someone knocking us up at this time of night isn't bringing good news, though.

First thing I reckon is it's our Gord, come to tell us that our mam's been taken to hospital. Or worse.

It could be Eddie's father, drunk too much and fell and cracked his head in the gutter.

I can hear voices down there, but it don't sound like someone we know. Then the front door closes and Eddie starts walking back up the stairs. When he comes in the room the look on his face sends the shivers right through me. 'What is it?' I say. 'What's happened?'

He doesn't answer me.

'Eddie?' I say, starting to feel really uneasy now.

'It's our Bob.'

'Your Bob? You mean that was him at the door? Blimey, his kids are all right, are they?'

He gives a little nod. 'It was Mr Gunter, Bob's next-door neighbour,' he says. 'Our Bob's gone and died.'

I just look at him, knowing I can't have heard right.

'He came home from work with a headache,' he says, staring at nothing. 'The doctor's been . . .'

I feel all the blood running out of me veins. It's like I'm going off me head or something, because this can't be real.

He starts getting dressed. He's like a robot, hardly seeming to know what he's doing.

'Are you all right?' I say.

He nods.

When he's ready he just stands there, looking at nothing, then he puts his hands over his face and takes a deep breath. 'It'll be all right,' he says.

'Yes,' I tell him.

'I don't know how long I'll be. You try and get back to sleep now.'

I listen to him going down the stairs and out the front door. There's the noise of him starting the car, turning the engine over and over until it catches. I think of him driving up through New Cheltenham in the dark, probably the only car on the road at this time on a Sunday night.

I can hardly bring meself to think of how poor Flo's coping up there now. If it was me, and Eddie went, just like that . . . But it's not me and I don't want to get me mind going off in that direction, because that won't do anyone any good.

Thirty-seven. Thirty bleeding seven. That's too young to die. I don't care what any of your vicars or priests have to say, Jesus, nor anyone else up there, don't need him yet. It's those girls who need him. And his wife.

And his brother, because they was close those two, lived in each other's pockets all their lives. For God's sake, we only saw him yesterday, and there wasn't anything wrong with him then. Right as rain he was, messing about with the kids, teaching Gary to drive a pretend bus, tipping Julie upside down, with Karen riding on his back. Full of life. A mischievous bugger, for ever teasing and joking, or getting worked up about the Union with Eddie, or sorting out someone else's problems because he has that kind of heart. Dads don't come much better than Bob and Eddie Lewis, and now to think those two lovely little girls have lost theirs. I can't seem to take it in. The world just don't make any sense when it does things like this.

It's six o'clock in the morning now. The sun's been up for a long time, and the birds are all out there singing. Eddie came back a couple of hours ago. By then he'd been to Flo's, to both his sisters' houses and his dad's, where he had to break the news to Beat because they couldn't wake the old man up. He got stopped by the police on the way home for not driving straight. Poor sod was worn out, and they was very understanding when he told them about his brother. We had a chat about things when he got back into bed. The only other time I've ever seen him cry was when his mam died. She wasn't all that old when she went either, but at fifty-five she had nearly twenty years on Bob. It just don't seem fair, do it? I mean, what have poor Flo and those girls ever done to anyone to deserve this?

Eddie says Flo don't seem to be taking it too bad, but she's probably still in a state of shock. Must have shaken her up terrible, to find her husband dead in his bed like that. Eddie's going back up there later to help her start sorting things out. If I was feeling a bit better I'd go with him, but I can't. No use to anyone when I'm as weak as this, and anyway, someone has to stay here with my two.

'Are you awake?' Eddie says.

'Yes.'

He's got his back turned and doesn't roll over. 'How are you feeling this morning?' he asks.

'Not bad. How about you?'

'All right.'

We don't say anything again, just lie there listening to the birds and trying to make ourselves believe what's happened.

'I suppose I'd better go round the phone box and tell work I won't be coming in today,' he says.

I know we're both thinking of the money he'll lose, but it can't be helped. He'll just have to ride his bike next week instead of driving the car, and I won't be able to go up our mam's on the bus. I don't go up there as much now anyway. I just can't do it. It's enough trying to keep me own house clean and tidy, and do me own shopping, while I'm having to go through this. But our Jacqueline's up our mam's a lot now, and she don't mind changing her bandages and making her a bit of dinner. I'll ask our Gord when he comes in for his chip sandwich at dinnertime, to pop in the offy on his way home tonight to get our mam her stout.

'I'll make us a cup of tea while you're gone,' I tell Eddie. 'What do you want for your breakfast?'

'Nothing. I'm not hungry,' he answers.

'You got to have something. I'll make some toast.'

After he's gone I get meself up, then sink straight back down on the bed again. Bloody legs. How the heck am I going to get downstairs if they won't even let me stand up? Come on you silly buggers. It's been three days already, you should be cavorting across Siston bloody Common by now, not buckling right out from under me like a couple of sodding straws. Still, at least Eddie wasn't here to see it. Don't want him fussing around me, when he's already got enough on his plate.

I try again, holding onto the bedhead, and after a bit of wobbling about I manage to get me balance. It's not too bad after that, a bit of a stagger here and there as I go out on the landing, but if I sit down on me bum and take the stairs that way, I should get to the bottom no problem at all.

It works.

I'm here now, back on me feet and going into the kitchen. And to tell the truth, I don't feel all that bad. It does me the power of good to get out of that bed, and back in me own kitchen. And what a blessing it is to make me own cup of tea. Not that Eddie's cups are bad, they're just not like I make them, nice and thick and strong with a little drop of milk and two spoons of sugar.

So, the kettle's on, the toast is under and I'm just lighting up when Eddie comes back.

'Everything all right?' I ask.

'Yeah. I said I'd be back in tomorrow. I could do with one of those, got any more?'

'Help yourself,' I say, offering him one.

He lights it off the gas and sucks the smoke all the way in. I can tell it's made him dizzy, well it would when he hasn't had one for over a year. It's a wonder he's not choking.

'Children awake yet?' he asks.

'Not a sound.'

He takes another drag and sucks it all the way in again. 'Bloody daft thing to do,' he says, starting to cough, 'but I've got to do something.'

'It'll make you feel better,' I tell him. 'Now go and sit down, I'll bring your breakfast in when it's ready.'

The bin under the sink needs emptying, so I take it out

the back and see there's a bit of washing that needs to come in. It's a lovely day already, warm and sunny, just what we needed a couple of weeks ago, down in Dawlish. Thank you very much God for letting us have it now, when Bob's gone. Laughing up there, are you, because that's what it bloody well looks like from down here.

After breakfast Eddie goes up for a wash and shave, while I do a bit of housework. I'm down on me hands and knees, halfway through scrubbing the kitchen floor, when there's a knock on the door and someone's head comes round.

'Hello! Anyone home?'

Bloody hell. It's old mother Weiner.

'Mrs Lewis! I didn't see you down there,' she laughs. 'You're up bright and early this morning.'

'So are you,' I comment.

'Oh, I always am. Busy, busy, busy, that's me. How are you feeling?'

'I'm all right, thank you. What can I do for you?'

'I just came to make sure everything's all right. I had a call out in the middle of the night, and when I came back I noticed your lights on, so I just popped in to see if there's anything I can do.'

Yeah, mind your own bleeding business, you nosy old cow, that's what you can do, I want to say, but I don't. 'We're all fine,' I tell her. 'Just a call of nature, that's why the lights was on. Got to finish this now, so if you'll excuse me.'

'Oh, yes, of course. Didn't mean to bother you. Well, you know where I am if you need me.'

How Eddie has time for that woman I'll never know, but seeing as he has time for everyone I suppose it's too much to expect him to make an exception for her. I bloody wish he would though, she might not be quite so ready to keep popping in here then.

He goes off back up Flo's about eight o'clock and just after the children start getting up. All that thumping and bumping around up there, makes you wonder what on earth they're up to. Give it five more minutes and one of them'll be crying. I wait for it, but it doesn't happen, so I wait for the sound of the flush instead, because I know one of them's in the bathroom, but that doesn't happen either. Lazy sods. I suppose Gary might not be able to reach, but Susan's old enough to stop being scared of witches gushing out by now.

I give them their breakfast, then tell them to stay at the table because I've got something to tell them. If you've ever seen such a pair of guilty faces you'll be looking at someone in front of a judge. You should see the pair of them. Makes me wonder what on earth they've been up to to be this worried.

'Your Uncle Bob . . .' I'm not sure how to put it now I've started. 'Well, your Uncle Bob died last night,' I say.

Susan's eyes grow bigger and bigger. 'Why?' she asks.

What a bloody question. Trust her. 'He just did,' I say. 'It happens like that sometimes. People die.'

Her face starts to crumple. 'I don't want him to be dead,' she says.

'Nor me,' Gary says, though I know he doesn't understand what we're talking about.

'It's not a case of what you want, my love,' I tell her.

'But he's not even very old and Dad said people don't die unless they're very old.'

'Well, usually they don't.'

'That means Julie and Karen aren't going to have a dad, and that's not fair.'

'I know it's not fair, but there's nothing we can do about it. We just have to be brave and say our prayers that he's gone to heaven.'

'I don't want him to go to heaven!' she shouts. 'I want him to stay here.'

'Now, now. That's just being silly.'

'No it's not.'

'Yes it is, and don't answer back in that tone of voice.'

Gary's mouth is a little O as he watches us, and I want to squeeze him. It makes me wish Susan was still his age, when she was a lot easier to handle.

'Come on, my love,' I say to her. 'Stop crying and go on out to play. I'll call you in when your dinner's ready.'

Off she goes, Gary trailing after her. That's the good thing about kids, they don't really understand what's going on, so it's all soon forgotten. Our Susan concerns me a bit though, because sometimes I think she understands more than is good for her. It's hard to tell, and I don't want to pry in case she starts asking questions I won't be able to answer. It's all best left alone where kids are concerned. The less they know, the less they can get their imaginations going, and God knows that girl of mine has got one of those.

I suppose we just have to consider it a blessing that Julie and Karen are still so young. They won't know any different after a couple of months, poor little loves, and though it's not very good for them to grow up without a father, you never know, Flo might get married again. She'll need to, or how the heck's she going to pay all the bills?

Susan

Julie and Karen are staying at our house today while Uncle Bob gets buried. It's happening up Kingswood church, and lots of people will be there, mainly from the

234

buses, but there'll be all his family, plus all his neighbours and other friends too. There's even been something about him in the paper, which goes to show how
popular he was, things like: *In loving memory of Evan
Robert Lewis, may you rest in peace, Eddie and Eddress*; or:
*To a dear husband and father, we'll miss you, Flo, Julie and
Karen*. There were lots and lots like that, taking up almost
all of one column, more than anyone else who died the
same day.

Because she's on Mum's side of the family Gran's here
looking after us. Mum hasn't gone to the funeral though,
only Dad's gone there, because Mum had to go to
hospital for one of her treatments. She wanted to go, but
Dad said no, she had to keep her appointment.

'Don't be daft,' she said, 'he's family.'

'Eddress, I'm not going to argue about it. Either you
go up that hospital on your own, or I'll miss the funeral
and take you there myself.'

Well, she couldn't make him miss his own brother's
funeral could she, so she's gone up Cossham now, and
Dad's going to pick her up on his way home, the way
he always does.

I keep trying not to mind about Uncle Bob dying, but
it's hard not to when I really, really want him to come
back.

'If we pray very hard,' I said to Dad, 'will God let him
come back then?'

'No my love,' he answered.

'Why?'

'Because God needs him in heaven now.'

'But Julie and Karen need their dad, can't we tell God
that? I think He'll understand. We can ask Canon
Radford to talk to Him for us. God listens to him.'

'I'm sure He does, but you know what it says in the
Bible, God moves in mysterious ways, so we have to

235

accept that God has chosen to take your Uncle Bob now, and not try to understand why.'

'Why?'

'Because that's how it is.'

I looked at Mum.

'It's best that you put it out of your mind now,' she told me. 'That's what me and Dad are doing, so you try to do the same.'

I keep trying, and sometimes it works, but then it comes back again and I feel angry with God for being so mean. I don't think I'll go to church any more, because if that's how He's going to be, He doesn't deserve to have anyone worshipping Him. I didn't mind saying my prayers with Dad last night though, because we were asking Jesus to bless Julie and Karen and take care of them.

I don't know if Jesus heard, but I'm helping to look after them this afternoon. They're sitting on the settee next to each other looking very little and lost, so I have to think up some jokes to make them laugh. Usually it's easy-peasy because they laugh at everything, but even my one about the earwig going over the cliff doesn't seem to be working today. Karen just wants her mum and Julie's trying to comfort her.

I know, Julie and Gary both start school next week, so I'm going to take them up to my bedroom and get out my blackboard to teach them some sums.

They get them all wrong, but I get them right, so I can tell them the answers. Then it makes them giggle when I tell Gary to go and stand in the corner with his hands on his head.

We do spelling next. I give Julie and Karen easy ones, like 'mum' and 'dad' and 'yes' and 'no' (Karen can't do it because she's only three, but Julie gets them all right so I give her a gold star). It makes them giggle again when I tell Gary that if he wants to come out of the corner he has to spell supercalifraglisticexpealidotious. He sings it instead, jumping up and down on my bed, until he falls off and bumps his head and goes crying to Gran.

After, we go outside to play ring-a-ring o' roses on the lawn, which they seem to like, then I let them play with my twin dolls' pram, and we have the good idea of putting Karen in, so she can be the baby. She doesn't hurt herself very much when the brakes don't work and the pram rolls off down the street into the wall. Just a bit of a bump as she got tipped out, which I rubbed and kissed better, then put a plaster on, because children always like wearing plasters. (She bumped her head, but I put the plaster on her knee so everyone could see it.)

By the time Mum and Dad come home, Julie, Karen and Gary have all fallen asleep and I'm sitting out on the kerb, getting worried in case God has decided to take my mum and dad to keep Uncle Bob company. It would be really mean if He did, so I must try to be extra specially good to make sure He doesn't.

When I see the car I jump up and wave, and run round to open Mum's door as soon as they've stopped.

'Hello my old love,' she says. 'Have you been a good girl for your gran?'

'Yes. She's asleep. So's everyone else.'

'Stand back,' Dad says, coming round to our side, 'let me give your mother a hand to get out.'

I walk up the garden path behind them, going slow because Mum can't go any faster. Dad's helping her, and I'm carrying her handbag. She goes straight up to bed to sleep off her headache, and when Dad comes back down he takes Julie and Karen home. Gary goes with him for a ride in the car, so I stay and help Gran to make some tea. She can't stand up for long though, so I have to do most of it. I'm not allowed to do chips, or fried eggs, or anything with hot fat, but I can make beans on toast, or grilled fish fingers and peas. Tonight though we're just having sandwich-spread sandwiches and a packet of smoky bacon crisps.

I take some up to Mum, but she's asleep, so I put it on the floor and sit down on the edge of her bed to have a think. I don't really know what I'm thinking about though, because I still don't understand why God had to take Uncle Bob.

'What are you doing there?' Mum says in a whisper.

'Just having a sit-down,' I say.

'Are you all right?'

I nod. 'Can I get in for a cuddle?' I ask.

'Come on then.'

When I'm lying down next to her I stare up at the ceiling and look along all the cracks, imagining they're roads that go through outer space to heaven. I wonder if Uncle Bob can see me, and tell what I'm thinking. He must want to come back, but people who are dead can't unless God says so.

'Did you play nicely with Julie and Karen today?' Mum asks.

'Yes,' I say.

'That's my girl.'

'Mum,' I say.

'Yes?'

'God's not going to take you away, is He?'

'No, of course not.'

I'm glad she said that. I feel a little bit happier now. Then I feel worried again. 'Mum, would you be sad if God took Daddy away the way He took Uncle Bob?'

'Oh my goodness, what a question,' she sighs.

'I would,' I tell her.

'God's not going to take any of us, so stop worrying

238

your head about things that are never going to happen.'

'But how do you know? He might, and if He won't let Dad come back . . .'

'Susan, that's enough now.'

I don't say anything else for ages, then when I think it's all right to speak again, I say, 'Mum?'

'What now?'

'I don't want anyone to die ever again unless they're very, very old, even much older than Gran.'

'All right then.'

'Is that a promise?'

She sighs again. 'Go on down with your gran now, there's a good girl. Let me get some sleep.'

I go back outside to sit on the kerb and wait for Dad again, but then I play hopscotch with Janet and Sarah, and 'May I' with everyone else. One of the boys says, 'I know, let's play doctors and nurses,' but that's rude, so I say no. I'm being good in case God's watching, I don't want Him taking me away for being naughty. But then a cloud goes over, which means He can't see, so I creep round to Janet's shed, where she's being the nurse and Geoffrey's being the doctor, while the others take it in turns to be patients.

When it's my turn I lie down on the floor, but then I get up again, because I'm afraid God might be watching. If He is, He might make me die, so I run home and tell Him I'm really, really sorry, and then I promise never to be wicked again.

I'm back at school now, in the third year, so I'm growing up fast, but I still have to wear these stupid glasses, and skirts all the way down to my knees. Some of the girls are wearing minis, but Mum says, 'absolutely not, and don't ask again.'

We're on playtime, so I'm in the playground, sitting

on the wall. The wind has turned bitter, so we've all got our coats on, and the teachers keep telling us to run around to keep warm. I want to, but I haven't got anyone to play with. Sophie told everyone that people who live down my way are as common as muck, so now no-one wants to be my friend. Anyway, I don't care. Just because she lives in a big house, and her parents are rich, she thinks she's better than everyone else, well she won't think that when I've smashed her head in. I can do it. I can beat her up any time, and all her stupid, stuck-up friends.

Kelvin Milton's teasing me again. He keeps running up and pushing me, then running away again.

'Ha, ha, ha, ha, Susan hasn't got any friends,' he sings.

'You smell,' I tell him.

'You mean you smell, that's why no-one wants to play with you.'

'You're just dumb and can't get any of the answers right in maths.'

'Who are you calling dumb?'

'You.'

'I'll smash your face in if you say it again.'

'You're dumb,' I say.

He comes and smashes my face in, and breaks my glasses. I don't care, it means I don't have to wear them now, and he's being sent to the headmaster. Serve him right. He's a nasty smelly little worm with spots on.

Mrs Fields, my new teacher, Sellotapes up my glasses and writes a note to Mum explaining what happened. I think she's afraid Mum might come and kick up a fuss, but Mum's in bed, so she can't. She's in bed nearly all the time now, but she'll be up and about again by Christmas.

At the next playtime, in the afternoon, someone says, 'Do you want to be my friend?'

It's Caroline Fry, the new girl who just started this term. She sits next to Kelvin Milton in class, about three rows in front of me. I'm sitting next to Paul Bridges who's all right, except for his great big nose and crooked teeth.

'I'll play with you if you like,' she says.

I shrug. 'All right. What do you want to play?'

'Chase? I'll be on it first.'

We run around, weaving in and out of everyone, jumping over skipping ropes, and whizzing round circles playing farmer's in his den. She catches me as I crash into a game of oranges and lemons, and bring two girls down on top of me. They kick and punch me for being so stupid, so I kick and punch them back, and start to cry.

'Cry baby, cry baby,' they chant, dancing around me.

'Get out of the way and leave her alone,' Caroline tells them.

'You don't want to be her friend, you should be ours,' Ruth Parker says.

'Yeah, why don't you be in our gang,' Lizzie Phelps pipes up.

'No, please don't leave me out,' I say. 'I'll do anything you want. Let me play too.'

Ruth and Lizzie go into a huddle with the rest of their gang and whisper. When they come up again they say, 'All right, you can play, but only today. We might not want you to play again tomorrow.'

That's all right. At least I've got someone to play with today, and they live down my way, so they might let me walk home with them too.

They do, and I can hardly wait to tell Mum when I get in, because we talked about all sorts of cool things, like boyfriends and kissing. Not that any of us has got a boyfriend, or ever done any kissing, but there are some girls in our class who have, and Ruth says one of them might be pregnant.

I don't think I'll be able to tell Mum everything we talked about, but she'll like to know that I've made some friends, because she's always asking, so I go running in through the back door, drop my satchel in the kitchen and race up over the stairs, shouting, 'Mum, Mum, you'll never guess what . . .' I push open her bedroom door. 'I've just been walking home with . . .' She's not there. Her bed's empty.

I'm really frightened. She's always there, except the days she goes to the hospital and today isn't one of them. 'Mum!' I scream. 'Mum!'

I run out onto the landing. 'Mum!' I scream again. 'Where are you?'

'I'm down here,' she shouts back.

I thunder down over the stairs, charge along the passage and into the living room. And there she is, sitting in her chair, next to the fire in her pink pyjamas.

She's laughing. 'There's a blinking noise you're making,' she says as I climb onto her lap.

'I thought you were gone,' I tell her.

'Gone where?'

'I don't know.'

'You're a silly nincompoop, sometimes, aren't you?' she says.

'Yes, I am,' I laugh. 'Can I have a spam sandwich?'

'Yes you can. There's some on the table that I made before you came in.'

'Oh cool. That's fab. And some lemon squash? I like that better than orange squash now.'

'I know you do, which is why I made you some.'

'Are you up for good?' I ask, tucking into a sandwich.

'I don't know. I might be. I feel a lot better, anyway.'

'Fab,' I say.

'All right, so what's happened to your glasses?'

I go to fetch the teacher's note from my satchel and hand it over.

'I see,' she says, after giving it a read. 'That boy's a damned pest if ever there was one. Did he hurt you?'

'Only a little bit, but I'm all right now. You don't have to go up there.'

'That's good, but I will if you want me to.'

'No. It wouldn't be cool, and I'm just making friends with some girls who are really cool and groovy. They might let me play with them tomorrow, as well.'

'Well, I'm glad to hear that. It's about time you made some friends. Now, let me hear you recite the Brownie Promise.'

'Why? It's not Brownies tonight.'

'It's Tuesday, so I think it is.'

'Oh yes. I forgot. Will you be taking me?'

'Not this week, but next week maybe. The Promise.'

'OK. I promise to do . . .'

'I beg your pardon? Was that an OK I just heard?'

I put a hand over my mouth. 'Oops, sorry. It just slipped out.'

'You know what I've told you about American slang. All your fabs and groovies are enough, thank you very much. Now, start again.'

I take a deep breath, and rattle it off in one go. 'I promise to do my best, to do my duty to God, and the Queen; to help other people every day, especially those at home.'

'Very good. And the Brownie Law?'

'A Brownie gives in to the older folk, a Brownie does not give in to herself.'

'Excellent. Now let's go up and get your uniform ready, then you can practise the piano for half an hour, because I don't think I've been hearing much of it lately, have I?'

'Half an hour,' I groan. 'That's ages.'

'This isn't your father you're talking to now, it's me, so you'll do as you're told. And leave those glasses on the mantelpiece, Dad can take them in to be mended during his lunch hour tomorrow.'

Fab, that means I don't have to wear them to school in the morning.

'Where are the little round National Health ones?' she asks. 'You'll have to wear them for the time being.'

'Oh no,' I say, shaking my head. 'I'm not wearing them.'

'You'll have to, until we get the other ones back.'

'I am *not* wearing them,' I tell her.

'I beg your pardon.'

'I'm not wearing them.'

'You'll do as you're told.'

'Mum, I'm not wearing them. They're stupid and everyone'll laugh at me. Even you laughed the first time I put them on.'

'I did not.'

'Yes you did, and you're laughing now.'

'No I'm not.'

'Yes you are, and it's not fair to make me wear them if you're going to laugh.'

'All right, all right,' she says, not hiding her laughing any more, 'you don't have to wear them. Now go and get on that piano before I change my mind.'

When I say my prayers tonight I'm going to say thank you to God for everything, because I'm really, really happy today. Best of all is being in a gang. It's fab, and I hope they let me stay in tomorrow. Oh yes, and I'm really glad Mum is feeling better, because it means God answered my prayers and probably didn't see me playing doctors and nurses in the shed.

Chapter Thirteen

Eddress

What a bloody relief to have all that treatment over. Knocked me for six this time, it did. Spoiled me summer, turned me bloody life upside down, and nearly stopped me taking my boy for his first day at school. I wasn't having any of that though. I told Michaels, 'I don't care what you say, my son isn't starting school without his mother being there on his first morning.'

He was quite good about it, and changed my appointment that week from Tuesday to Wednesday. Vi Dickens, across the road, took him for the rest of the week, because her boy David was starting at the same time. After that, they wanted to walk on their own. Don't want mummies coming and holding their hands, only sissies do that.

It's only been a couple of weeks since it all stopped, and already I'm feeling a hundred times better. They've changed me tablets too, but I'm still on the bloody steroids so me weight hasn't gone down. Don't matter though, just as long as I can get out of bed in the morning and take care of me kids, that's all that's important. And believe me, they need taking care of. Little perishers, been running rings round their father, they have, getting away with blue murder.

They've gone blackberrying with him now, up Siston Common, and seeing if they can find some sticks for the runner beans out the back. It'll save us a couple of bob if we don't have to buy canes. I can't say Eddie's that much of a gardener, but he tries, and to be fair, we haven't done too bad with the potatoes, or the cabbages this year. Got a few onions too, and believe me, every little bit of savings helps when he's been having to take so much time off.

He's better with flowers. We've got a lovely front garden, with hydrangeas, foxgloves, delphiniums, peonies, glads, chrysanths, you name it, he's got them popping up all the way from spring till the end of summer. It's late autumn now, so it's not looking quite so colourful out there today.

I'm in the middle of giving the bedrooms a good clean. Now I've got me energy back I can be nice and thorough, getting into all those mucky corners, under the beds, in all the cupboards and drawers, and all round the skirting boards. You wouldn't believe how the filth builds up, and I'm not one to put up with filth. Speak to anyone and they'll tell you, spick and span we are, in our house. Floors you can eat off and furniture you can see your face in. I wouldn't be surprised if ours was the cleanest house in the street.

It wasn't this summer though. A right bloody pigsty it turned into then. Eddie just doesn't have a clue when it comes to housework, because one look at these carpets and anyone can see, he can't tell one end of a vacuum from another. And he probably thinks a duster's for blowing his nose, or wiping his arse, because it definitely hasn't been making any contact with me ornaments or glass shelving.

About four o'clock they all come bursting in through the door, looking like a bunch of bloody golliwogs. Blackberry juice everywhere, all round their mouths, up over their cheeks, in their hair and all down their fronts.

'I might have expected it of them,' I tell Eddie, as I

scrub Gary's face with the dishcloth, 'but you! You big kid. Just look at yourself.'

He's grinning from ear to ear. 'But we had an awfully good time, didn't we, children?'

I forgot to mention. He's started talking posh. Don't ask me why, he just started a couple of days ago and now we have to put up with him sounding like a right bloody charlie every time he opens his mouth, which isn't so bad at home, but honest to God, you could clobber him when you're out. Makes you feel proper soft, he does, going on like Lord bleeding Muck just off on a tally-ho round his estate.

'Are you going to make a blackberry pie?' Susan asks. 'Can I help with the pastry?'

'Yes, you can. I think with all this lot, we'd better make some jam too.'

You should see what they've brought home, there must be at least four pounds here, enough to feed half of bloody Africa.

'We'll have to give some away,' I tell them.

'Not the ones I picked,' Gary says. 'I got the biggest and fattest.'

'Yeah, and then ate them,' Susan responds.

'No I didn't.'

'Yes you did.'

'All right, all right. Go on upstairs now and get out of those clothes. And don't throw them on the floor, put them in the linen basket.'

'We managed to find some sticks,' Eddie says, like a toff. 'A couple of them might not be long enough, but I rather think they'll do the trick. I'll go on out there now, before it gets dark.'

'Oh do bring some coal in first, old thing,' I say, 'the fire could do with stoking up.'

'Righty-oh. Chop, chop.'

He's a berk, but his heart's in the right place. Anyway, it's good to see him like this, because he's been proper down since his Bob went, proper down. Nearly six weeks it's been now, and to be honest, I still keep expecting him to walk in the door any minute, or be driving the bus when I go up Cossham, so what it must be like for Flo God only knows. With her own family all living down Wales she must be finding it hard, coping on her own, so I'm going to make the effort to see a bit more of her now I'm feeling more meself, do what I can to help.

'Mum?' Susan says when we're rolling out the pastry later.

'Yes?'

'Do you know a horrible man called Michael?'

'No. Why?'

'I just wondered.'

'Who is he?' I ask, closing up the cookery book and popping it back in the drawer.

'No-one.'

'So why did you ask?'

She shrugs. 'I just thought . . .' She shrugs again.

'What did you think?'

'Nothing. Can I eat some of this pastry now?'

'Wait till we've lined the dish and made a circle for the top. Get a big plate out of the cupboard, we'll cut round that.'

I don't know, she's a funny thing sometimes, my daughter, talks in riddles so you never know what's going round in her head.

'Has Susan ever mentioned anyone called Michael to you?' I ask Eddie when we're upstairs on our own.

'No, darling, not that I recall,' he answers, still sounding like a berk. 'Why?'

'She asked me just now if I knew a horrible man called Michael.'

'What horrible man called Michael?'

'I don't know, that's why I'm asking you.'

'Do you think she could be referring to Mr Michaels?'

'Mm, maybe. I've never mentioned him to her though. Have you?'

'No, but you're always saying she has ears like a bat.'

'That's her all right. Check my nylons, will you? Are the seams straight at the back?'

'All looks tickety-boo to me. What time are you going out?'

'In about five minutes.' I check in my handbag to make sure I've got me money and lipstick. 'See that they only have one piece of that pie each,' I tell him, 'I don't want them up in the night, being sick.'

'One piece each,' he repeats. 'Anything else?'

'Yes, put out some clean pants for our Gary tomorrow, and stick an apple in his satchel. Susan doesn't want one, but see that her reading book's in there, she left it at home on Friday.'

'Pants, apple and reading book. Ah ha, that must be your friends knocking on the door. Do you have enough money?'

'I've got ten bob, that should do me. I'll bring you home some fish and chips if we get the number eight back. Now make sure they're in bed by seven, or no, *Dr Who*'s on tonight, instead of last night, so I said they could stay up and watch it. Keep an eye on our Gary though, I don't want him having nightmares. Have you seen me fags?'

He don't answer that, which is no surprise, but when I turn round I find him looking at me in one of his daft ways that always makes me heart melt. He's as happy as I am that I'm feeling better, and it does us both good to have a bit of a cuddle, because God knows, we do have the living daylights scared out of us when I'm bad. Silly

249

buggers we are really, because we both should know I'm going to be all right . . . Oh, look at that, he's gone and smudged me lipstick now, so I'll have to put it on all over again.

By the time we get downstairs our Susan's already opened the front door to Betty and Brenda Lear, who live the other side of us. We're going to meet our Jacqueline on the bus up Soundwell, if she can get someone to look after the baby. Poor cow could do with a night out after all she's been going through with that swine of a husband. Mind you, she can be a bit of a handful herself when she wants to be, so half the time she probably has it coming.

'Off you go then, my beauties,' Eddie says, holding open the door. 'Have a topping time, what?'

'I'm going to clout you,' I tell him, trying not to laugh. 'Take no notice of him,' I instruct the others as we walk off down the path, 'he's gone a bit soft in the head.'

We're off down the Gaumont to see the film everyone's been talking about, *Doctor Zhivago*. They say it's very good, so I hope the bloody bus turns up on time, because we don't want to miss the start.

None of the men was interested in coming, except Eddie of course, what with it being set in Russia, but he's baby-sitting so I can go out, and he took some new books out the library yesterday, so he'll be happy enough staying home and having a read. If it turns out to be really good, I'll go and see it with him again. Not next week, because we're going dancing over the Staple Hill Legion with our Jean and Gord, but maybe the week after.

You know, I can hardly put into words how happy I'm feeling. On top of the bloody world, that's what I am, because there's nothing like being ill to make you appreciate everything you've got in life, and believe me, I've got a lot. I might not have known it before, but I bloody well do now. Your health, that's what matters, not bloody money, or big houses, or flash cars, it's your health, and I don't mind admitting there was times over the past couple of months when I wasn't too sure I was ever going to get mine back. All that radium, and the drugs they gave me, it makes you feel that bad, that sometimes you come close to wishing you could close your eyes and never open them again.

But that's all behind me now. The doctors are happy with the progress I've made, and I don't have to go up the hospital again until the beginning of December. Course, I still have to go and see Tyldesley every week, but that's only so's he can keep an eye on how I'm getting on. Any bad signs of anything, and they'll have me back in, but I'm not worried about that. The worst is over, I can feel it in me bones. We can get on with our lives now, like a normal family, and put all this down to an experience that was hard, but worth it in the end for how good it's making us all feel now it's over.

Susan

I've decided God is very nice, because He's answered my prayers. Mum's not in bed any more, she's up and about, doing the cooking and cleaning, and going up Gran's and making sure we brush our teeth and wash behind our ears. She's always in a really good mood too, and keeps making us laugh the way she plays jokes on Dad. He plays them on her too, and then she teases him about the way he talks posh. Sometimes he reads to us like it, but then he has to stop, because we laugh too much, and Mum says we mustn't get overexcited before going to sleep.

I think I'm doing a bit better in school now. The teacher said I was when Mum went up to see her. I've got lots of friends as well, but really I want to be in Ruth Parker and Lizzie Phelp's gang. They might let me if I buy them some sweets, or give them my tuck, but I haven't tried yet. I feel a bit shy, which happens to me sometimes.

I'm not worried about Mum going off with her other family any more, because I think she loves us the best of everyone. Anyway, I don't really think she's got another family, because she's too busy with us, and she's probably not pretending to go to hospital when she's bad, I expect she's really there. Well, she could be pretending, because I don't ever see her – no-one lets me go in, but Dad does, so she must be there, unless he's pretending too. I think grown-ups have too many secrets, which isn't very nice, because us children ought to be told the truth, or how are we going to learn?

Mum and Dad have gone dancing tonight with some of my aunties and uncles, so me and Gary are up Gran's playing with our cousins, Geoffrey and Deborah. We've got this deck chair to put in our den, which we're building with blankets and coats draped around the table and a big wooden clothes horse. We're in it now, eating our midnight feast of tomato sauce sandwiches, even though it's only half past eight, but we were getting a bit hungry so Gran wound the clock on.

It's Gary's turn to have a sit in the deck chair now. He's the youngest so he's had to wait till last. We can't see him very well, because it's dark in our den, but he's jumping about and being silly as usual, and Geoffrey's poking him and pretending to pull the deck chair out of the way. Then suddenly Gary's screaming and screaming, and Gran's tearing the roof off our den, and I'm shoving Geoffrey out of the way, then I see Gary's little finger is trapped in the deck chair, and there's blood everywhere, and the finger's all flat and soggy.

'Oh my Lord, what's your mother going to say?' Gran cries, opening up the deck chair so he can get his finger out.

He's sobbing and screaming, and so am I, because his finger looks like it might come off. 'We have to get an ambulance, Gran!' I shout.

'Stay here, all of you,' she tells us, 'I'm going to send Nelly from next door up the pub to use the phone,' and because she can't run she goes as fast as she can out of the door.

Gary's still crying and shouting for Mum, and Geoffrey looks really scared, because it was his fault. I go to put my arms round Gary, but he's afraid I'm going to touch his finger and screams even louder. It looks really strange now, like a lump of bubbly red wool.

After a while Gran comes back, all out of breath and worried. Then not long after Mum and Dad come running in the door. Straight away Dad picks Gary up and takes him out to the car. Mum goes too, but they make me stay at Gran's, even though I cry and plead to go with them.

'We're going to take him to the emergency at Cossham,' Mum says, 'so we won't be long.'

'Lucky they was only at Hubert and Hetty Bright's dance school,' Gran says as they leave. 'Where's me stout? Got to have a drink after that.'

Geoffrey gives it to her, then still looking scared he takes Deborah home, because they only live next door with their mum who Gran doesn't speak to.

When Gary comes back he's got a whopping great bandage on his finger, and a lollipop in his mouth that one of the nurses gave him. He lets me have a suck, and then he falls asleep on Dad's shoulder, so I climb up on

253

Mum's lap to snuggle in with her while she talks to Gran about what happened.

When we go home we all sleep together in Mum and Dad's bed. I'm on the outside, next to Dad, and Gary's on the other outside, next to Mum, and because I think Mum and Dad are having a kiss I close my eyes really tight so I won't see. I don't mind them kissing, but it's a bit embarrassing really, and when they start laughing I feel all sort of funny inside.

'Stop making so much noise, I can't get to sleep,' I tell them crossly.

Everything goes silent for a few seconds, then Dad turns over and blows a raspberry on my cheek.

'Kids, who'd have 'em,' Mum grumbles, but I can tell she doesn't mean it.

We all go off to sleep then, and when I wake up in the morning it's only me and Gary in the bed, because Mum and Dad have gone into my room. When I find them I start to giggle, because they look really silly all squashed up in my little bed, then Gary comes in and starts to cry because his finger is hurting. I offer to kiss it better, but he thumps me out of the way, and goes to sit on the pillow right next to Mum's face.

With her eyes still closed Mum says, 'If you fluff now, Gary Lewis, you'll be in big trouble.'

Gary and me start to laugh, then next thing he's trying really hard to fluff. Boys are so disgusting, but it's ever so funny, especially when he does it and Mum dives under the covers to get out of the way.

We have a really nice Sunday then, because instead of doing the ironing the way she usually does, Mum takes me up Kingswood Park to play on the swings and run round the bandstand, while Dad drives Gary back to the hospital to have his finger looked at again. Later, when Mr Softie comes round, we all have a 99, and then

Dad lights the fire while Mum makes herself a nice cup of tea. I get a bit worried when she lights up a fag in case Dad starts on at her and everything gets spoiled, but he doesn't, so everything's lovely, and it's really easy to make Mum laugh, so we keep on doing it.

She's the very best mum in all the world, except when she's telling me off, or making me have a bath, which I have to today, because it's Sunday. I don't mind really though, I don't want anyone calling me smelly, and Mum goes extra careful when she's washing my hair to make sure she doesn't hurt, so I'm all squeaky clean and smelling of baby talc when I get into bed ready for Dad to read us a story.

Eddress

Four weeks it lasted. Right as rain I was, back to me old self and never been happier, then I wake up one morning and it's all I can do to get meself out of bed. Course, I did. I made meself, but the minute the kids left the house, hair not properly combed, coats hanging off their shoulders, shoelaces ready to trip 'em up, I had to go and sit down. I cried at how scruffy they looked. My kids, scruffy. It's never happened before, but honest to God, I didn't have it in me to sort them out that morning. I didn't even have it in me to get back on me feet for the rest of the day.

When he got home Eddie went straight round the phone box and called the doctor. I didn't want him to. 'I'll be all right tomorrow,' I told him, but he wouldn't listen, and the next thing I know they've got me back up Cossham for more tests and poking about, then another bloody session of radium. I can't tell you how much it upset me. I reckon I must have cried for a week, not that I let anyone see. No point is there, nothing they can do, and if you keep blubbing in front of the doctors they just ignore you anyway.

I'm back home again now, and spending more time in bed than out of it. It's never right is it, for a mother to be lying about like this. I should be downstairs in the kitchen, like every other kid's mother. Believe you me, it's where I'd be if I could, making their tea, sorting out their squabbles, doing all the normal things a mother does.

They never complain, bless their hearts. They've just come to accept this is how it is for now. It won't go on for ever though, I tell them. It'll all change by Christmas. I'll be up and about again then, good as new. And I will, I've made me mind up about that, so those bleeding doctors who don't know what the bloody hell they're doing better get used to the idea. In fact, I told Michaels that the last time I was there.

'You don't know what the bloody hell you're doing,' I says. 'You got me on radium and steroids and God knows what else, and none of it's working, is it? You give me a rest from it, change me drugs, and then it all comes back again. So what kind of treatment's that, I want to know?'

'I understand your frustration, Mrs Lewis,' he answers, 'but I do assure you the treatment's necessary to deal with your condition.'

'I never felt like I had one until you got going,' I tell him. 'Everything was all right till then.'

'I'm sure it seemed that way, but if we hadn't taken action when we did, your condition would be at a far more severe stage than it is now. So please, just be patient, and I'm sure we'll start seeing some positive results again very soon.'

Well, we'd better, that's all I can say, because if I'm still feeling as bad as this by Christmas I'm going to put a stop to it all. I swear it's all these damned pills, and everything, that's making me worse, and I've got to be all right by the time our Maurice comes across in the middle of December.

Meantime, Eddie's talking about making up a bed for me on the best settee in the front room. That way I can be downstairs when the kids come in from school. I think they'll like that better than having to put up with me lying about in bed all the time. I can watch them playing, when I'm not dozing off that is, and Eddie's going to put the telly in there too, so I can get back to *Coronation Street*, and *Billy Cotton's Band Show* and all me favourites. That might perk me up a bit too. God knows how Eddie's going to get me up and down the stairs though, because I'm no lightweight now, I can tell you that. Never was, of course, but honest to God, you should see me now. Well, it's probably better no-one has to, because I don't feel good, oh no, I don't feel good at all. Bloody steroids. I'd like to tell that damned doctor to stick 'em down his own bloody throat then look in the mirror, see how he likes it. He'd have himself off 'em quicker than you can say, 'Who's that fat sod looking at me?' I'll tell you that.

We had Bonfire Night last night. The kids made a guy to put on top the bonfire, and Eddie went out in the garden to set off the fireworks. Murder, it was, watching from up here, because our Gary kept getting too close to the flames trying to light his sparklers, and our Susan ran back up to a Catherine wheel that wouldn't go round. Luckily Eddie spotted her, and pulled her back. No emergency though, because the bloody things never work anyway. The rockets were worth the money, soaring up out of the milk bottles, and the Roman candles went off well. Course Gary loved the bangers and the jumping jacks. You should have seen them all out there, having the time of their lives they were.

Anyway, I ought to start thinking about what to get them for Christmas now. If I can't go out shopping, I can always buy what they want from the club book.

Did I already mention, our Jacqueline's been coming down a lot lately? Good as gold she is, going up Kingswood to get me shopping, and taking the kids to the dentist and optician, so Eddie doesn't have to take any time off work. I wonder what we'd do without her. She even makes Eddie's tea on a night sometimes, so it's on the table when he comes in from work. Her baby Vanessa's a cute little thing. No trouble. Chuckles away with the kids and goes off to sleep when you want her to, no fuss at all. Can't say my two were ever like that, little perishers. Still aren't. Love 'em to bits though. Don't know what I'd do without them. Won't think about that though, cos it don't do no good to.

Oh well, I suppose I ought to think about taking me next lot of pills, and getting meself out to the bathroom. Eddie's always telling me not to do it on me own, but I can't keep relying on Betty and I want it over before that nosy old cow, Cissy Weiner, calls in on her rounds. Of all the people, they had to go and give me her as a nurse. I reckon someone's having a bloody joke on me, I do. Either that or she wangled it herself, so she could come in here and have a good look round.

Honest to God, getting off this bed and standing up is so bloody hard that for two pins I'd just lie here and wet the damned thing. That'd give old Weiner something to gossip about, wouldn't it? She'd like that, I bet.

Oooh, blimey. Me head's spinning, me limbs are like lead, but at least I'm up. I just got to make one foot move in front of the other now, to get me out to the bathroom. It'll be all right tomorrow, I'll be able to do it no trouble by then, it's just today, after the treatment. Feels like they've filled me veins with concrete, it does, and stuck a brass band inside me head. Boom, boom, boom. I can hardly think for that bloody boom.

Here we go. One step, two steps . . . It's like walking a baby, or a bloody cripple. I can do it, I know I can. It's just keeping me balance that's hard. Bloody head's lolling about like a football and it feels like someone's nicked the bones from me knees.

I make it to the door, then out onto the landing. Kids' clothes hanging out of the linen basket, curtains not all the way open. Carpet could do with a vac. Think I'll have a rest a minute and sit down on the stool Eddie put there in case I need it.

Oooh, ow, bloody hell. I missed, and now I'm lying here on the damned floor with the bloody stool on top of me. I don't think I can get up again yet, but it's too cold to go on lying here. Crying's not going to do me any good, so I'm going to bloody stop that right now. I must look a right bloody charlie, sprawled out here across the landing. A beached bloody whale in pink pyjamas.

'Yoo hoo! Anyone home?'

Oh Christ, it would be her, wouldn't it, Cissy bleeding Weiner. Trust her to come now, before I've managed to get meself up again.

'Are you up there, Mrs Lewis?' she calls out. 'Can I come up?'

'No, I'm all right, thank you. No need for you to stop today.'

'Have you taken your pills?'

'Yes.'

'How are you feeling?'

'A bit tired. I'm having a lie-down.' Well, it amuses me.

'That's good. You need lots of rest. Have you done your bathroom business today?'

'Yes, thank you.'

'All in order, was it?'

Why doesn't she just bugger off? 'Yes, all in order.'

'Good girl. That's what we like to hear.'

I can see her down there now, checking for dust, turning her nose up at the bits on the carpet.

'I saw Eddie at the school last night for parents' evening.'

'Yes, he said.' Annoys me how she calls him Eddie and me, Mrs Lewis.

'How's Susan doing?'

Not as well as she was, but I'm damned if I'm going to tell her that. 'Very good thank you.'

'Our Wendy came second in the class, did your Susan tell you? She's doing ever so well. The teachers can't say enough good things about her. They don't think she'll have any trouble getting into the grammar school when she's eleven.'

'Lovely.'

'Our Tina's doing well too. Very sociable, the teacher said when I was in there this morning, helping with the vaccines. Your Gary had his. Brave boy he was, didn't even murmur.'

If I stop answering will she think I've fallen asleep? No, knowing her she'll creep up the stairs to check. 'I'm glad to hear that,' I say.

I'm bloody freezing and this floor's as hard as rock. Bugger off, you old bag, please, just bugger off.

'All right, I'll be on my way now then,' she says. 'Send one of the children up if you need anything. You know where I am.'

She slams the back door behind her and I heave a sigh of relief. Thank God she's gone. I'd rather die than have

260

her come up here and find me like this. Trouble is, I've got to get meself up again now, and back into bed. I can do it though. It might take all I've got, but I can do it.

Turns out the easiest way is to crawl. I even manage to get into the bathroom then, and onto the toilet. I lean against the wall as I'm doing me business and close me eyes. When it starts to come it's like giving birth. Sometimes I think it's worse. We buy soft toilet roll now, even though we can't really afford it, but I can't use that Izal any more. Susan and Gary moaned that they didn't have any tracing paper, so Eddie bought some up Woolworth's to keep them quiet.

Ow, ow, ow, ow, bloody ow. You can't help but cry when it hurts like this. Tears just stream down your cheeks and sweat out of your pores. There I am like a block of ice, with sweat coming out all over. I'll catch me death of cold if I don't hurry up.

Thank God that's over. I thought I was going to pass out come the end, but I managed to finish and pull the flush. Blood everywhere, as usual. Now I better fill a glass with water to take me pills.

It probably don't do me any good to flop onto the bed the way I just did, but I didn't have the energy to hold meself up any longer. It's about all I can do now to pull the blankets over me to try and get warm again. I'll be better tomorrow though, it's always the day after that's worse.

Told you I'd feel better today. I'm propped up on the pillows now and, would you believe, Eddie's reading me a story. No need to tell you it was his idea. Daft bugger, but I'm enjoying it. The kids are up our mam's for the night, and he's just come back from the Union. They're hoping Tony Benn'll come and give another talk in the spring. If he does I think I'll go. It'd please Eddie to have me there, and I'm interested in what the old git's got to say. He's for us workers, or as for us as anyone of his class ever is. Like I said to Eddie, he can afford his socialism, question is, can we?

This is a saucy book Eddie's reading. Everyone was talking about it a few years ago, and I can see why now. That Constance Chatterley's a bit of a floozie with the Mellors bloke, doing it under bushes and in the backs of cars. Dirty little devil she is, but I have to admit, it could put you in the mood if you weren't weak as a fish, like me. Blimey, just listen to it . . . I'm surprised Eddie's not blushing, because he's a bit of a prude when he wants to be, but he's just reading away, getting proper carried away by the look of him. What about the washing-up, I want to know. Has he done that yet? I hate to think of my sink being full of dirty dishes, just in case someone pops in.

That hasn't been happening much lately. They've all stopped coming as regular as they used to, my brothers and sisters, me mate Nellie who I used to work with, the neighbours, they don't drop in for cups of tea and a chat any more. Well, they can't can they, when I'm not down there to put the kettle on. Eddie says it's because they don't want to tire me out, but I know it's more to do with them not knowing what to say. I don't blame them, I don't suppose I'd know what to say in their shoes either. I mean, this isn't something you want to talk about, is it? It's a bit like Cissy Weiner, you just wish it wasn't there.

She was in here again earlier, fussing about and getting on me nerves. Luckily I didn't need to go to the bathroom, though it'd serve her right if I made her wipe my arse, the way she shoves her bloody kids down my throat. I'd never tell her this, but it was a bit of a boost having someone to chat to for five minutes, and a relief having someone to get the water for me pills. Down they all went, every last one of them. I just wish I knew what bloody good they was doing, because I'm not seeing any end to this yet.

'Are you asleep?' Eddie says.

'No. Just got me eyes closed.'

'How are you feeling?'

Like I want to have a fag, but I better not say that. 'All right.'

'Fancy a cup of tea?'

'Yeah. Why not?'

Shall I ask him to empty the ashtray? It's stinking a bit.

'Mr Flowers, over the back, is going to let me borrow his ladder for the weekend, so I can get up on the roof to sort out the aerial,' he says.

'That's good.'

'Do you think you'll be comfortable enough down there on the settee?'

'It'll be better than being stuck up here.'

'What about getting upstairs to the bathroom?'

'I'll manage.'

By tomorrow, or the next day, I'll be going up and down right as rain anyway.

Chapter Fourteen

Susan

I wish Ruth Parker or Lizzie Phelps would be my best friend. I keep asking them, but they say no, they're already each other's best friends, and they don't need any one-eyed twits to be their friend, thank you very much. That's mean, saying that, because I've got two eyes, like everyone else. Anyway, they're still sort of letting me be in their gang, so that's all right.

Caroline Fry's gone over to Sophie's side now so we don't speak to her any more. Really, I wish I was in that gang, because they're all going on a school cruise next June, and I am too. Mum and Dad talked it over, and decided they'd put away a bit each week so I could go to Norway and Denmark on a ship called the *Devonia*. I've seen pictures of it, and of the places we're going to see. There are glaciers (mountains of ice) and fjords (blue lakes at the edge of the sea) and a mermaid sitting on a rock.

'Oh, I'm sure you'll all be friends by then,' Dad said, when I told him about the others who are going.

'But what if we're not? They might push me overboard.'

'Don't be silly. Anyway, you've got your junior swimmer now, so you'll be all right.'

I hit him and he caught my hand and pulled me into one of his scratchy-chin hugs.

He's coming up the school later to have a word with Mrs Fields about how well I'm not doing in class. I'm trying, but it's all really hard. When Mum does it with me at home it's all right, but when I get to school I can't do it any more. Except spelling. I'm quite good at that.

Kelvin Milton keeps calling me a dunce. I just do as Dad says and ignore him, because I know I'm not. Last year, at the end of Spring term I was sixth in the class. I know I dropped down to twenty-sixth by the end of Summer term, but that happens sometimes, Dad said. I was just having a few problems paying attention, but we're going to get that sorted out this year, which is why he's coming to talk to Mrs Fields, because I'm still not paying attention.

We don't tell Mum any of this because we don't want her to worry. She's got enough on her plate at the moment, what with still trying to get these headaches sorted out, thinking about Christmas, and preparing for Uncle Maurice coming over at the beginning of next week. She says she's going to get up for that, but Dad says, 'We'll see.'

She's got a bed on the settee in the front room now. The telly's in there too, and Dad's seeing about putting in a gas fire, so she doesn't have to worry about keeping going out in the cold to get some coal. I like the front room, it's our best room, with pictures of the Queen and Prince Philip in round brass frames, a big, cosy green three-piece suite and a furry rug in front of the fireplace. There are little wooden camels on the mantelpiece joined together by chains, and a cabinet in the corner where Mum keeps our bit of bone china, and some costume dolls Aunty Kathleen sent down from London.

'All right class, close your exercise books now and bring them to the front.'

I feel a bit worried because I haven't finished. We're

supposed to be writing a composition on Christopher Columbus, who discovered America in 1492, but I've only written down that he sailed across the Atlantic with three ships, the *Santa Maria*, the *Pinta* and the *Nina*. I couldn't think of anything else, but we're meant to fill a whole page.

I take my book out the front and put it on the pile with the others.

'Please miss, I don't feel very well,' I say.

'What's the matter?'

'I've got a headache.'

'Then stay in the classroom during break, and don't try climbing out of the window again. You could have had a nasty accident last time.'

'Yes miss. I mean, no miss.'

I did it for a dare.

'We dare you to jump out of the window,' Lizzie and Ruth said. 'If you do, you can be number three in our gang.'

I would have won if Mrs Fields hadn't walked in and grabbed me before I jumped down into the playground. It wasn't all that high, only about as tall as Dad, so I could have done it, easy-peasy, without breaking my neck and going to hospital in an ambulance with the siren blaring.

I wonder if she'll tell Dad about it tonight. I hope not, because I'm in enough trouble already for not doing my work and talking in class. Still, it wouldn't be as bad as telling Mum, I'd really be in for it then.

I've just come in from school now and Mum's asleep on the settee, so I sit down next to her and wait for her to wake up. She doesn't though, but I wait a bit longer, just in case. She's got the pink candlewick eiderdown from her bed over her, and some pillows with pale pink and blue stripes. I run my finger along the lines, not making any noise, but quite close to her face. Her eyes don't open so I lean right down to her, until my nose is almost touching hers. Then I stare out of the window and watch the bush outside bobbing about in the wind.

I'm getting a bit bored now so I go and find something to eat. Gary's already out in the street playing, so I think I might start making the tea. I can't find anything to cook though, so I go upstairs to play with my dolls. I put my record player on really loud, and when that doesn't wake Mum up I jump up and down on the bed.

I go back downstairs. She's still asleep, so I take my glasses off and poke out my tongue. She'd go really mad if she could see me, but she can't, so I keep on doing it. Then I go and get my bike and take it out for a ride.

I cycle round the green twice, very fast without falling off and grazing my knees and knocking my teeth out. Then I take my bike home and into the front room.

'What are you doing?' Gary says, coming in through the door. His lips are nearly blue he's so cold. 'That's not allowed, to have your bike in here.'

'So?'

'You'll get told off.'

'See if I care.'

He looks at Mum, then back at me. 'Is there anything to eat?' he asks.

'Only some celery.'

'Ugh, yuk, yuk, yuk. Makes me feel sick. When's Dad coming home? I want some tea.'

'I know, we could go round the shop and get something. There's money up in the cupboard, for the rent. We could use that.'

'All right. What shall we get?'

'What are you two going on about there?' Mum says, coming awake.

'We're going round the shop to get some tea,' Gary tells her.

'Oh, are you now? And whose bright idea was that?'

'Susan's.'

'I thought as much. And what's that bike doing in here, madam? Get it out, now.'

I do as I'm told then go back to sit down on the floor next to her knees. Gary's next to her head so I can't get in there. She lights up a fag and I wait for her to say something about my glasses not being on, but she's too busy chatting with Gary about what he did in school today. I don't want her to ask me, so I go back upstairs and get into bed.

I hardly ever get told off now. I can do almost anything I like and no-one ever says anything. It makes me feel brave and scared. I wonder what would happen if I did something really bad, like rob a bank or murder some-one. I could strangle Kelvin Milton to death, and they wouldn't hang me, because it's been banned now. I'd go to prison for the rest of my life though, and live in a cell, or a dungeon and only have bread and water to eat. I wonder if Mum and Dad would come to visit me. I think Dad would. Mum would just go on lying on the settee, drinking tea and smoking fags, because that's all she ever does now. She's not interested in us any more. Well, she is in Gary, she's just not in me.

Gary and I are up Gran's, making toast in front of her new gas fire. My cousin Jacqueline's out in the kitchen, peeling some potatoes for dinner and having a chat with my other cousin, Brenda, who's about nineteen, the same age as Jack. Brenda's got a mini dress on that's so short you can see all the way up to the top of her big fat legs. I was wondering why you couldn't see her suspenders, but then she showed Jack that her nylons have got knickers attached, so they don't need suspenders. It's really clever that, but I bet she's freezing, because it's nearly snowing out. You can see it whisking about in the wind.

Our Jack's in the doghouse with Gran at the moment, because Andy, her husband, came round earlier to try and take their little girl Vanessa away. They had a terrible row, Jack and Andy I mean, me and Gary heard it all, we even saw her whack him round the head with the vacuum pipe. I don't know how much damage it did to his head, but it broke the pipe, and Gran's mad now, because she can't afford another. Me and Gary thought we might go and sit outside on the wall and ask people to spare a halfpenny as they walk past so we could help her buy a new one, but it's too cold, so we're making some toast instead.

Gran's having a bit of a snooze in her chair, so we can put on as much butter and jam as we like. *Watch with Mother* is coming on in a minute. It's Friday, so it'll be *The Woodentops*. I love Spotty Dog, but I always want to punch Baby Woodentop. I don't know why, because usually I like babies. Oh no, just a minute, *The Woodentops* come on after dinner, that's right. I think it should be *Andy Pandy* or Bill and Ben in a minute. Pob-bop little weed!

Oh yes, I nearly forgot. Uncle Maurice is here from New Zealand now. He came down our house last night, but it was late so we were already in bed and asleep. Dad told us he'd been when he was driving us up Gran's on his way to work this morning. He said Mum was very happy to see her brother for the first time in nearly fifteen years, but it had worn her out a bit, which is why we're up Gran's today, so Mum can have a rest.

Uncle Maurice is upstairs in the bath now, so we still haven't seen him. Gran says his hours are all upside down because he's come from the other side of the world. He's in the air force, so he might have flown the plane back himself and landed it over the BAC in Filton. We'll be able to ask when he comes down for his breakfast. Well, it'll be his dinner now, and we're having a nice roast chicken especially for him, that Jack's making, if she gets on with it and stops gossiping with Brenda.

'Get on with it and stop that bloody gossiping out there,' Gran shouted at her just now. 'And make sure you peel the spuds thin, we're not millionaires.'

After she put the spuds on to boil, Jack took a kettle of hot water up to Uncle Maurice, to warm up his bath, and we could hear them laughing and joking up there, carrying on like a pair of bloody lovebirds, Gran said. They're not though, because he's her uncle, and he's ten years older than Mum, so that makes him more than twenty years older than Jack. It's a bit rude though, for her to take him some water when he hasn't got any clothes on. I wonder if she saw his dicky di-do.

It's Andy Pandy, Looby Loo and Teddy Bear.

When Jack and Andy were courting they used to come and babysit for us sometimes, and they'd kiss right in front of me. I never knew whether to look or not. I wanted to, but it felt naughty to watch, so I just used to steal little looks and hope they didn't catch me. They kissed the way people in films do, for a long time on the mouth, with their heads going round and round. I've been practising on my dolls, but I don't think I'm moving my head right yet.

'All right, you two,' Jack says, coming into the room, 'say a nice hello to your Uncle Maurice.'

We both turn round and look up. He's not anything like I expected. He hasn't got a uniform on, the way he has in the photo Mum keeps, and he isn't even as tall as Dad. His hair's wet, but I think it's the same colour as mine, and his clothes are all creased, like they need a good iron.

'So you're Susan and Gary,' he says with a great big smile. 'I've heard all about you.'

'Stand up,' Gran tells us, making us jump because we didn't know she was awake.

'How do you do?' Uncle Maurice says, holding out a hand towards me to shake.

No-one's ever said how do you do to me before, so I take his hand and do a little curtsey. 'How do you do?' I say back.

He laughs quite loud, then swings me up and gives me a great big kiss on the cheek. I don't like it very much, but I don't say anything, because it wouldn't be polite. 'You're a lovely thing, aren't you,' he says, 'behind those funny old glasses.'

I've just noticed something very strange about him, he's got one blue eye and one brown.

'Why have you got one blue eye and one brown?' I ask.

'Susan! Where's your manners?' Jack cries.

'Sorry,' I say, going really red.

Uncle Maurice thinks it's funny and laughs loud again. 'One of them's false,' he tells me. 'Can you guess which one?'

I guess the blue, but it's the brown.

'Why didn't they give you two eyes the same colour?' Gary asks, as he gets scooped up for a kiss.

'Because they'd run out of blue ones the day I went in,' he answers. 'I can see yours are nice and blue.'

'Just like Dad's,' I inform him.

He puts his eyebrows up and says, 'That's right, just like your father's.'

'Do you want a cup of tea, Maurice?' Jacqueline asks

him. 'The kettle's already on, so it's no bother.'

'That'd be lovely,' he tells her. 'No milk, two sugars. What about you, Florrie, are you going to have one?' Fancy calling his mum by her first name. I wonder if she's going to tell him off.

But Gran's scowling at Jacqueline. 'Not if she's making it,' she says.

'Oh, Gran, don't be stupid,' Jack grumbles. 'What difference does it make . . .'

'It makes a difference to me. You broke my bleeding vacuum, then you come in here, behaving like a bloody trollop . . .'

'What the bloody hell are you talking about?'

'You know what I'm talking about, and you can cut it out my girl, do you hear me? You too.' She's glaring at Uncle Maurice now.

He gives her an air-force salute. 'Anything you say, Florrie.'

'She's going off her head,' Jacqueline mutters.

'You can stop all that muttering, thinking I can't hear you,' Gran says. 'If these two weren't here I'd give you a piece of my bloody mind, I would, carrying on the way you are. It's no wonder your husband kicked you out.'

'He didn't kick me out. I left, and you know very well why, so just shut up, all right? You'll wake our Vanessa up and I don't want her hearing your bloody lies.'

'I'll be kicking you out next if you give me any more lip,' Gran warns. 'Now go and make that tea before I put me boot up your ass.'

'Dear old Florrie,' Uncle Maurice chuckles, going to put an arm round her. 'Haven't changed a bit, have you?'

'Nor have you, more's the pity.'

His laugh is loud and long. 'You'd be disappointed if I had, and you know it,' he tells her.

'I just don't want any of your shenanigans going on under my roof, is that understood? We had enough of them before you went off to New Zealand. I'm not putting up with it again.'

He gives her another air-force salute, then a big smackeroo on the cheek, which seems to make her smile. 'You're a good boy, when you want to be,' she tells him, 'sending me that money, taking care of your old mam, but it's time you learned how to behave yourself with the ladies.'

Gary and me are hardly breathing. This is better than *Andy Pandy* any day.

'I don't know what you're talking about,' he teases her.

'Yes you do. Now, that's enough while innocent ears are listening. Tell me how you found our Ed last night, and be careful again,' she adds, giving a nod towards us.

'She didn't seem too bad,' he answers. 'All rosy cheeks and bright blue eyes.'

'Her eyes are brown,' Gary and I say together.

'Of course they are. I was just testing you.'

'Was she in bed?' Gran asks.

'No. She was downstairs in the front room. Had her best dress on for the occasion, she did.'

'A blue one with white dots?' I ask.

'That's the one. And lovely she looked too. Your dad's a lucky man, you two, do you know that?'

We look at Gran, not sure how to answer.

'How was Eddie?' she asks. 'Did he say anything?'

'Like what? He was civil, if that's what you mean, and why wouldn't he be? I'm a pretty civil sort of bloke myself when I want to be.'

'He didn't tell you anything about how it is?'

'Florrie, it's the first time I've ever met the man, so

he's not going to be telling me the ins and outs of it all, now is he? Anyway, why are you asking me? Doesn't he tell you?'

'He never tells anyone anything. Carries it all, he does. I don't think he even tells her everything that's going on.'

'Gran?' I say.

'Yes my old love?'

'What's going on?'

'Nothing. You shouldn't be listening. Go on out and give our Jack a hand with the dinner. Tell her I said you can have a biscuit to keep you going. And tell her to hurry up with that bloody tea.'

'Gran says hurry up with the bloody tea,' I say to Jacqueline as we walk into the kitchen.

'Oi! That's enough of that language, young lady.'

'We're allowed to have a biscuit,' Gary tells her, tripping over the cat on his way to the biscuit tin.

'Just one each, mind, we've got to make sure there's enough for Uncle Maurice.'

After she's gone with the tea, I put my finger over my lips to warn Gary to be quiet, and we tiptoe to the living-room door to have a listen. It turns out they're just talking about boring things, so I take Gary back to the kitchen.

'What do you think of him?' I ask.

'Who? Uncle Maurice?' He shrugs. 'He's all right.'

'I don't like him,' I say.

'Why not?'

'I just don't. I don't think Gran does either.'

'She has to. She's his mum.'

'What are you two whispering about?' Jacqueline snaps, making us jump.

'Nothing.'

'Then go on upstairs Susan and fetch Uncle Maurice's

newspaper, there's a good girl. He wants to have a read before the news come on.'

I feel like telling her to go and get it herself if she likes him so much, but I'm not brave enough, though I could have said it, because no-one ever tells Mum these days, when I'm rude. Dad didn't even tell her when I said Father Christmas was just a silly old bugger who isn't real anyway, so I couldn't care less if I don't have any presents for Christmas.

'You won't, if you carry on like that,' he told me. 'You'll just get a thick ear and sent straight to bed.'

'That's your answer for everything,' I said back.

'Susan, don't be difficult. All I said was, Father Christmas might not bring you as much this year, because he's got a lot of houses to get round.'

'He can miss me out altogether if he likes, see if I care.'

'Don't be silly now. He's not going to miss you out, he's just going to concentrate more on the children in Africa who don't even have anything to eat, never mind presents.'

'Shall we make them some presents, for him to take?'

'That would be a lovely thing to do.'

'I can send them my pocket money too.'

'We'll see. But when we've got some time, we'll think of what we can make.'

We haven't made anything yet, because he's never got any time, and everything I've tried to make on my own never looks like what it's supposed to be. Dad said I might have a future as an abstract artist which made Mum chuckle and me mad, because I don't like it when they use words I don't understand.

Uncle Maurice's bedroom's a bit of a mess, with his clothes hanging out of his suitcase and the bed not even made. The paper's on the floor, next to an ashtray that's

275

only got one cigarette end in. I don't take much notice of it at first, then I realise it's got red lipstick on the tip.

'I told you he was strange,' I whisper to Gary after I've delivered the paper. 'He wears lipstick.'

Gary's eyes go big and round. 'That's silly. Men don't wear lipstick,' he says.

'They do if they're Danny La Rue.'

'But he's not Danny La Rue.'

'He might be like him though, you know, wearing women's clothes and high-heel shoes.'

Gary giggles.

'Ssh,' I say, giggling too. 'Come on, let's go upstairs and see if we can find anything else.'

We creep up as quietly as we can, freezing every time a stair creaks, and holding our breath in case anyone hears. No-one does, but Gary stays on watch at the bedroom door while I go and have a look in the suitcase to see if there are any frilly knickers or ladies' brassieres.

'Huf, look,' I cry in a whisper. 'Nylons. He's got nylons. See, I told you. And there's a bottle of scent here too.'

'Quick, I think someone's coming,' Gary says.

I drop the bottle and flee across the landing to Gran's room.

We wait and listen, but no-one comes up the stairs.

'He's a queer,' I whisper.

'What's a queer?'

'A man who dresses up as women. And it's against the law. He could go to prison if anyone found out.'

Gary's eyes blink up and down. I can see he doesn't really understand what I'm saying. I wonder if I should tell Gran what we know. I could tell Lizzie and Ruth at school, because I bet they don't have an uncle who's queer, or even know anyone who has. They'll be really shocked and want to know all about it, and I can say, 'If one of you'll be my best friend, I'll tell you.'

Eddress

'What have you two been out there chatting about?' I ask Eddie as he comes back in the front room with a fresh pot of tea. 'Thought you'd gone round the pub, or something, you were gone so long.'

'Oh, Maurice was just telling me how he's thinking about packing in the air force and going to Rhodesia,' he answers.

That takes me back a bit. 'He never said anything to me.'

'He's just thinking, that's all. He was asking me what I thought about all the troubles they're having over there.'

'Where is he now?'

'Gone to the toilet. Where're the children?'

'I sent them upstairs to play, all their noise was giving me a headache.'

He fills up my cup and passes it over. 'Are you warm enough? Do you want me to turn the fire up a bit?'

'No. I'm all right. So what did our Maurice have to say about me?'

'What makes you think he said anything about you?'

'Because I know our Maurice.'

He picks up his cup and goes to sit in the chair next to the fire. 'He just said it's a shame you're not up and about and more yourself.'

I have a closer look at him. 'What's the matter with you?' I say. 'If I didn't know better I'd think you'd been bloody crying. What's happened to your eyes?'

'Got some dust in them. Now come on, drink that tea up, before it gets cold.'

To tell the truth I don't want it, which isn't like me at all. Usually, I love me cup of tea, but I've gone right off it lately. No point making a fuss though, he'll only start reading something into it, so I force a drop down and leave the rest to go cold.

I'm just about to light up a fag when our Maurice opens the door and quick as a flash flicks out his lighter.

'Haven't lost your touch then,' I comment.

He chuckles and it makes me smile, because it sounds just like it always used to. Me smiles aren't lasting very long tonight though, which is a shame, but I'm feeling a bit down and I can't seem to shake it off. But wouldn't you in my shoes, if you'd been waiting fifteen years for your brother to come home, and when he does you can hardly get up off the settee, never mind do any of the dancing and going to the races like you used to? I've been really looking forward to him coming, and now, I have to be honest, I almost wish he wasn't here.

'So how's our mam?' I ask him. 'I haven't seen her all week.'

'She's not too bad. Same old Florrie. Worried about you though.'

'What's she worried about me for? She should be worrying about herself, that's who she should be worrying about.'

'That's what I told her, but you know what she's like.'

'Fuss, fuss, fuss, that's all she does. Gets right on my bloody nerves.'

He looks at his watch.

'What's the matter?' I say. 'Got somewhere else to go?'

'As a matter of fact, I have. It came up last minute, you know how it happens.'

I roll my eyes. 'So what's her name?' I say, feeling

jealous, even though I'm not in the mood for going out to have a bit of fun.

He laughs. 'Did you hear that, Eddie? She's got me down as some kind of Romeo, she has, and it couldn't be further from the truth.'

'Spot on it, more like,' I tell him. 'I know you, remember? In fact, I'd go as far as to say no-one knows you better.'

'Now you could be right about that,' he laughs, coming to give me a kiss. He's the only one of my brothers who goes in for all that kissing and hugging business, and to be honest, I wish he wouldn't, not in front of Eddie. It just don't feel right.

'I'll see you to the door,' Eddie says, getting up.

'Are you coming again?' I ask him.

'Course I am. I'm over till the end of January, so plenty of time to see my favourite sis. And I expect to be taking you out down the Legion, getting those legs twirling again, before I go back, so buck your bloody self up a bit, my girl. You don't want to go on lying there for ever, now do you?'

'Get away with you,' I say, trying to laugh so he won't notice I'm nearly bloody well crying.

Him and Eddie stay out by the front door chatting for a bit, which gives me a chance to pull meself together. I can't hear what they're saying. Something about me again, I expect, which gets me all riled up because I don't want them out there gossiping about me. Anyone would think I was a bloody deafo, or an invalid, the way they're carrying on, but let me tell you, I still got all me faculties and they ain't going anywhere in a hurry, so they better watch out, those two out there, saying things about me that they've probably got all wrong anyway.

Eddie comes back in the room and sits down. Neither

of us says a word, well, there's nothing to say, is there? We sit here night after night, pretending everything's going to be all right when both of us are scared stiff it won't be. No point dwelling on it though. It'll only make it worse, and why do that, when I was reading in the *Woman's Weekly* the other day about someone up north who had what I've got, and now she's right as rain. She even said how scared she used to get, she even got to the point where she was ready to give up, but she didn't, and now look where she is. Fighting fit and writing her story in a magazine. Don't suppose I'll ever do that, write I mean, but it just goes to show, don't it, I'm not the only one who's ever been in this position and though it can take a bit of time, it does get better.

I just wish it would in time for Christmas.

'Why don't you go and see what they're up to,' I say to Eddie. 'They're too quiet for my liking.'

He goes off without a word, and I shut me eyes. Our Maurice's visit has left me tired right out again.

He's up to something, our Maurice, I can tell. He's got himself involved with some woman already, and it wouldn't surprise me one bit to find out she's married. It wouldn't be the first time, but if our mam gets wind of it he'll be out on his ear. She chucked him out when he did it before, and I know her, she'll do it again.

'What are you doing down here?' I say as Susan comes in the door.

'Dad sent me down to say goodnight,' she answers.

'All right, goodnight then.'

'Mum?' Gary says, coming in behind her. 'Can I wear my Batman cape to school when we go back after Christmas?'

'Your what?'

'My Batman cape.'

'I don't know, ask your father.' I rest me head back

down on the pillow and try to keep me eyes open.

'Mum, can we put up our Christmas tree on Saturday?' Susan asks.

Oh, bloody hell, the tree. How could I have forgot? And bless their hearts they're only just reminding me, when they must be dying to get on with it. What's wrong with Eddie, for God's sake, why didn't he say something? 'Course we can,' I tell her. 'Ask your father to fetch it down from the attic in the morning.'

'Can we light a fire in the other room too?' Gary says, 'so we can send our notes up the chimney to Father Christmas.'

'Come here,' I say, holding out my arms. 'Both of you.'

They come and we have a good old cuddle. 'I'll light the fire meself,' I tell them. 'First thing tomorrow. So how's that?'

Their faces light up and excitement starts rushing out of them.

'All right, all right,' I laugh, 'don't get carried away. It's time for bed now, so up you go.'

'Goodnight,' Susan says.

'Goodnight. Sleep tight.'

'Goodnight,' Gary says.

'Goodnight. Sleep tight.'

As they go I lay me head back down and start thinking about dancing with our Maurice and winning at the races; unwrapping Christmas presents and lighting up the tree. I can see Dr Michaels with his X-rays, and Eddie with the starting handle of his car. It's all getting jumbled up. What's our mam doing riding a bloody horse? She'll fall off and break her neck. Here's our Susan coming in with the coal, and Gary trying to help her. They're setting theirselves on fire! Eddie! Where's Eddie? The kids are on fire. I've got to get to my kids. I'm trying to get up, but I can't. The flames are swallowing them up, and I still can't get there. Eddie! Where are you? Eddie! Susan! Gary! Why can't I get there?

I come awake with a bit of a jump. Me heart's racing and I'm feeling all hot. Thank God it was a dream, frightened me half to death it did, not being able to get to them. Too much bloody rubbish going round and round in me head, I'll end up down the loony bin if I go on like this. I'll just lie here now and think about Christmas. The kids' presents are all up our mam's, waiting to be wrapped. Just thank God for the club books, is what I say. Got nearly all our presents off John Myers and Littlewoods this year, and we haven't taken too much on the never-never either, only about twenty-five quid's worth, which I don't like doing, but we're a bit short, with Eddie not being able to get in much overtime lately. What shall we have for dinner on the day? Turkey, or another goose? I don't feel up to roasting a goose. We can just have turkey. Our mam can go to our Phil's, or our Gord's for a change, not so much work if it's just us four. Why was Eddie's eyes red just now? Is this him, coming back in the room? Yes, it's him. I'll pretend I'm asleep.

Thank God that last lot of treatment's over. A couple of days ago I thought I was on me way out, honest I did, and now here I am, still a bit weak and tired, but managing to stuff a turkey ready for our Christmas dinner tomorrow. I've even made a dozen mince pies and the tree's all lit up in the front room with presents piling up all over the place. Eddie tried to warn the kids that there wouldn't be much this year, you know, with me not being able to get out much, then it turns out our families have all rallied round, and have been traipsing up and down to our house for the past week, bringing a damn sight more than any of us deserve, I can tell you that much.

Notes have gone up the chimney now, and our mam's

stocking drawer's been emptied (her fault for having so many grandchildren), and we've got so many bloody cards streaming in through the letter box every day I'm running out of space to hang 'em all.

I've been wondering how Flo's managing up there with her two girls, this being their first Christmas without Bob. Breaks your heart, don't it, to think of them coping all on their own. Makes me glad I got Eddie, but I wish I'd been able to get up there more. I just haven't been feeling up to it, and I don't blame Flo for not coming here, she's got enough on her plate without having to be bothered about me. Eddie's been taking the kids up regular though, which is where he is now, finding out if Flo and her girls want to come and have some Christmas dinner with us.

Funny how I keep thinking about Bob, you know, wondering if he can see us, or hear us, and what it's like being where he is. They say everything's better when you're dead, that it's all happiness and no pain, but it's hard to imagine that when the poor bloke left two young kids behind, innit? Must be tearing his bloody heart out, if he can see them but can't do anything to help them. If it was me I wouldn't be able to stand it. I don't even want to think about it, because not being here for my kids . . . Tell you what, I'll just get on stuffing this turkey and have a bit of tea ready for them all when they come in.

'Mum! Mum! Wake up, Mum!'

'What? What's going on?'

'Father Christmas is coming tonight,' Gary's shouting at me. 'You have to go to bed.'

'Blimey, what time is it?' I say, looking at the clock. 'I must have dropped off.'

'It's time to go to bed!'

I start laughing. 'It's only ten past four,' I tell him. 'Where's your father? And get that wet coat off.'

'I ran on and beat them,' he says. 'They're slowcoaches.'

'Is Aunty Flo coming for Christmas? Ugh! Don't throw that wet coat at me. Go and hang it on the bottom of the stairs.'

'Can we go to bed then?'

'No we cannot.'

As I follow him out to the kitchen Eddie and Susan come stomping in, dripping more rain all over the floor. 'Look at the pair of you, wet right through,' I grumble. 'You'll catch your blooming deaths and then who's going to eat the lovely Christmas dinner I've got for you all tomorrow?'

'I'm going to get Daddy a new car for Christmas when I'm older,' Susan informs me. 'One that works all the time, and he's going to teach me to drive it. Why don't you learn too, Mum?'

'Your father keeps saying he'll teach me. Full of promises he is, so let's make sure he keeps them. Now, do you want a mince pie, all of you? They're still nice and warm.'

'Yes,' they all cheer. 'With lots of clotted cream,' Susan adds.

'Tell your mother what we saw on the way down from Aunty Flo's,' Eddie says, hanging all the wet coats on the back door.

'Oh yes, we saw a lighting-up reindeer in someone's garden,' Gary gushes.

'And there was an elf too,' Susan says. 'And a Christmas tree that looked as though it had real candles on, but Dad said they were only pretend. Can we get some like that, for our tree?'

'When we can find a tree that money grows on,' I tell her. 'Come here, let me look at you.' I tilt her face up to the light. 'Is that chocolate round your mouth, young lady?'

'Oh yes, we had some Christmas log at Aunty Flo's. She's coming tomorrow with Julie and Karen, isn't she Dad? They'll be down about one, she said. Ow, Mum, that hurts.'

'A girl your age should be washing her own face by now,' I tell her. 'Here, put some soap on this flannel and get yourself clean.'

I look at Eddie, who's rubbing Gary's hair with a towel. Funny, but I've got this urge to go and put me arms round him. Can't do it in front of the kids though, so I just give him a bit of a smile. I hope Bob, wherever he is, can read me mind, so he knows how pleased I am to have his family here on Christmas Day. I'll take care of 'em all, don't you worry, Bob. They'll be all right here with me.

'How are you feeling?' Eddie says, as the kids trot off down the passage with their mince pies and big dollops of cream.

'Not bad. Had a bit of a doze just now, but I got the turkey stuffed, and a few more presents wrapped up. Just the spuds to peel and vegetables to get ready.'

'I'll give you hand with all that,' he says, slipping an arm round me waist. 'Fancy giving us a kiss?'

'I might.'

'Come on then.'

'All right, that's enough,' I say, before we start getting too carried away. 'Anyone'd think it was Christmas the way you're going on.'

He laughs and bites into me neck before picking up a mince pie. 'How did I manage to get myself a wife who's as gorgeous as a film star and a better cook than Fanny Cradock?' he teases.

'A wife who's fat as a blooming house, more like,' I grumble.

'All the more of you to eat up,' he tells me, chomping into a mince pie.

Someone knocks on the front door, which brings Susan and Gary racing out of the front room.

'If it's carol singers can I pay them?' Susan cries.

'Can I?' Gary cries.

'There's two ha'pennies in my coat pocket, one each,' I tell them.

'I want them to sing "Away in a Manger", Gary decides, after they've scrabbled about to find the money.

'No! "Silent Night"'s better,' Susan insists.

'It is not.'

'Yes it is. Or "Once in Royal David's City".'

'Just answer the door,' Eddie calls after them.

I go on getting the potatoes out of the pantry, and start running the water. Then instead of hearing carol singers, I hear adult voices out at the door. I look at Eddie, he looks at me, and we both look round as our Maurice comes down the passage, no coat and soaked right through to the skin.

'Happy Christmas,' he grins.

'What the bloody hell are you doing here?' I say. 'I thought you'd be out dancing. And what's the matter with using the back door, or have we got too posh in our old age?'

'Thought it was only polite to come the front way, seeing as we weren't expected . . .'

'We? Who's we? Oh, Maurice, you haven't brought your girlfriend round now, have you? You could have given us some warning. And where the bloody hell's your coat?'

As I finish speaking a woman comes out of the shadows behind him.

'All right Ed?' she says. 'Happy Christmas.'

It's our Jacqueline, wet through too, hair all plastered to her face.

I'm a bit flummoxed, so I look at Eddie.

'I'll put the kettle on,' Eddie says.

'Good idea,' Maurice agrees. 'I reckon we're all going to need it.'

'Why? What for?' I say. 'What's going on?' I'm starting to get a bad feeling about them dropping in like this. 'Our mam's all right, is she? Nothing's happened to her?'

'The old bird's right as rain,' Maurice answers. 'Never changes, does she? Bloody clouted me one, she did, just like I was still in short trousers.'

'Why, what did you do?'

'I didn't do anything. You know what she's like.'

'She wouldn't have clouted you for nothing, so what's going on?' I'm eyeing our Jack now, who's looking very sheepish behind him. 'Just what the bloody hell have you two been up to?' I demand.

'You better tell her, Maurice,' Jack says.

'I'm going to.'

I'm waiting for him to go on when someone else knocks on the door. 'Who the bloody hell's that now?' I cry. 'This place is turning into Bristol bloody Zoo. If it's carol singers, tell them to go away.'

Ten seconds later our Gord and Jean are coming down the passage. I can hardly believe me eyes. Here it is, Christmas Eve, and never mind they've got seven kids at home, they're coming down our passage.

'You're here,' Gord says to Maurice.

'Looks like it,' Maurice answers. 'What are you doing here?'

'We just left our mam's.'

'And thought you'd call in to tell Eddress the news?' Maurice says sarcastically.

'What bloody news?' I shout.

'Oh you haven't told her yet,' Gordon says.

'I'm going to throw something at the bloody lot of

287

you if someone doesn't tell me what's going on.'

'Florrie's chucked us out,' Maurice says. 'Shoved us right out in the street and slammed the bloody door on us, she did. You should have heard her, carrying on like a bloody fishwife, had half the bloody neighbourhood out, and wouldn't listen to a word we had to say, would she Jack?'

'No,' Jack confirms.

'Haven't got a bloody stitch to our names,' Maurice goes on, 'apart from what we're standing up in, and she won't let us back in to get anything. Christmas bloody Eve and she goes and throws us out on our ears. Now what kind of mother is that, I ask you?'

'So what did you do?' I ask, feeling like I don't want to know the answer.

'She caught him in bed with our Jack, that's what he did,' Gordon tells me.

'You should be ashamed of yourselves, the pair of you,' Jean chimes in.

I'm just staring at them.

'Milk, everyone?' Eddie says.

'Our mam caught you in bed with *her*?' I say, pointing at our Jack. 'What the bloody hell's the matter with you? She's your bloody niece, for God's sake!'

'Not strictly speaking,' he reminds me. 'I mean, we're not blood related, like me and you, and we was . . .'

'I don't care if you're blood related or not,' I say. 'She's still your niece, you're over twenty years older than her and she's married. For God's sake, she's got a baby. And where the hell's Vanessa now, will someone tell me? What have you done with her?'

'Andy's got her,' Jack answers. 'I said he could have her over Christmas.'

'So you could be with Maurice?'

She shrugs.

I look at Jean. 'I know,' Jean says. 'Florrie's in a dreadful state up there.'

'Well what do you expect? How could you do this to her, Maurice? She hasn't seen you in over fifteen years, and now you're back in her house giving how's-yer-bloody-father to your own bleeding niece.'

'I'm not his niece,' Jacqueline shouts. 'Him and my mother had different parents.'

It's true, they did, but I can see very well why our mam's so upset.

'Hey, come on, up to bed you two,' Eddie suddenly barks.

'Bloody hell,' I groan, only just spotting Susan and Gary standing behind the crowd, boggle-eyed.

'Take them up,' I say to Eddie.

'Tea's brewed,' he tells us. 'Gord, can you carry the tray in the front room?'

'We'll have to go then,' Jean says. 'We've got our lot to sort out tonight. We only popped in Florrie's to take her present. Phyllis is up there now.'

A few minutes later, with Gord and Jean gone, and Eddie upstairs with the kids, there's only me, Jack and Maurice in the front room. What a bloody picture we make, sitting here lit up by coloured fairy lights, like a bunch of Santa's bloody elves, presents all round our feet and faces longer than fiddles.

'Turn the fire up a bit,' I tell Maurice. 'You must be perished the two of you.'

'She wouldn't even let us have our coats,' Jack says.

'Not a brass farthing to rub between us,' Maurice adds. 'We came here because we didn't have anywhere else to go, what with it being Christmas Eve and all.' He takes a sip of his tea. 'It'd only be for a couple of nights, just till I can sort us something out.'

'What are you talking about? You can't stay here.'

'We got nowhere else to go, Ed.'

I don't know what to say. I can hardly sling them out when they've got no coats and no money, but staying here . . . ? 'I'll have to talk to Eddie,' I tell them.

'Oh come on, we all know he'll do whatever you want him to,' Maurice jeers.

'Don't take that for granted,' I warn. 'He'll have some strong views about this, if I know him. It's not right, Maurice, and you know it's not.'

'It might not seem that way to you, but it does to us.'

'But you've hardly known each other five minutes. What's going to happen when you go back to New Zealand? What's she going to do then?'

'I'm going with him,' Jack says.

'What? Don't talk stupid. You can't go with him. You've got a child to bring up.'

'We'll take her with us,' Maurice chips in.

My head's starting to spin, and I wish Eddie would come back down. Or do I, because he's not going to like this, not one bit.

'We only need a couple of blankets, and if you've got any air beds we can sleep in the other room,' Jack says. 'We won't be putting you out, at all. You can pretend we're not there.'

'Pretend you're not there? Have you gone a bit simple in the head or something? The kids are hanging their stockings in there tonight, and we're having our Christmas dinner at the table tomorrow, so how are we going to pretend you two great lummoxes just aren't there?'

'It's only for the night,' Maurice reminds me. 'We'll get up before you in the morning and make you some breakfast. We'll even go out for Christmas dinner if you like, provided you can lend us a few bob. You know, just till Florrie lets me back in to get what's mine.'

'I reckon it'll have to be me who goes in to get your stuff,' I tell him, 'because if she's as mad as I expect she is, you won't be going back over her threshold again for another fifteen years.' I start shaking me head, as it sinks in all over again. 'What the bloody hell got into the two of you? You're not animals, for God's sake. Couldn't you have had some control? Or at least gone somewhere else to do it?'

'It's called passion, Ed,' Maurice answers. 'It just took us over. You know how it is, you can't help yourself when you feel like that.'

I sigh wearily and shake me head again. 'Well, I suppose you better go and get some more coal and stoke up the fire next door,' I tell him. 'And while you're out there, have a look in the shed to see if there's any air beds. They're either there, or up in the attic, but I'm not asking Eddie to go up there tonight.'

'I'll come and give you a hand,' Jack says, getting up.

'No you won't, young lady,' I snap. 'You're going to sit right there where I can have a word with you.'

'Oh Ed, don't start getting on at me now,' she grumbles. 'I feel bad enough already, but it's not going to change anything.'

I decide to let her go so I can have a couple of minutes on me own, to think how I'm going to break this to Eddie.

'No, I'm not having it,' he says, when I tell him. 'They're not staying here committing their sins. She's married, Eddress, and what they're doing is bloody incest. I'm not having that going on in my house.'

'It's not incest. Our dad already had Maurice by another woman when he married our mam, so he's no blood of our mam's. And our Ivy is our mam's by her first husband.'

'It's still not right.'

'I know, but it's happened now, and we can't just chuck 'em out.'

'You might not be able to, but I can. You're not well, for heaven's sake, so I'm not having this putting any more strain on you.'

'I'm all right. I can cope.'

'That's what you think, but you're already worn out, look at you. Hardly a drop of blood left in your face.'

'Look, Maurice already knows you don't like him, he can sense it, so don't go and make it worse . . .'

'I don't give a damn what Maurice thinks, you're what I care about and I don't want him bringing his bad ways into our house . . .'

'Ssh, he'll hear you.'

'Let him. He's a grown man, he should know better than to think he can come here, when you're ill and we've got two young children waiting for Christmas . . . And what about our Bob's two? Flo's coming tomorrow, you don't think I want all those kids sitting round the table with sinners, on Christmas Day, do you? No, Ed, I'm not having it.'

'Listen. Let them stay tonight, while it's raining, then we can lend them a few bob tomorrow to go out round the pub for some dinner. That way, they won't be at the table with us, will they? And we'll have done the charitable thing by giving them a roof over their heads when they've got nowhere else to go. I mean, if you think about it, it's what Christmas is all about really, innit? Making some room at the inn. All right, I know our Jack and Maurice don't exactly qualify as Mary and Joseph, but we've got a living room they can sleep in – and don't you go saying we've got a shed, because I'm not telling them to sleep out there. Just do this for me, eh? One night, that's all. It's not going to hurt, is it?'

'There's always the Sally Army. They can go down there.'

'Eddie.'

He's not looking very happy, in fact I can see it's upsetting him quite a bit, but I know he'll do it, because he hasn't really got it in him to throw anyone out on the street, no matter what he says.

'We found a couple of air beds,' Maurice announces, coming into the room and rubbing his hair with a towel. 'Looks like they belong to the kids, but they'll do fine. Just need a bit of a cleaning up. Jack's out in the kitchen doing it. Don't want to be any trouble, Eddie. Good of you, man, to let us stay.'

'I'm doing it for Eddress,' Eddie tells him bluntly. 'And I'll lend you ten bob tomorrow to go round the pub. I can't have you here with my sister-in-law and the kids, it wouldn't be right.'

'No, no, I understand. We'll do whatever you want.'

Susan and Gary start shouting out, asking if they can come down now.

'I'll go,' I say, grabbing Eddie's hand so he can pull me up. 'Maurice, don't you put anything in that living room until they've hung up their stockings, do you hear me? I don't want them thinking Father Christmas is going to be scared off by you couple of sinners in the middle of the night. And while we're at it, I don't want any bloody hanky-panky going on in there either, or you'll be out that door a lot faster than you came in it.'

'We'll be pure as the driven,' he promises, giving Eddie a wink.

'Come on,' I say to Eddie before he changes his mind, 'let's both go up, then we'll have to see about where to put all their presents.' I just hope Christmas in't going to be bloody ruined now, though I can't see how it won't be – I almost wish our Maurice hadn't bothered to come back.

Chapter Fifteen

Susan

Christmas is all over now, and I don't really want to tell anyone about it, because it wasn't a very nice time. Well, it was when we opened our presents on Christmas morning, and found everything we wanted, like a new record player for me and a bike with stabilisers for Gary. I had a Beatles LP too, and some other records by Herman's Hermits and Lulu . . . Well, we had lots of things, and it was lovely when Julie and Karen came down with Auntie Flo for dinner, which I helped cook. But then, on Christmas night Mum and Dad had a terrible row about Jack and Uncle Maurice staying, and after that it wasn't a very nice time. Even Dad's birthday, on Boxing Day, was horrible, because him and Mum weren't speaking (I don't think she even gave him a present, so we wrapped up one of our selection boxes from Christmas Day to give him with the bar of nougat we already had), and when we got back from Grampy and Aunty Beat's on the night, Jack and Uncle Maurice were there again.

They're still here, and I wish they'd go away, because they're making everyone unhappy, but Mum says they can stay as long as they like. I don't think it's really up to Mum though, because dads are the boss, and now that Mum's not very well again, Dad says she has to do as he tells her.

'But Eddie, he's my brother and she's my niece,' Mum keeps saying. 'I can't just chuck 'em out on the street.'

'Your mother did, and he's got enough money that he can go to a bed and breakfast.'

'That's not the way you treat family. You wouldn't do it to yours.'

'If they were making you ill, I would.'

'They're not making me ill, you silly bugger, I'm already ill, and you carrying on like this is making me worse. Now, just shut up about it will you? They'll be gone soon, back to New Zealand, then God knows how long it'll be before I see them again. So I'm not throwing them out and having it on my conscience for the next twenty years.'

I slept with Mum last night, while Dad slept in my bed with Gary. I like it when it's just me and Mum and we have a chat about when she was growing up, or when I was a baby. She told me how I popped out of her tummy and screamed so much blue murder that she tried to pop me back in again. It's funny the way she says pop, it always makes me laugh. Then she told me how Dad cried when he picked me up for the first time, the soppy old thing.

We were just falling off to sleep when Jack and Uncle Maurice came creeping up the stairs and into Gary's bedroom. I lay there listening to their noises, whispering, going to the bathroom, opening and closing the wardrobe door. Then the bed creaked as they got in, and went on creaking for a bit until they settled down. I can hear them much better in my room, because it's right next door. I was just wondering if Dad had heard them when the bedroom light goes on and he comes in.

'Susan, go to your room,' he says, sounding really cross.

'What the hell's going on?' Mum grumbles, sitting up.
'Susan! Do as you're told.'

I look at Mum.

'Do as your father says,' she tells me.

I'm really cross as I throw back the bedclothes and stomp across the room. When I get out on the landing Dad closes the door.

'She starts back to school tomorrow,' I hear Dad say. 'She should be in her own bed, having a proper night's sleep. Now, I'm going to get Gary, he can come in with us, and tomorrow they better be gone, do you hear me? If they're not I'm taking the children up our Nancy's and we'll stop there until they do go.'

'I'm lying here, sick in this bed, and you come in, shouting and swearing . . .'

'I'm not shouting or swearing. I'm just telling you what's going to happen. Susan has to have a good night's sleep before school, and you've got her in here talking till all hours, while your *brother* is in there committing adultery with your own bloody niece. I don't know what's got into you Eddress, I really don't.'

'Oh just shut up! I'm sick of you carrying on.'

'And I'm sick of them carrying on. They're out tomorrow, or you'll be living here with them, and we'll be gone. Now, I'm going to get Gary, so move up and make some room for us both.'

Quick as a flash I dash into my bedroom and under the covers. Gary's down the bottom end, fast asleep. I pretend to be too, as Dad comes in and picks him up.

'It's all right, sssh,' Dad says as Gary starts to murmur.

I lie as still as I can, but I'm still shivering after standing out on the landing.

'Are you all right, my love?' Dad whispers.

'Yes,' I say. I think about telling him that I don't want to leave Mum and go up Aunty Nance's, but then he'll know I was listening. *Please God make Jack and Uncle Maurice go away.*

Now I'm back at school and everyone's in the classroom showing off their Christmas presents before Mrs Fields comes in to call the register. I forgot to bring anything, so I just watch as Lizzie shows us her posh pen and pencil set, and Ruth rolls up her sleeve to tell us the time on her new watch with a leather strap. Everyone else in the gang has got something too, and I'm starting to feel cross and silly that I haven't. In the end I say, 'I didn't have anything for Christmas, because my mum's ill and she couldn't go out to get us anything.'

'Oh, no, that's really sad,' Lizzie says. 'Here, you can have a go with my pen and pencil if you like. You can be the first one to use it, except for me.'

'You can have a wear of my watch too, up until playtime,' Ruth offers. 'Look, if you put it next to your ear, you can hear it tick.'

I think that's really nice of them, and say thank you, but it's all right, I don't mind not having any presents.

'Did you have any dinner on Christmas Day?' Ruth asks.

'Yes. I cooked it. My mum wasn't well enough.'

'She's a liar,' Kelvin Milton shouts out. 'She didn't have any dinner because her mum and dad are too poor to feed them. And that's why she's smelly, because they can't afford any soap either.'

'You're a nasty, stinky, disgusting little bogey,' I tell him.

'You mean you are.'

'Just shut up,' Lizzie shouts at him. 'You're always picking on her.'

'Because she's a stupid one-eyed monster,' he jeers and all his friends laugh.

'I've got a secret to tell you,' I whisper to Lizzie and Ruth.

Their eyes go round.

Kelvin Milton shouts, 'Do you know why her mum and dad don't buy her any presents? Because they can't stand her. I know, because my Aunty Beryl told me. And who can blame them when she's so ugly.'

'Kelvin Milton, I heard that,' Mrs Fields barks. 'Go to the back of the room and put your hands on your head, and a fine way to start the new term, I must say. Good morning the rest of you.'

'Good morning Mrs Fields,' we chorus.

'All right, sit down. I hope you all had a lovely Christmas and we're going to do lots of good work this term.'

'Yes Mrs Fields,' we say.

'Diane Meadows, would you like to call the register today?'

After that's done we take out our maths books and open them to page forty-three. It's a bit mean to make us do maths on our first day back, but it's better than PE.

At playtime we wrap up warm in our hats and coats and skip over to the girls' toilets and round the other side. Everyone knows I've got a secret, so everyone wants to hear it and they all gather round.

I start by telling them how my gran threw out Jack and Uncle Maurice on Christmas Eve.

'But why?' someone asks.

'Because she caught them doing it,' I answer.

'Doing what?' someone near the back calls out.

'*It*,' someone else answers.

'What's it?'

They all look at me.

'It's two people being in bed with no clothes on,' I tell them.

Everyone gasps and giggles and moves in closer to hear more.

'Why didn't they have any clothes on?' someone asks.

'Because they were doing it, stupid,' Lizzie answers.

'But it's not allowed unless you're married.'

'I know,' I say, 'that's why my gran was mad. But now, they're in our house, sleeping in my brother's bed, and my dad's really angry with them. He says they're committing a sin, and they have to leave, but my mum says they can stay.'

'Are they doing it in your brother's bed?' Ruth wants to know.

I nod.

'Is your brother in there too?'

'No. He's sleeping with me, or with Mum and Dad. I'm in the next room to them, so I can hear them when they're doing it.'

They all gasp again.

'What are they saying?'

'Things like ooooh, and darling, and ooooh and . . .' and we all collapse laughing.

'How long are they staying with you?' Lizzie asks.

'Well, my dad says they have to leave today.'

'Where will they go?'

'To New Zealand I think.'

'Where's that?'

'Somewhere up near Scotland,' Ruth answers.

'No it's not, it's down by Australia. They'll go there in my uncle's plane, because he's in the RAF. It's parked over the BAC, where he left it when he came.'

'Your uncle's got a plane?' Ruth gasps. 'That's really groovy.'

'I know. And he's got loads and loads of money, and his own servants and a great big house in New Zealand.'

'If he's so rich then why didn't he buy you anything for Christmas?' Kelvin Milton shouts out.

'Because, if you must know, my gran kept all his money at her house, and she won't let him have it.'

'He should shoot her,' one of the other boys pipes up. 'If he's in the RAF he'll have a gun, so he should shoot her to get his money back.'

'He can't shoot his own mother,' Lizzie argues.

'She's not his real mother,' I tell her. 'She's his step-mother.'

'Then he should definitely shoot her,' Kelvin says, 'because all stepmothers are wicked.'

'My gran's not, and you can just shut your mouth if you're going to say horrible things about my gran.'

'You can shut yours.'

'Are you going to make me?'

'Stop, stop, the teacher's coming,' Lizzie warns. 'Come on Susan, you're my best friend now,' she adds, putting an arm round me.

'No, she's not, she's mine,' Ruth snaps.

'I'll be both your best friends,' I tell them, and we go off to play some French skipping.

Mum's upstairs in bed when I get home, so I go and sit next to her and wait for her to wake up. I've got something to show her that she's really going to like. She'll know I'm here in a minute, so I count the patterns on the wallpaper and make sure they all match up at the joins, then I look at her again and wish she'd wake up, because this is going to make her really pleased with me.

I decide to write my name in the dust on the dressing table. After I've done that I pick up the hand mirror and look at my face. I purse up my lips like a model, and suck in my cheeks, then I put the mirror down again.

Mum's handbag is there, so I open it up and take out a fag. I'm pretending to smoke, watching myself in the big mirror. It makes me look like a film star. I put the fag away again and look down at Mum's face.

'Wake up,' I whisper. '*Pleeease* wake up.'

Her eyes come open.

'I've got something to show you,' I tell her, and I open my exercise book so she can see. 'I got a gold star for my geography.'

'Oh, that's lovely.' She strokes my hair with her hand. 'Well done, my old love.'

I close the book, then hang my head.

'What's the matter?' she says.

'Ruth and Lizzie were my best friends today, but now they're not speaking to me any more.'

'Why's that then?'

'They said I tell lies, but I don't. I only said that Uncle Maurice has a plane, because he's in the RAF, and it's true, isn't it? Because everyone in the RAF has a plane.'

'Well, not really, my love. He flies in one, but he doesn't fly it himself. Only the pilots do that.'

'Isn't he a pilot?'

'No.'

'Oh. Are you coming downstairs?'

'If I can find me dressing gown. Where is it?'

'Here, on the floor,' I say, picking it up.

It's blue and yellow, with a twisty rope belt and a satin collar. After she puts it on she lights up a fag.

'Are Jack and Uncle Maurice sleeping here tonight?' I ask, as she pushes her feet in her fluffy yellow slippers.

'Why do you want to know?' she says, squinting down at me through the smoke.

I shrug. I can't tell her I heard what Dad said last night, but I'm scared now that he might take us away

301

and make us live up Aunty Nancy's, while Jack and Uncle Maurice live here with Mum. I don't mind Aunty Nancy's, because she's got a lot of ornaments from all the places she's been, like Bournemouth and Barry and Blackpool, that are quite interesting to look at, but a lot of work to dust, so I don't want her turning me into a slave.

'Where's that Gary?' Mum says as we go down the stairs. She has to take it steady, because her headaches make her legs a bit weak.

'Out the front playing football,' I answer.

'In this weather? Doesn't that boy feel the cold? Come on, let's get that gas fire going, and make a nice cup of tea.'

'I don't like tea.'

'I didn't mean you, I meant me. You can have some drinking chocolate.'

'*Hot chocolate, drinking chocolate. Hot chocolate, drinking chocolate,*' I chant like the advert. 'Can we bake some cakes?'

'No, not today. Bloody hell, it's freezing in here. Where's me matches, let's get this place thawed out a bit.'

I watch what she's doing as she puts her cigarette out in the corner of the grate, then uses the same match to light up another and then the fire. The gas makes the flames go poof! and whooshes a little curl of flame out towards us.

'Blimey, nearly lost me bloody hair there,' Mum laughs. 'Now, you stay here and get warm, and I'll go and boil the kettle.'

After she's gone I put the telly on, but it takes even longer to warm up than the room so I start getting bored. I want to go out to play, but instead I follow Mum out to the kitchen. She's standing against the pantry door, leaning her head back on it with her eyes closed.

'All right?' she says, when she sees me.

I nod.

'So what do you want for your tea?'

'Nothing. I want Dad to make it.'

'Why?'

'Because.'

She sighs. 'Your father's tired when he gets in from work, so he doesn't want to be cooking your tea now, does he?'

'He does it all the other times, when you're in bed, or laid on the settee.'

'That's because I've got a headache. I haven't got one tonight, so I'm making your tea.'

'I want Dad to do it.'

'Stop being silly. Now, snap out of that mood and get practising on that piano.'

'I don't want to.'

'I don't care whether you want to, you're going to. Now off you go.'

'Why should I?'

Her eyes go all big. 'Because I'm telling you to, and if you answer me back again you'll get a good hiding.'

'I don't like you. I want you to go back and be in bed.'

'I beg your pardon?'

I'm nearly crying now. 'I don't like you,' I shout, 'and I don't care if you're not very well, because you don't like me anyway, and you're only going to bed so you don't have to see me.'

'What? Where on earth did you get that nonsense?'

'Kelvin Milton told me, his Aunty Beryl told him that you don't like me, so you pretend to be ill. Well I don't care, because Dad likes me, so there.'

'Susan Lewis, if you weren't so bloody daft . . .'

'No, I'm not listening,' I cry, putting my hands over my ears. 'I'm fed up with it now. One day you're in bed, and the next day you're not, so I don't know where you're going to be, and I don't care where you're going to be. You're just being mean to me, and I'm not going to put up with it any more.'

'Susan,' she says, trying to pull my hands down. 'Susan, listen to me. Sometimes people don't feel very well and . . . Listen to me! Susan, don't run away when I'm trying to talk to you. Look, here's your father coming down the path, do you want him to see you being naughty?'

'I'm not being naughty.'

'Yes you are.'

'It's not my fault if you don't like me.'

'Stop being ridiculous and come here.'

'No.'

'Brrr,' Dad goes, as he comes in the door and starts wiping his feet.

'Talk to this girl, will you?' Mum says. 'She won't listen to me.'

'What's the matter?' he asks, taking off his cap and gloves and stuffing them in his pockets.

'Dad! Dad! Come and play football,' Gary shouts, bursting in the door behind him.

'Come here, you little scoundrel,' Dad laughs, and turns him upside down.

'Help!' Gary cries.

I hate them all so I charge up over the stairs and slam my bedroom door behind me. I put my new Beatles record on my new record player and get into bed to keep warm. I feel like crying, but I just think about all the nasty things I can do to Kelvin Milton to make him sorry for all the horrible things he says about me and my mum and my dad.

Someone knocks on my door, but I just ignore it. They knock again, then Gary comes in.

304

'Who said you could come in?' I demand.

'Can I?' he asks.

'All right then.'

He comes to sit on the bed next to me. 'Can I get in, it's cold out here?'

I throw back the covers and let him snuggle up next to me. 'You're freezing,' I tell him crossly.

'Sorry.'

'What are Mum and Dad doing?'

'Having a row.'

'What about?'

'Mum said you've got a lot of nonsense in your head, and Dad says she should stop shouting at you all the time and listen for once.'

'Are Jack and Uncle Maurice down there?'

'No.'

'Go and turn the record player off,' I tell him. 'And don't scratch the record.'

He does as he's told and comes back to bed.

'You're the best brother in all the world,' I tell him.

'So are you,' he says.

We lie very quietly, listening to the raised voices downstairs, but we can't make out what they're saying. Then we hear Dad coming up the stairs, and I hold very tightly to Gary.

'He might be coming to take us away,' I whisper.

'Why?'

'Ssh. Pretend you're asleep.'

The door opens and Dad comes to stand next to the bed.

We go on pretending we're asleep.

'Fe, fi, fo, fum,' Dad roars. 'I smell the blood of an Englishman.'

We start to giggle.

'Come on, time for tea,' he says.

When we get downstairs Mum's next to the stove, shaking the chips over the pan. 'Go and lay the table,' she tells us, 'and ask your father if he wants beans or peas with his.'

'Do you want beans or peas?' Gary asks Dad.

'Peas,' Dad answers.

'Peas,' Gary tells Mum. 'I want beans.'

'You've got beans.'

'Tell your mother to go and sit down and I'll finish off out here,' Dad says.

'Tell your father to mind his own business.'

Gary's taking knives and forks out of the top drawer. He's not really tall enough so I go to help him. 'One, two, three, four,' he counts. 'Mum, are Jack and Uncle Maurice coming? Shall we lay the table for them too?'

'There's just the four of us,' Mum answers.

I look at Dad, but he's washing his hands under the tap.

Gary takes the knives and forks into the room.

'Susan, ask your mother if Jack and Uncle Maurice are staying here tonight?' Dad says.

I look at Mum.

She just goes on as if she hasn't heard.

'Susan, tell your mother I'm waiting for an answer.'

I look at Mum again, but she still ignores him.

I'm getting really mad again now, because they're just being silly.

'Tell your father,' she says, 'that if I never see my brother again, it'll be all his fault.'

'Tell your mother to stop talking rubbish.'

'Tell him I'll give him rubbish, right round his bloody earhole in a minute.'

'Stop it!' I shout, stamping my foot. 'Just stop it!'

'I beg your pardon?' Mum snaps.

'I said stop it. You're always being mean and horrible

to each other, and I want you to stop, because it's really upsetting me.'

Mum looks at Dad. He wipes his hands then puts the towel down and goes to take the chip pan off her. Mum comes over to me and tilts my face up to look at her.

'You've got a lot going on in that little head of yours, haven't you?' she says. 'Too much, if you ask me. So now you just stop worrying about things that don't matter, and give me a nice big hug.'

'No. Not until you answer Dad's question.'

Her eyebrows go up in the way that means I'm going too far.

'You've got to answer him,' I tell her. 'Are Jack and Uncle Maurice staying here tonight?'

'All right. No, they're not,' she says. 'Now, does that make you happy?'

I nod. 'Now you have to say you're sorry.'

'What for?'

'So you and Dad can be friends.'

She gives one of her sighs then says, 'All right. Sorry.'

'Now you, Dad. You've got to say sorry too.'

'I'm sorry,' he says.

'That's better,' I tell them. 'Now we can all be friends.'

Mum doesn't ask this time, she just wraps me up in a great big hug. 'I don't know what to do with you sometimes,' she laughs. 'You're growing up so fast, I forget you're not still a baby.'

I've got my arms all round her, and she smells so lovely that I want to go on staying there, but I'm getting hungry now, and Dad's just put our chips on a plate.

We're about halfway through our tea when Mum says she's not feeling very well so she's going back to bed. After she's gone I put my knife and fork down because

I'm not hungry any more. When everyone else has finished and we've helped clear the table, I go to practise the piano because it might make her feel better. She'll be able to hear, because her bedroom's above where the piano is.

When it's time for bed I put my pyjamas on really fast to stop myself getting too cold, then I go in to say goodnight to Mum. Her light's not on, but I can see her in the light from the door and her eyes are open.

'Come on,' she says.

I go and sit next to her.

'You did very well on the piano,' she tells me. 'You're a good girl. I'm very proud of you, and Dad's going to give you sixpence for getting a gold star.'

'Will you get up again tomorrow?' I ask.

'We'll see. I'll tell you what though, if you go and jump into bed now, I'll come in and lie down with you for a while. How's that?'

I rush into my bedroom to move all my dolls to make some room. Dad's already put a hot-water bottle in for me, so I lie it on the space next to me to warm it up for Mum.

'Mm, that's lovely,' she says, as she slides in next to me. 'Are you comfortable?'

'Yes.'

'We haven't had a little song from the walls for a long time, have we?' she whispers.

'Shall we have one now?' I whisper back.

'Come on then.'

> Little Bo Peep has lost her sheep
> And doesn't know where to find them,
> Leave them alone, and they'll come home,
> Wagging their tails behind them.

It's a bit babyish, but we don't mind, so we sing it again.

Mum falls asleep before I do, so I go on singing to her for a while, in case she can hear, then Dad comes in and tells me it's time for me to go to sleep now too.

Chapter Sixteen

Eddress

It's been a funny old couple of months since Christmas, I can tell you. And what a bloody Christmas it turned into, didn't it, thanks to our Jack and Maurice's shenanigans. Still, that's all behind us now, thank God. They've gone off to New Zealand, leaving the baby here with her father, because the courts wouldn't allow her out of the country. How on earth Jacqueline brought herself to leave the poor little mite I'll never know, but she did, and it seems her and Maurice are settling in nicely over there – if you call upsetting the natives settling in, which sounds about right for our Jack. Never could abide foreigners, so why she wants to go and live amongst 'em I'll never know. In his last letter our Maurice was talking about Rhodesia again, so I suppose they might end up there where she can have a go at upsetting the blacks. Whether our mam'll ever have anything to do with them again, God only knows. She never let them back over her threshold before they left, and she still swears she never will.

We've had a few other things to be worrying ourselves about though, like our Susan not doing well at school, and me having to go back in hospital for a couple of weeks at the start of February. I don't know what gets into that girl when I'm not here, honest I don't. One minute she's as good as gold with Eddie, helping him with the tea, making her own bed and Gary's, the next she's cheeking him back, being difficult and even telling him there's nothing wrong with me, and that I've just gone off and left them. How she gets these things in her head, I'll never know. He ended up giving her a good smack and sending her to bed or she was going to frighten Gary with all her nonsense. I suppose it's got something to do with her worrying about me, but we keep telling her, she should put it out of her mind and concentrate on her lessons.

Now, to cap it all, Eddie's been hauled up in front of the management at work to be told he's taking too much time off, and if it goes on any longer they'll sack him. Bloody furious he was when he told me, and of course he ended up blaming our Maurice, because he blames him for everything now.

'It's his bloody fault you ended up back in that hospital,' he ranted at me when he came home that night, still all in a lather after his ticking off. 'If it weren't for him and all his carrying on you'd be all right by now. I told you it wasn't doing you any good, having them here, but you wouldn't listen, would you? Oh no, you had to have it your way, and now look where we are, being bloody punished for allowing his sinning to go on under our roof.'

I argued back a bit, because it's not in me nature not to, but I have to admit (not to him, mind you) that all that business with our Maurice did wear me out a bit, and I'm always in two minds about God, so I have asked meself once or twice if He might be punishing me, not just about our Jack and Maurice though, but about everything else I've done in me life. There's a lot, believe me, enough to make me glad I'm not a Catholic, because I'd never want to confess to anyone else what I've done, especially not a bloody priest.

Anyway, whether or not it was a punishment, it bloody well felt like it when I was in hospital this time round. Don't know what the hell they did to me, but it's taken me until now – the middle of bleeding March – to get back on me feet again. To be honest, I got to a point when I was in there where I could see meself coming out in a bloody box, I felt that bad. Never said anything to Eddie mind, don't want him thinking like that, or we'd all be bloody done for.

He's been having a chat with the doctors again. He thinks I don't know, but I do. I don't say nothing though, what you don't know you can't worry about, is my motto. I just wish it was his, because it can't be doing him any good. I mean, he's not a bleeding doctor is he, so what's the point in finding it all out? I've got a feeling they've told him they might not have got it in time. Turns my bloody insides straight to ice just to think it, I can tell you. Can't eat, can't sleep, can't even bloody think straight when it comes over me what's going on inside me. It just don't seem right that they can't do anything about it. Makes you feel so helpless that you want to do something . . . Well, something bloody drastic, if only you could think what. Honest, you got no idea how bloody angry it makes you, knowing your own body's letting you down. It's like having a brand spanking new car and finding out it's all rusty inside. Cheated, that's what it makes you feel, downright bloody cheated. Trouble is, you can't take your body back, can you, or send someone round to sort out the bloke who shafted you, because God's never home when you need Him to explain what the bloody hell He's doing, and if the mechanics you're left with haven't got the tools to put you right . . .

It's a load of old bunkum. That's what it is. I mean, if they have told Eddie they can't cure it, it's a load of old bunkum, because they could discover a new drug any time, or it could just get better of its own accord, or we could all get bombed by the bloody Russians for all I know. They just landed theirselves a rocket on Venus, so chucking the odd bomb over here shouldn't be too much trouble, should it? So it don't make any sense to listen to all that nonsense. It just gets you all worked up about something that might never happen, and it don't get you nowhere that.

Anyway, I'm up and about again now, good as new. All right, I'm not as fast on me feet as I was, got to take me time over things, but that's improving as I go on, so I should be back to normal I reckon, by Whitsun, or at least by summer. We're even talking about going up to Wembley to watch the World Cup in May, if England manages to get through that is, and providing we can get tickets. Eddie knows a bloke down the Rovers ground who might be able to get some, and there's someone else down his work who's got a brother-in-law who's supposed to have an in at Wembley. We haven't been to a football match since we had kids, and we used to love going down the Rovers on a Saturday afternoon with our blue and white scarves and rattles, then stopping up the Shant on the way home for a drink with our mates.

I've been thinking about the past a lot lately. Well, I suppose it's hard not to when your number's looking like it might be up. It's better than thinking about the future and knowing you won't be there. That's bloody hard, that is. Breaks you right up. You don't want to do it to yourself, not when you got kids. Honest you don't. Still, it's all right now. The worst is over, and I'm sitting here in the front room on a lovely spring day, looking at the most beautiful white lacy dress for our Susan to wear at Whitsun. It's just turned up from the club book, along with some new shoes for Gary and a Fair Isle pullover for Eddie. Usually I knit all our jumpers meself, but I haven't been able to this past while, so I ordered a few from John Myers. We can do it on the weekly, now Christmas is all paid off.

It's a funny feeling I've got today. Don't know where it's coming from, but here I am, sitting in me own house, where I've been every day this past I don't know how long, yet it's like I've just come back after months and months of being away. Now isn't that strange? I reckon, if you ask me, not that I'm getting me hopes up too much, you understand, that it could mean I'm finally back on the real road to recovery. Something inside me knows that I've turned the last corner now. I'm not like someone lost in a wilderness any more, crashing about, not knowing whether I'm coming or going, or even bloody dead or alive. I'm back here now, right where I belong, and that sun out there today is the light at the end of the tunnel. I've come through. I'm on the home bloody stretch, so just you watch me romp past that finishing gate come May or June. Whitsun! The World Cup! Dawlish for our holidays! It's a lovely time we're going to be having, just you wait and see.

'Yoo hoo! Anyone home?'

'In here.'

I'm in too good a mood to try and dodge Cissy Weiner today. Anyway, I have to admit she's been bloody good to Eddie and the kids these last couple of months, and to me too, which is why I've invited her to come and see *The Sound of Music* with me and Betty next Wednesday night. We're going up the caff in Kingswood after, if they're still open that late, so she'll probably drive us mad with all her talking, but I can always tell her to belt up if she starts getting on our nerves.

'Hello Eddress,' she says, bustling in the room like the fussy old bag she is. 'Oooh, look at the lovely colour in your cheeks. I can see you're feeling well today.'

'Not bad,' I assure her. I never actually told her she could call me Eddress, but I suppose after all she's had to do for me these past couple of months, it wouldn't seem right to go on calling me Mrs Lewis, now would it? 'Did you put the kettle on while you were out there?' I ask her.

'No, I'll just go and do it now. Don't put that dress away. I want to have a better look. It's the prettiest thing I ever did see.'

Her and her Scarlett O'Hara talk. Silly cow. 'It's for our Susan at Whitsun,' I tell her.

'She'll look a picture, she will. I just wish I could find something like that for one of mine.'

I don't tell her where I got it, in case she has the bright idea of sending for one too. Really bloody upset me that would, if one of her girls turned up in the same dress as our Susan for the Whitsun parade.

'Right,' she says, coming back in. 'Kettle's on, tea's in the pot. Dr Tyldesley been in today, has he?'

'About half an hour ago, so he took me temperature and checked everything that needs it. I've taken me pills too. I reckon these new ones are a lot better than the others. I don't feel half as bad as I used to.'

She goes on smiling and blinking, and looking like she doesn't have a clue what I'm talking about. Oh well, maybe Tyldesley didn't tell her he changed my pills. I mean, he didn't actually tell me either, but you've only got to be me to know something's different.

'Eddie getting ready to vote, is he?' she asks. 'They reckon Labour'll sweep the board this time.'

'Oh, he'll be out there all right. He's offered to do a bit of canvassing, when he's got time, and he's doing an hour at the polling station after work on the day.'

'What about you? Are you going to vote?'

'Course I am. I don't want those bloody Tories getting in, do I?'

'None of us do.'

That takes me back a bit. 'Don't you vote Tory?' I ask her. 'I thought you did.'

She chuckles. 'We're as Labour as you and Eddie in our house,' she tells me. 'I'm doing a shift down the polling station too, on the day. Mine's in the morning, just making some tea and generally lending a hand. If you're feeling up to it, why don't you come along too?'

'Yeah, I might,' I say. 'There'll be a lot of faces there I know, and I haven't seen anyone since I can hardly remember when.'

'That's settled then. I'll put your name down, you can do the same shift as me. Now, I've got to ask you if you can spare a couple of pennies for the blind dogs.'

She's always collecting for one good cause or another, bloody do-gooder that she is. Worse than Eddie. Anyway, I got no objection to helping train a dog so some poor blind person can get around a bit. God knows, enough's put in the collections for people who've got what I've got, so it would be a bit bloody rich if I refused to help anyone else, wouldn't it, even if I have only got one and three in me purse. I'll borrow a couple of bob off Betty to buy some fags later, rather than ask Eddie for any more before Friday.

Cissy stays for about an hour, chatting on and on the way she always does, boasting about her girls, and what she does for her patients, who it seems wouldn't be alive, half of them, if it weren't for her. The woman never bloody stops, but I don't suppose she means any harm. To tell the truth I reckon she's a bit lonely, because it can't be easy making friends when you're married to a German, can it? Eddie says he's a nice bloke, but I've hardly ever spoken to him meself, and I don't know how

316

Eddie manages it without mentioning the war. It's all I can ever think about when I see him. And the Jews – though Eddie says Mr Weiner hates the Nazis as much as we do. Well, he has to say that now he's living here, doesn't he? But maybe he does hate them, or he'd still be in Heil Hitler land pinning yellow stars on poor sods with big hooters. I don't suppose a lot of it goes on now though, does it? It wouldn't be allowed.

Twenty to four prompt Gary comes crashing in through the back door, bursting for the toilet and shouting back down the stairs for a chocolate-spread sandwich and a coconut marshmallow. Never ceases to amaze me how that boy manages to remember what's in the cupboard. Down it all goes, with a glass of squash, while he tries to tell me what he did in school. He's in too much of a hurry to get back out to play to make much sense, but I manage to talk him into a hug and a kiss, which he immediately wipes off his face in case I'm wearing any lipstick.

At five past four Susan bounds in, full of her new best friend, Diane Meadows, who's going on the school cruise in June, so they're going to make sure they have beds next to each other, and matching bags to carry their luggage. (Where does she get all these ideas?) She wants a sandwich-spread sandwich and a glass of Ribena. She has to go running back outside then, because she's promised Janet and Sarah across the road that she'll play skipping with them and they're out there waiting.

'Don't you want to see your new dress?' I ask her. 'It came from the club book today.'

Her face lights up. 'The white one?'

I nod.

'Where is it?'

'Hanging up in your wardrobe.'

She charges up over the stairs, sounding like a herd of elephants. I follow her up and find her standing in front of her mirror holding the dress up against her.

'It's the best dress in the whole wide world,' she declares. 'Can I try it on?'

'I think you'd better, because we don't want to leave it till Whitsun to find out it doesn't fit.'

But it does, perfectly. Or it will by then, she's growing that fast. Just a tiny bit big across the shoulders and under the arms, nothing a little tuck here and there won't sort out if need be come the day. She's going to look like an angel.

She turns and gives me a hug all round my neck.

'How did you get on in school today?' I ask her.

'All right.'

'No tellings off for chatting, or not paying attention?'

'No. Well, I did have to put my finger over my lips once, but that's because I was asking my best friend Diane if I could borrow her rubber. That's all I was saying, so I shouldn't have had to put my finger over my lips for that, should I?'

'Are you sure that's all you were saying?'

'Honest. I just told her that Gary borrowed mine last night and forgot to give it back, so that's why I didn't have one today. And she said her brother does that too, forgets to give things back. And I said brothers are a nuisance, I'd rather have a sister.'

'So you were chatting?'

'Yes, but only about the rubber.'

What can you do but laugh. 'You've got to try a bit harder,' I tell her. I'm thinking about the final test she'll have to sit next year for Red Maids now. I definitely don't want her failing that.

'Can my best friend Diane come here for tea one night?' she asks.

'If you start doing a bit better with your lessons. Where does she live?'

318

'Up by New Cheltenham park, not far from Aunty Flo. Oh yes, I've got a note from school asking if we can go on a trip to the Roman Baths. Can I go? I want to.'

'Let's find out how much it is first. You've got the cruise coming up in June, don't forget, and you've had this new dress.'

'Can I wear it outside now, to show Janet and Sarah?'

'Don't be silly. Take it off before it gets dirty.'

'Can I wear it up to show Gran on Saturday?'

'No. It's for Whitsun. Now go on out to play, you can practise the piano after tea.'

As she thunders back down over the stairs, I hang the dress up again and tidy up some of her dolls. She don't do badly, considering the little bit of money we've got. Neither of them do. It's just me and Eddie who do without, really, but we've got decent clothes on our backs, and food on the table, so we mustn't grumble, must we? No, mustn't grumble, but it's bloody hard not to.

The days and weeks have gone on. It's nearly the end of April now, and I'm starting to feel a bit worn down again. I have to have a rest in the afternoons, and sometimes I don't get up again till the next morning. But like I tell Dr Tyldesley when I see him on Wednesdays at half past ten, it's nothing to get worried about. I mean if I can get up to his surgery, instead of him calling in on his rounds, there can't be, can there? Carry me samples on the bus I do, tucked inside me handbag so no-one can see. He's gone and banned smoking in his waiting room, so I generally stand outside having a chat with the others out there, until me name is called.

I always know I'm in for a telling off when I get in his office. 'You shouldn't smoke, you know how bad it is for you, it's not helping you to get better, you should try to give up.' I've heard it all a hundred times before, and today's no different, so I just let him get it off his chest before I remind him of how much better I am, so it can't be doing me that much harm, can it?

Anyway, he goes on then about me latest tests and the letter he's just had from the hospital. I can hear what he's saying, but I don't think I'll take any notice. I'm not going to have him spoiling things now, when everything's just starting to go right again. Instead I have a think about where to go when I leave here. I'm supposed to be going up our mam's, but I don't fancy it now, so I think I'll call in and see Flo on my way back down the hill. Yeah, that's a good idea, because I want to pop in the post office to get meself a provisional licence and it's on the way. Eddie said he'd teach me to drive, so now let's see if he really will. Blimey, if I pass me test, I could be driving us down Dawlish in the summer.

Dr Tyldesley walks to the door with me. 'You'll be hearing from them in the next few days, I expect,' he tells me.

'All right,' I answer. 'Thanks then. Cheerio,' and I skedaddle before he can say any more.

Flo's in when I get there, which is lucky, because she's got herself a little job as a home help now, just mornings, but Karen's got chicken pox, so she's had to take the day off.

She puts the kettle on and makes us a nice cup of tea, which we drink in front of the fire in her living room. It's looking very nice in here. I remember when Bob put the wallpaper up and Eddie gave him a hand. Doesn't seem all that long ago, but it must be a couple of years now. It's a horrible thought, knowing Bob won't be putting any more up – I wish it hadn't come into me head. I wonder if Flo ever thinks like that. I suppose she's bound to, but it don't do any good to dwell on it, does it? You can't help but admire how she keeps every-thing up together though, when she has to cope on her own. Must be hard not having a man about the place. I know Eddie wishes he could do more, but with me being under the weather all that time, he just couldn't manage it. She's got some good neighbours though, so I expect they help. They bloody better, or I'll be knocking on their doors wanting to know why.

We chat about the kids and this and that, you know how you do. In the back of me mind I keep wondering about Bob and whether she still misses him at all. She must, I mean, it's not even a year yet, is it? He has to have left a great big hole in her life. I know Eddie would, if anything happened to him. I'm feeling a bit tempted to ask her about it, but that would be prying, and anyway, she probably doesn't want to be reminded. She's a lovely woman, quiet, never pushes herself on anyone, makes you wonder why God had to go and do this to her.

When I leave her place I walk on down the hill and stop outside the park where I stare in at the swings and sliders. No kids there today, they're all at school. Just old Bert, the caretaker, picking up some bits of rubbish. He gives me a wave, so I wave back then go on walking down to the post office. The sun's gone in a bit now, but it's still not cold. I keep me scarf tied up though, just in case the wind picks up from nowhere, the way it does sometimes, when you're not expecting it. It'll be handy when I can drive. Our car's been quite reliable lately, so Eddie might even be able to give me a lesson tonight. He reckons we'll end up having a row. He could be right, we usually do, about one thing or another.

I wonder if he'll be glad when I'm gone, no more arguing and fighting then.

*   *   *

The letter turned up a few days ago, and now I'm sitting here on the edge of me bed with me coat on, staring down at me feet. Me little case is next to me, on the floor, me handbag's already over me arm.

'All right?' Eddie says, coming in the room.

'Yes,' I say, and crush out me fag in an ashtray.

He picks up me case, then puts a hand under me elbow to help me up.

'I can manage,' I tell him.

I check me lipstick in the dressing-table mirror and decide to put on a bit more. I see him watching and try to give him a smile. 'You can't afford to take this time off,' I tell him. 'The last thing we need now is for you to go getting the sack.'

'We'll worry about that if it happens. I'll take this on down then.'

I watch him go, then I look down at me bed again and start remembering the night I had our Gary. No good thinking about that now though, is it? It's time to go.

'At least it's a nice sunny day,' I say to Eddie as we get in the car.

'They're saying it could go up to sixty-five later,' he tells me.

'That's nice.'

The engine starts after about the third go, and we reverse back up the street.

'Have you told the kids?' I ask him.

'Not yet. I'll tell them when they come home from school.'

We drive on round past the Anchor and up New Cheltenham Road. We see a couple of people we know, walking, but we don't stop to offer them a lift.

'Make sure our Susan don't wear that white dress before Whitsun,' I tell him, 'because if she has her way she'll have it on tomorrow.'

322

'You'll be back home long before then,' he tells me.

'Yeah, course I will. I'm just saying.'

'I'll come in as often as I can.'

I nod. 'Shame the kids can't come too, but it's not allowed, so that's that. Probably be too upsetting for them anyway.'

'They'll be all right.'

'Yes.'

When we get to Cossham I feel like I'm going to start sobbing, or screaming. I don't though, I just pull meself together as we drive on by. You see, it's not Cossham I'm going to this time, it's back down the bloody General, the place where I had me first big operation. Never ever wanted to go there again in me life, but it don't seem as though I've got a choice now, does it? That's where they want me, so that's where I have to go. Thing that keeps going round and round in my head is, they can't remove me liver the way they did me bosom, can they? I've only got one of them, and if it's no bloody good any more, well then, I've had it, haven't I? It's all going to be over and I'll never see me children again.

Susan

Mum's gone back in hospital. She went last Thursday, and we don't know when she's coming out again, so Gran's been staying with us, helping to get us ready for school in the morning, and making our tea at night. Gary's been sleeping in with Dad, so I creep in too, and we all sleep in the big bed together. It's not the same without Mum being there, but she'll be home soon, Dad says, and I know she will because she's come home all the other times when I was afraid she wouldn't.

She's not up Cossham this time, she's in the General, down town. Dad goes in to see her most nights, and sometimes we go too, but we have to wait out in the car. When she was up Cossham she could wave to us from a window, but she can't down the General, so we just sit there with Gran, in amongst all the other cars, waiting for Dad to come out again. We play I-spy-with-my-little-eye, and sing 'Ten Green Bottles', or 'One Man Went to Mow'. Then we sing on the way home with Dad.

Tonight when he came back Dad said Mum was getting a lot better, so she could be coming home at the end of the week. I'm glad because she said my best friend Diane could come for tea. Dad wouldn't let her, because it was too much for Gran. I've been up Diane's house though, and I was even going to sleep there, but then I wanted to go home, just in case Dad was missing me, or Mum came back, so Diane's dad drove me down in his car.

We're doing French in school now, so I can say *bonjour* to Mum when I see her, and *comment allez-vous?* She'll like that, because she says it's good to speak another language, even though she doesn't like the French very much. They eat frogs' legs and snails, which is really disgusting. Lucky we don't have that for tea or we'd be sick.

I'm trying out for the choir again next week, so I can be in the school concert. I'm going to sing my very, very best, so they don't turn me down again, because I really want to be in it. Everyone else is, so I don't want to be left out or Kelvin Milton will make fun of me again. I haven't told Dad, because I want to surprise him.

Gary's in his school choir, and he's done lots of

paintings for Mum that Dad takes into hospital. I haven't done any, because mine are no good, but I'm making her a card saying 'Get Well Soon' with bows and stars on it, which is nearly ready, I just have to make some more glue. I'm doing it in secret, up in my bedroom, so no-one else knows.

'*Bonjour frère*,' I say as Gary comes in the living room where I'm helping Gran wind some wool.

'What?'

'It means hello brother,' I tell him. 'It's French. And you'll never guess what the word for yes is. It's *oui*.'

He starts to laugh. 'No it's not, is it Gran?'

'Yes it is,' she answers.

'You mean, *oui* it is,' I tell her.

'*Oui* it is,' she repeats and Gary and I laugh our heads off.

'What's all this noise?' Dad says, coming down from the bathroom where he's been having a shave. He's got little bits of paper stuck to his chin where he's nicked himself, with spots of blood seeping through.

'Susan keeps saying wee,' Gary tells him. 'And Gran did too.'

'It's French for yes, isn't it Dad?'

'*Oui*,' he answers and we start laughing all over again.

'Are you going down the hospital now?' I ask him.

'Yes, do you want to come?'

'I don't know. Can I go in and see Mum?'

'You know children aren't allowed in.'

'I don't think she's in there,' I say.

'Now don't start that nonsense again. Of course she's in there, and we should find out tonight whether or not she can come home at the weekend.'

'What's wrong with her?' Gary asks.

He always asks that question and Dad always says, 'She's having a little operation.'

'You mean like having her tonsils out?'

'Yes, a bit like that.'

'Will she be able to speak after?'

'Yes, but she'll probably have to be in bed to recover.'

We have to go through what recover means then, and after that we try to guess what the score's going to be when England play Germany at Wembley in the World Cup.

I didn't go with Dad to the hospital the other night, but I'm going now, because Mum's coming home. I've got my card ready to give her, and some scent I made with rose petals and water. It's in a pickled-onion jar that Gran washed out for me, because it's the only one we could find with a lid.

I'm sitting in the back seat of the car, all on my own, while Dad goes in to get her. Gary's got choir practice tonight, so he couldn't come, and Gran's gone to watch him so she can bring him home when he's finished. I still don't know if they're going to let me be in my school choir. I did the audition, and I sounded really good, except for when Kelvin Milton and his friends starting wailing like cats outside and put me off.

'It's a pity it's raining,' Gran said when Dad and I left earlier. 'The weather's been lovely while she's been in.'

'Forecast is good though,' he told her, and he must be right because the rain's stopped now, but the sun still hasn't come back out again yet.

They've been in there a long time, and I'm starting to get worried that Dad can't find her. Or that they've forgotten all about me. The car doors are locked, but I can always climb out of a window to go and find them. If the windows won't go down I could end up living here, in the back of the car. I expect one of the nurses would give me a blanket to keep warm, and I might be able to beg some scraps of food from the kitchens. It'll be handy if I get ill.

A man and woman come across the car park and get into a car behind me. I turn to watch them out of the back window and the woman gives me a little wave. I don't wave back though, because I'm not allowed to wave to strangers.

I jump as the passenger door opens and turn round as Dad starts to help Mum get in.

'Take it steady now,' he's saying. 'It's all right, I've got you. There you go, are you down?'

'Yes, I'm down,' she says. 'I just got to get me feet in now.'

'Don't worry about that, I've got them,' and he lifts her feet inside.

'All right to close the door now?' he asks.

'Yes, I think so.'

She tilts herself to one side a bit and the door slams closed.

'I'm here, Mum,' I say from behind her.

'I know you are,' she says. 'How are you, my old love?'

I start to say I'm all right, but then she turns round to look at me and I want to scream. She's got a funny-colour face. It's all grey and dark and the whites of her eyes are yellow.

'Look a bit of a fright, do I?' she says as Dad gets in. 'I'll be all right when we get home.'

'I've got a card to make you better,' I tell her, but I don't want to give it to her because I don't think she's my mum.

'There's lovely.'

'And some scent.'

'Oh, that's good, get rid of the horrid hospital smell, eh?'

I pass it over and she unscrews the lid to have a sniff.

'Whew!' she says, jerking her head back. 'There's nice. I'll put some on after I've had a bath, eh? And look at this lovely card. Did you make it yourself?'

'Yes. All on my own, didn't I Dad?'

'No help from anyone,' he answers.

I want to climb on Dad's lap and whisper in his ear if he's sure it's Mum, but he's driving the car, so I sit back on the seat and stay quiet. She should have put some lipstick on, and some powder, because it's scaring me to see her that horrible colour. I don't want her to be like that. It makes her look like a ghost.

When we get home Dad takes her straight upstairs, and Gran goes to help her undress and get into bed. When she's ready Gary goes in to see her, but I stay downstairs with Dad and Gran.

'Aren't you going up too?' Dad asks when I go out to the kitchen to see what he's doing.

I shake my head.

'What's the matter?' he says.

'Nothing.'

'Are you hungry?'

'No.'

'Go on up and see your mum. She's missed you.'

I shake my head again. 'I don't want her to be in bed,' I say. 'I want her to get up again.'

'She will when she's better.'

'But she's never better. She's always ill. Why can't she be like other people's mums and be all right?'

'Ssh, now, or she'll hear you, and you're old enough to know that she doesn't want to be ill. That's why she's had an operation, to make her better again, but it takes time to get over it.'

'How much time?'

'We'll have to wait and see.'

* * *

Mum's been home from hospital for nearly two weeks now and she still hasn't got out of bed, except to go to the toilet, when Dad or Gran have to help her. We're not allowed to go into her room very much, in case she's asleep and we wake her up. We just pop in to give her a kiss before we go off to school in the morning, and then again when we come home to let her know we're back. Sometimes we go in and say goodnight, it depends how she's feeling.

The doctor comes nearly every day, and Mrs Weiner, but she doesn't seem to be getting any better. I wish she'd hurry up though, because we want her to watch the World Cup with us, and to come up Kingswood for the Whitsun parade. I don't care about the school concert, because they won't let me be in the choir anyway. I hate them, and their choir's just stupid. So's Diane Meadows, because she's gone off with Caroline Fry, and I don't want a best friend anyway, so there.

Gran's gone back home again for a couple of nights, so Dad's making the tea tonight. He's standing in front of the stove, checking the boiled potatoes to see if they're done. They're always crunchy when he makes them, so you can't mash them properly, and they go a funny colour too. I wish Mum would come downstairs and make our tea.

'Dad?' I say.

'Yes?'

'Is Mum going to die?'

'No, of course not,' he says. 'Don't be daft. Now go and lay the table, like a good girl.'

I'm happy now, because it's taken me days and days to pluck up the courage to ask, and now I know it's going to be all right. Anyway, I didn't think she was going to die really, it was just worrying me a little bit.

Chapter Seventeen

Eddress

The days all seem to be running into one now. Haven't got much idea when one finishes and another starts. Too weak to do more than just lie here, drifting in and out of sleep, and thinking, though most of the time I'm too tired even to do that. There in't much pain, not now they've got me on the morphine. Reckon I'd be climbing up the walls otherwise.

No-one's come out and told me there's no more they can do, but I d'know. It's a feeling that's all about me, and has been ever since I went into that bleedin' General. While I was there they opened me up and had a look round, but it was all too far gone, so they just stitched me up again, gave me a bit of time to get over the oper-ation, then sent me home. They don't say the words like, 'We're very sorry, Mrs Lewis, we've done all we can,' or 'Bad luck, Mrs Lewis, we didn't get it in time,' they just say, 'We think she'll be more comfortable at home now, Mr Lewis.'

Not sure if I am more comfortable here. It's hard to tell when I'm out of it most of the time. Can't be very nice for Eddie though, having to put up with me like this. Obviously the kids don't know anything. Couldn't bear it if they did, poor little mites. Sometimes I hear them charging about, up and down the stairs, in and out of the bathroom, whispering at the tops of their voices so they don't wake me up. Love 'em to bits, I do. Just love 'em to bits. It's tearing out me heart to think of leaving 'em, it's so bad I can't let meself do it. Got to think of something else.

Daft part of it is, I've managed to give up smoking. Either that, or I just don't have the energy to do it. Whichever, don't make any difference, because it's a bit bloody late now, innit?

Funny how me head seems a bit clearer tonight. Don't expect it'll last long, but it's nice that Eddie's sitting here next to me, holding me hand. I can't get up the wind to speak, or even move much, but I can hear him telling me poems. He's got a lovely voice. Me eyes do flicker open every now and then, but everything's all blurred, and it wears me out trying to see, so I just close 'em again. The kids is in bed. I can't remember if I said good-night to them or not. I hope so, because I got to be honest, I reckon it'll have been me last chance. Don't want to go without giving them a kiss and saying cheerio. I want to ask Eddie if I did it, but I just can't manage it.

I can hear meself breathing. Or is it him I can hear? In and out. In and out.

Thought I'd be scared stiff when the time came, but turns out I'm not. I was, mind, right up to this morning, or was it yesterday morning? I don't know what happened to make it go away, but I'm not scared now. Not for me. It's Susan and Gary I'm scared for, and Eddie, and how they're going to get on without me.

Haven't got it in me to argue or plead with God any more, but I still don't understand it, honest I don't. I hoped I would before I went, but it still don't make any sense to me, that He'd take a mother away from her children. Why did He give 'em to me in the first place, if this is what He intended? It's cruel, innit? That's what it is, downright cruel. They need me. Nine and five,

that's all they are. They're not even old enough to understand why I won't be here any more.

Funny thing is, when I was younger I never thought
I'd have any kids. Never thought I'd get married even.
Always afraid no-one would want me, I suppose. It
would be better now if no-one had.

I think Eddie knows how much I love him. I hope so.
I've never been any good with those sort of words, not
the way he is. Look at him. Can't open me eyes, but I
can see him in me mind's eye, sitting there. Is there a
better man in all the world? He's here with me now,
making sure I'm not on me own, or in any pain. How's
he going to cope when I've gone? Who's going to take
care of him then? Who's going to make sure he becomes
a writer, and help him with the kids? He can't do it on
his own.

Think I must have drifted off for a bit, because I can
hear the birds now, just coming awake. What day is it?
I think it's a Wednesday. Eddie's still sitting here, next
to the bed. He's asleep, I think, but his hand's still
holding mine.

I manage to get me eyes open. He's watching me. Eyes
all blue and filled with tears. He knows the moment's
here. So do I.

Goodbye then, me old love, I say to him in me mind.
I'm off now. Take care of my children. I know you will.
Make sure they do well.

He's got tears running down his face, the daft sod. I
try to squeeze his hand to let him know it's all right.
This is what I want now. I'm ready to go. I don't know
if he felt it. I hope so . . .

Susan

It's Wednesday morning, and Dad's just brought in my breakfast, the same as he does most mornings now. Toast, cornflakes and a cup of milky tea. I don't really want to go to school today, but I suppose I'll have to.

After I've washed and dressed I pop in to say cheerio to Mum. She's still asleep, and the blankets are over her face, so I pull them back and give her a kiss. She doesn't wake up, so I go on out to the landing and open the curtains. I'm trying to remember if I need my PE bag today, but I can't. Anyway, if I forget it, I won't have to do games, so that's all right.

Dad hasn't gone to work yet, so I suppose he must be going in late. He's washing Gary's face and combing his hair in the bathroom.

When I get to the bottom of the stairs I pick up my satchel, shout cheerio and go out the door. All the other children are coming out of their houses now, on their way to school, so I walk up the hill with Janet and Sarah.

Our first lesson is English, and after that, at quarter to eleven it's French. We're outside the French room waiting to go in, when the school secretary comes along and calls out my name.

'Yes miss?' I say, stepping out of the line.

'Come with me, there's a good girl,' she says.

Everyone's watching me, and I'm trying to remember what I did wrong as I follow her along the corridor.

'Have I been naughty?' I say when she stops outside the headmaster's office.

'No my love,' she answers. 'Go on in now,' and she opens the door.

The first person I see is Dad, then Mr Dobbs. Now I'm really frightened, because if they've made Dad come up the school I must have done something very bad. Then I see Mrs Preddy, who's the headmistress down at Gary's school.

'Hello my old love,' Dad says.

I look at them all and wait for them to tell me off.

'We're going to go down to the infants' school,' Dad says. 'The car's outside. You can go with me, or Mrs Preddy.'

'Why?' I ask.

'Just go and get your coat, there's a good girl.'

I do as I'm told and come back to find them waiting on the front steps.

'I'll go with you,' I say to Dad.

He lets me sit in the front seat as we drive down Alma Road to the infants' school. I don't understand what's happening, but I feel very afraid.

As we get out of the car, Dad comes to hold my hand across the road.

We go inside the infants' school, where Mrs Preddy's already waiting outside her office.

'Where's Gary?' I ask.

'In his classroom.'

Dad takes me into Mrs Preddy's office and closes the door. He then tells me to sit down, and comes to sit on a chair in front of me. I think I know what he's going to say, but I don't want him to say it, so I wonder if I can run away, or block my ears so I can't hear.

'You know you asked me the other night,' he says, 'if Mummy was going to die.'

I sit forward. I'm really, really frightened now.

'Well, the angels came last night and took her to Jesus.'

'But I don't want them to,' I tell him. 'You can't let them Dad. Please. She has to stay here with us.' Big fat tears are running down my cheeks.

'I know, my love, but she can't.'

'Dad, please.'

He pulls me onto his lap and puts his arms all round me. 'Ssh, now,' he says, 'you have to be a big, brave girl now.'

'I don't want to be. I want my mum.'

'I know, I know.'

He rocks me back and forth and holds me tight.

'Come on now,' he says after a while. 'Stop crying. You don't want all the little ones to see you, do you?'

I shake my head, and wipe the tears away with the backs of my hands.

Anyway, it doesn't matter that she's dead, because I know she's going to come back. She will. I know she will.

'Do you want to come home now, or do you want to go back to school?' Dad asks.

'Um, I think I'll go back to school.' If I do everything normal, then it'll all be normal again.

'All right. Mrs Preddy'll drive you up the hill, while I have a little chat with our Gary.'

In Mrs Preddy's car I'm thinking about what it'll be like if Mum really is dead. I mean, I know she's not, but if she is, I'll be the only girl in our family, so I'll have to do all the cooking and cleaning, and take care of Gary, and make sure Dad's sandwiches are cut, and do the shopping, and all the other things Mum used to do. But only until she comes back. I won't have to do it after that, until I'm grown-up and I'm a mum myself.

The French class is nearly over when I get there, so Mr Dobbs lets me wait in his office until the bell rings for dinner. He takes me over to the canteen himself, holding my hand, which makes me feel really silly. After he's gone everyone comes crowding round me, wanting to know why I was called out and what I did wrong and did I get the cane.

'My mum's dead,' I tell them.

All their faces go strange. 'How?' Lizzie asks.

'She just died.'

'What was wrong with her?'

'She wasn't very well, so she died.'

'That's really horrible,' Diane says. 'I'll be your best friend again if you like.'

'No I will,' Lizzie tells her.

'No, I will.'

'No, I will.'

Everyone wants to be my best friend.

'She's a liar!' Kelvin Milton shouts. 'Her mum's not dead, she's just left her, because she can't stand her.'

Mrs Fields snatches him up by the ear and marches him out of the canteen. We don't see him again until class starts in the afternoon, when Mrs Fields makes him stand up in front of everyone to say sorry to me.

'He had six strokes of the cane from Mr Dobbs,' one of his friends whispers to me.

Good. I hope it hurt.

We do some lessons then go out to play. Everyone's crowding round me again, being my friend. I think Mum can probably see me, but I'm not really sure. Then Mrs Jeffries comes up and tells me I can be in the school choir.

'There won't be any time for you to rehearse for the concert,' she says, 'but we'll get round it.'

I'm really happy now, and can't wait to tell Mum. I expect she'll be back by the time I get home. I mean, I know she's dead, but really she's just gone to her other family for a while, so she can always come back whenever she likes.

When I get home from school lots of my aunties and uncles are sitting round the table in the dining room. I go upstairs to see Mum, but she's not there, so I go into my room and have a sit-down on the bed. It all feels really funny and I wish it didn't.

'Can I come in?' Gary says.

'Yes.'

He comes and sits next to me on the bed. 'What does dead mean?' he asks.

'Nothing,' I answer. 'It doesn't mean anything.'

'Oh.'

I put my arm round him, because he's little and he doesn't understand. 'Let's go and find Dad,' I say.

When we get downstairs one of our aunties comes into the passage. 'There you are,' she says, 'we were all wondering where you'd got to.'

'Where's Dad?' I ask.

'He's in the front room, but you're not to disturb him. He's having a bit of peace and quiet.'

'We want to see him,' I say.

'No, you can't. Come and have some tea. We've got some nice cakes and lemonade.'

'I want to see my dad,' I shout. 'Dad! Dad!'

'Sssh. Oh my goodness, you always were a handful.'

'It's all right,' Dad says, coming out of the front room, 'they can come in.'

We go in and climb up on his lap. He gives us a great big hug and asks what we did at school today. I tell him I'm going to be in the choir for the concert and he smiles. Then we don't say anything for quite a long time. We just sit there, being quiet.

'She'll come back, Dad,' I tell him. 'Don't worry, she will.'

Lots of days have gone by now and Mum still hasn't come back. They had a funeral, but it was only a pretend one, because she's still with her other family somewhere. It's all right though, she'll come back when she's had enough of them.

I had a funny dream last night, that I was in her

bedroom, carrying her around on my back. She was really heavy, so I was glad when I woke up.

I think she might be back today, because I'm singing in the choir tonight. There hasn't been enough time for me to learn all the words, so I have to go 'Rhubarb, rhubarb,' to make it look as though I know them. I'm going to wear my white lacy dress, even though it's supposed to be for Whitsun. This is a special occasion, and Dad agrees that if Mum was here, she'd say I could. I'm not going to wear my glasses either, or a ponytail. I want to look really lovely for my first time in the choir.

Gran's coming to the concert, and two of my aunties. One of them keeps stopping me from going in the front room to see Dad. She says he has to have some time to himself, so I'm not to go bothering him with all my talk. She even slapped me the other day for cheeking her back. I hate her. Just let her wait till I tell Mum she hit me, she'll really be in for it then.

If Mum is in heaven she might be watching me now, standing here at the edge of the choir, with the curtains swinging back so everyone can see us. We're already singing, and I'm going 'Rhubarb! Rhubarb,' with all my heart, in case she can hear me. We're about halfway through the second verse when Mrs Jeffries pulls me off into the wings and whispers, 'You're supposed to be miming the word, dear, remember?'

'Oh yes,' I say. 'Sorry.'

But it's hard when everyone's singing at the tops of their voices, and I'm not allowed to. It's not fair, so I bellow it out again, and at the end everyone in the audience claps and claps and claps, and after, when I go to find Dad everyone says what a lovely dress I'm wearing, and how proud my mum would be of me if she could see me now. Lots of them are crying, but I don't know why, because our songs weren't sad. Anyway, Mum can see me, but I don't tell them that.

England won the World Cup and there was a party out in the street, with lots of flags and lemonade and everyone cheering and jumping up and down on the tables. I don't care that Mum didn't come to celebrate with us, so there. Me and Dad and Gary went out for a bit and joined in, but then Dad came inside again, so we did too.

He's in the front room on his own again now, and Gary's gone out to play with his friends. My aunties have been trying to persuade Dad to give us away, because he can't bring us up on his own, but he says, 'We belong together, and that's how we're going to stay.'

I'm glad about that, because everyone wanted to take Gary. No-one wanted me, so I might have ended up in a home like Oliver Twist, beaten and starved and turned into a pickpocket and never allowed out to play.

I decide to go outside. Everyone's playing up on the green, but I don't want to go that far away from Dad, so I draw a hopscotch on the path outside our gate and play on my own. I'm just turning round to hopscotch back again when I look up and see Mum, standing at the corner of our house. She's got her pink pyjamas on and she's laughing.

I feel all happy and then really strange, because she's not there really, I just thought she was. I don't want to play any more, so I go back inside and listen by the front-room door to see if I can hear Dad. There's no noise, so maybe he's asleep. There are some parcels on the floor, with some new coats in from China. Mum ordered them ages ago, and they've only just got here. I think about putting one on, but instead I skip up over the stairs and into my bedroom.

I've got lots of toys, but I don't feel like playing with them, so I lie down on the bed and stare up at the walls. If I sing, the way we used to, I wonder if she'll come back.

Little Bo Peep has lost her sheep,
And doesn't know where to find them,
Leave them alone, and they'll come home,
Wagging their tails behind them.

I sing three more songs, then I go quiet. I know I'm not supposed to cry, that I'm supposed to be strong and brave, but I can't help it. I want my mum. I want her to come back.

I think I'd better speak to Jesus again, so I get down on my knees and put my hands together. 'I'm sorry, Jesus,' I say. It comes out as a bit of a sob, so I have to say it again. 'I'm sorry, Jesus, for all the bad things I've done and said and thought. I'm really, really sorry, so if you've got Mum there please will you let her come home now. If you do I promise to be good for ever and ever and ever, amen.'

I'm not sure, but I think He might have heard me this time. I hope so, because Dad's really missing her and I don't know how to make him feel better. It'll cheer him up a lot if Jesus would let her come back in time for the Whitsun parade next Monday. She can see me in my new dress then as well. And watch Gary marching with the Cubs. And in winter we can wear our new coats from China.

Acknowledgements

Firstly I would like to thank my cousins Alwyn Brabham and Karen Shields, as well as my friends Sheelagh Cullen, Ruth Thomson, Pamela Salem, Denise Hastie and Fanny Blackburne, who each in their own way supported me so generously during this often painful, but occasionally hilarious journey. I'm also extremely grateful to Don and Betty Williams for sharing their memories of my mother, and of me as a child, as did my aunts Jean and Flo, and uncles Gordon and Maurice.

Most of all though I would like to thank my agent and good friend, Toby Eady, for so much humour, encouragement and enthusiasm throughout the writing of this book, as well as all his sensitivity and support during the crafting of many others.

To anyone else who knew Eddress, I hope you feel I've done her justice here and managed in some small way to recapture a little of her indomitable spirit.

Susan Lewis
Bristol 2005

A daughter trying to make sense
of a shattered world.

A father who's desperate to help.

Susan Lewis continues her story
in the deeply moving follow-up to
Just One More Day

Susan was only nine when her mother was
cruelly taken from her. No one spoke of it,
no one dared. Susan was left frightened,
angry and confused.

When she is subsequently sent away to school she
finds herself an outsider. And in her struggle to
cope with an uncertain world she pushes away
the one person she loves best – her father. As they
try to find a way back to each other, they are
forced to learn one of the hardest lessons of all –
to take one day at a time …

SUSAN
LEWIS

One day
at a time

Chapter One

Susan

I saw a film once, or part of a film anyway, where two prison officers were walking a murderer along this creepy dark corridor to where he was going to have his head chopped off. Actually, they might have been going to hang him, or shoot him to bits, or fry him up in an electric chair. I never found out, because my mum caught me hiding behind her chair watching the film I was too young for, and packed me off to bed, lucky not to have a clip round the ear for sneaking downstairs.

Anyway, the point is, I'm that person now, being walked along a creepy corridor to the end of my life. I know they don't put eleven-year-olds to death, but they do lock them up, and that's definite, because it's happening to me right now. My dad and Auntie Nance are marching me along like prison warders, and I – even though I haven't done anything wrong – am going to be shut away in this stinky, horrible, really scary place that's full of ghosts and evil witches and probably has secret passageways all gummed up in spider's webs and rat nests that you can never find your way out of.

And you should see my shoes.

Even my gran wouldn't wear shoes like this. Well, actually she does, and that's my point. She's really old and I'm not, so it's just mean to make me wear these black lace-ups with a round toe and big thick heels like a man's. They even squeak, and they hurt, but no one cares, because no one asked me if I wanted to come here and I *don't*. I cried and cried and begged my dad not to make me, but he kept saying it would be for the best.

'You'll get a good education and go to university and I'll be very proud of you,' he said, over and over again.

'I don't want you to be proud of me,' I shouted, over and over again. 'It's stupid being proud. It's a sin, even, because it says so in the Bible.'

'She's got an answer for everything,' my auntie muttered. I could tell I was getting on her nerves and I was glad, because she was getting on mine. I wished she'd go home, and my mum would come back. Mum might have been strict, and it might have been her idea for me to go to this stupid school in the first place, but I knew she thought it was creepy too – and stuck-up and not somewhere she'd ever really want to send me. Would she? When I came to think of it, I decided that perhaps it was a good job she wasn't there to ask, just in case her mind was still made up, because there was never any getting round her. Not like Dad.

'Please Dad, I want to stay home with you and Gary and all my friends,' I begged. 'I'll be really good, I promise. I'll do all the housework and the washing, I'll make your tea every night and wash up all the dishes and dry them and I'll never answer back.'

'My love,' he said, in the voice he uses when he's sorry and upset, but he won't back down, 'you've won your place there now, which is marvellous, because it goes to show how clever you are. Not everyone can go to Red Maids...'

'I don't care. I don't want to go. I'm not clever, I'm really dumb and I want to stay here with you.'

He gave me a big hug, mainly because I was crying, and he never likes it when I cry. 'I can't let you stay here,' he told me (I think he was close to crying too, which just went to show that he didn't want me to go really). 'People might start saying things, because you're a girl and there's only me and Gary...'

'Then we'll bash them up. What sort of things?'

'Bad things, and if they do, someone might come and take you away and we don't want that, do we?'

'So you're sending me away instead?'

'To a place where you'll grow up to be a proper lady, the way your mum wanted.'

I didn't say anything else after that. I just put on my cross face and stormed off, because I didn't see why we had to do anything Mum wanted when she wasn't even there to tell us what she thought any more. I wanted her to come back, more than anything. Sometimes I felt as though all my skin was going to explode I wanted it so much. It made me really mad that she'd gone. I mean, some days it was all right, I'd just get on with things and it would be like normal, but then it would suddenly become all horrible and wrong, and I would feel really afraid to think that I might never see her again. I'd hide under the sheets so no one could hear me crying – or stand by my bedroom window and look up at the sky in case she was there, looking down. 'Please come back,' I'd whisper. *'Please.'*

They keep saying she's dead, and I know it's true, but then suddenly I'm not all that sure. You see, I found a photo once, when I was about nine and she wasn't dead. It was tucked inside her cookbook and it was of a man called Michael. He'd even signed it, *To Eddress, with love.* I remember feeling really scared and angry, like everything was going out of control. I ended up tearing it into little bits so she wouldn't be able to look at it any more. Because she had a wicked temper I expected her to go on the rampage after that, demanding to know what had happened to the photo, but she never said a word, which just goes to show it must have been a secret. Apart from once hearing her say to Mrs Williams – her best friend and our next-door neighbour – that she had to see Michael, I never heard her mention him, and I never asked who he was in case she told me it was someone she loved more than Daddy.

The next time she went into hospital I asked her if it was where she was really going and she said, 'You're a dafty, aren't you? Where else would I be going?'

'I don't know,' I answered. 'When will you be coming back?'

'Soon, I hope, but you have to be brave for Daddy and Gary and keep your chin up while I'm gone, all right?'

'Are you taking your cookbook?'

She gave a cry of laughter. 'You do ask the funniest things at times,' she said. 'What am I going to be needing that for?'

I only shrugged, because I couldn't give her a proper answer, and because I felt glad she didn't need it I put my arms around her.

'Oh, what's all this nonsense now?' she said as I started to cry.

'I don't want you to go,' I told her.

'I know, my old love, and I don't want to go either, but it's the only way I'm going to get better.'

'But there's nothing wrong with you, not really.'

'Just a little bit, but we'll get it sorted out, and if it turns out to take a bit longer than we think it'll still be all right, because whatever happens you'll still be my best girl, and nothing's ever going to change that.'

I don't know if I'm still her best girl now, because I don't know if it counts when people are dead. Unless she's not really dead and she did go off with Michael. I hope she did in a way, because then she'd be able to come back. The trouble is, I saw them carrying a coffin out of our house just after Daddy told me the angels had come to take her to Jesus, and I think she must have been in it. I was next door when it happened, and I saw, because I peeped out of their landing window. They put the coffin in a big black car and drove off. It could have been a trick, of course, and if it was I don't know where she's living with her other family, I just think it's really mean to leave your husband and children, especially when they haven't done anything wrong.

It's worse for Gary, because he was only five when she went. (He's seven now.) Everyone felt really sorry for him. I heard my aunts and uncles talking about him one night, well, arguing really. They all wanted him to go and live with them. No one wanted me, which was good, because I wouldn't go and live with any of them if they begged me. I just want to stay with my dad, because he's the best person in the whole wide world with loads of stories up his sleeve and great big hugs any time we want one. He's really clever and funny, and everyone likes him and says hello to him, and offers to do things to help him. The only thing he's not very good at is cooking, but that doesn't matter. We don't have to eat much, beans on toast will do, or fish fingers and chips. I quite like corned-beef mash too, except when the potatoes are still hard. On Sundays we usually have a roast dinner with one of my aunties, followed by tinned peaches and condensed milk for afters – my favourite.

Wonder what poison we'll be served up here in this bloody school.

We've just reached a prison bed, which is the last but one in a row of about twelve going down one side of the dormitory. Opposite is another row of twelve and at the end are two private rooms where, apparently, sixth-form girls live. All the beds have blue iron frames (and snakes under, I expect), with a cubicle behind that has a curtain across the front so no one can see in. Inside the cubicle is a dressing table with two drawers for our brassieres and bags (that's what they call knickers here, or so it said in the information they sent – *bags*, what a stupid name), and a wardrobe to hang up all our uniforms. There are loads of them. One for school, another for evenings, a different one for Saturdays, and one that's actually quite mod for Sundays. (The Sunday uniform is a bit like a Mary Quant dress, because it's straight with long sleeves, a zip up the front and a white collar that can be unbuttoned off the dress so we can put it in the wash. If it was short it would be really fab, like one I've seen my cousin Alwyn wearing, but it comes right down to the knee and we have to wear these thick granny stockings under it that are as old-fashioned and vile as our shoes. Honestly, I'm so glad no one can see me.)

There are lots of other girls arriving with their parents, and by the sound of it they all speak really posh. I'm not going to speak posh for anyone. The girls in the beds either side of mine are first-formers too, and the one whose name turns out to be Laura has a sister up the other end of the dormitory who's a year older. Her name's Cheryl.

'Are you all right then?' my dad asks in his best chirpy voice. He's trying to look jolly and jokey, but I think he looks a bit worried and shabby in amongst all these tall, stuck-up people with their smart hairy overcoats and bri-nylon shirts. He's taken his cap off now and put it in his pocket, but Auntie Nance's scarf is still tied up under her chin like it's trying to stop her mouth falling open. No one else is wearing a scarf – or a cap.

'No,' I say.

'I know, why don't we put your things in your dressing table?' he suggests.

'No.'

'Come on, I'll do it,' Auntie Nance tells him.

So they open up the curtain behind my bed and

start stuffing my smalls, socks and nighties into the drawers. Everything has a name tag on it – Susan Lewis RM 74. My dad sewed them in himself, so they're a bit wonky, but who cares? I was going to help, but then I thought, why should I when I don't even want to go there?

'We've put a nice writing pad in your top drawer,' Dad tells me. 'You'll be able to send us lots of letters telling us what's happening.'

My stomach's starting to go all funny now and I think I might cry. 'I'm not writing to you,' I tell him sharply.

'Well, that's a shame, because I'll be writing to you.'

'I won't read them.'

Auntie Nance is taking something out of her handbag. 'Here's a couple of mint humbugs,' she says, passing them over. 'Don't tell anyone you've got them, because you're supposed to hand in your sweets.'

I look at my dad, but he's not looking at me. He's watching what everyone else is doing. Some parents are starting to leave now, and some of the girls have already changed into their uniforms. Our own clothes have to be laid out on the end of our beds ready for collection, and we won't get them back again until the next time we're allowed home. 'Please don't make me stay,' I say, catching hold of Dad's hand.

He's starting to look all worried and ruffled.

'That's enough of that nonsense now,' Auntie Nance butts in. 'You're a lucky girl to be here, and don't you forget it.'

I don't think my mum liked Auntie Nance very much, and I can see why.

Suddenly an alarm starts shrieking around the walls like a witch's scream. Fab! There's a fire! Let's move! I start grabbing my things, but then I realise no one else is reacting the same way.

'That'll be it then,' my dad says. 'Time for us to go.'

I look at him again. He's not really going to leave me here. I know he won't, because he loves me, or he's always said he does, so he wouldn't be so mean as to go home without me. He can see how horrible this place is with its stink of BO and cabbage and great big windows that are too high to see out of, even if you stood on a chair. There are all sorts of rules and regulations we got sent that I still don't understand, and I'll only get to see him on Sundays after church, and that's not fair when all my friends are seeing their mums and dads every single day. I want to see my mum. Where is she? Why doesn't she come and save me?

Daddy won't leave me. I know he won't.

'All right then, my love,' he says, and puts his arms around me.

I turn away.

'I'll put your suitcase here, at the end of the bed,' Auntie Nance says. 'They'll probably tell you what to do with it later.'

'Dad,' I wail.

'Oh, come on now, you're a big girl,' he chides.

I don't want anyone to see me crying, but it's really hard to make myself stop. I steal a quick look round and see that the other girls are unpacking, or chatting to one another, or lying on their beds reading comics and magazines. I like *Dandy* and

Beano, but *Jackie*'s the best, even though I'm not supposed to be old enough to read it. All I've got now is a copy of Lambs' *Tales from Shakespeare* which I don't like reading myself, because it's always better when Dad reads it out aloud.

'Do I get a kiss then?' he asks.

I shake my head.

'That's not very nice now, is it?' Auntie Nance says.

I don't look at her, because I've really stopped liking her now. She used to be my favourite auntie once, but not any more.

'I'll be up next Sunday,' Dad tells me. 'I'll bring Gary to the church with me and we'll see you after.'

'I don't want to go to church,' I reply. 'I don't believe in God.'

'Now, now. You won't go to heaven if you say things like that.'

'I don't want to go to heaven, I want to go home.'

'Try to be a good girl,' Auntie Nance says.

I want to tell her to bugger off, the way my mum did once, but I don't have the guts. So I look at Daddy and say, 'Please let me come with you.'

He takes both my hands in his and says, 'All you have to do is take one day at a time and everything will be fine.'

He said that after Mummy died and it wasn't, and now it never will be again.

He plonks a kiss on my head and gives me a great big hug, then I stand next to my bed watching him walking away. I keep staring at his back, willing him to give in and come back to get me. I know he will. He won't be able to leave me on my own,

12

because he's too kind and always gives me everything I want – well, most of the time anyway. Anything could happen to me in a place like this, so he must be scared too. I wasn't supposed to be a boarder. I was supposed to be a day girl, and I would be if my mum hadn't died. It's all her fault really and now there's nothing I can do to change it.

Daddy goes out through the double doors at the end of the dormitory and disappears, Auntie Nance following him. I'm still standing next to my bed. I don't know what to do. I'm so full up with unhappiness that I can hardly move.

I clench my hands really tightly. I don't care that he doesn't love me. I always knew he was just pretending, like everyone else. I expect him and Gary would rather be on their own, without me. They might not even write me letters, or come to see me, or let me go home for holidays.

Why doesn't anyone want me?

I'm all on my own now, like an orphan in an orphanage.

I have to try and be brave, like Oliver Twist.

Keeping my head down, I go into my cubicle and close the curtain before anyone can tell I'm crying. I can hear them all talking out there, but I'm too afraid to go and join in. They all seem to know one another and no one's interested in me. Why would they be when they're all posh and I'm dead common?

I wish I was dead with Mummy, but knowing her she'd only send me back again and tell me to go and make Daddy proud.

I don't want to make anyone proud. I just want to go home.